Contesting the
Master Narrative

Contesting the

Master Narrative

ESSAYS IN SOCIAL HISTORY

EDITED BY JEFFREY COX AND

SHELTON STROMQUIST

UNIVERSITY OF IOWA PRESS ⊔ IOWA CITY

University of Iowa Press, Iowa City 52242

Copyright © 1998 by the University of Iowa Press
Printed in the United States of America

http://www.uiowa.edu/~uipress
Printed on acid-free paper

Library of Congress Cataloging-in-Publication Data
Contesting the master narrative: essays in social history /
    edited by Jeffrey Cox and Shelton Stromquist.
        p.   cm.
    Includes bibliographical references and index.
    ISBN 0-87745-624-0
    1. Social history.   I. Cox, Jeffrey.   II. Stromquist,
Shelton, 1943–   .
    HN13.C655   1998
    306'.09—dc21   98-24439

98 99 00 01 02 C 5 4 3 2 1

CONTENTS

ACKNOWLEDGMENTS

The essays in this volume were first presented at the University of Iowa Workshop on the Rhetoric of Social History, supported in part by a grant from the National Endowment for the Humanities, an independent federal agency. The workshop was one of a series of Scholars Workshops in the Rhetoric of Inquiry held under the auspices of the University of Iowa Project on Rhetoric of Inquiry, with financial support from the University of Iowa. We would like to acknowledge the support and assistance of Kate Neckerman of POROI and Deirdre McCloskey, Allan Megill, Linda Kerber, and John Nelson.

This volume is published with a subvention from the Graduate College of the University of Iowa. We would like to thank Bryan Palmer and David Roediger for helpful comments.

Contesting the
Master Narrative

JEFFREY COX & SHELTON STROMQUIST

INTRODUCTION: MASTER NARRATIVES
AND SOCIAL HISTORY

The interdisciplinary essays in this volume, by literary critics, sociologists, and historians, illustrate the possibilities of social history at a time of some disarray in the field. Drawing attention to alternative narrative practice both in the past and among contemporary historians, they call into question the persuasiveness of both "objective" and "synthetic" master narratives. While reflecting on the much-debated linguistic turn in scholarship, these essays suggest ways in which social historians may transcend some of the dilemmas in their field through a greater sensitivity to diverse narrative strategies and a wider assemblage of audiences.

For some time, but notably since the publication of Peter Novick's *That Noble Dream* in 1988, the historical profession in the English-speaking world has contemplated its lack of a unifying principle to guide professional practice.[1] Novick unmasked a rhetorical tradition in scholarship, all the more persuasively by working within the rhetorical conventions being unmasked. He made explicit what had been hidden by a shared but usually unspoken assumption of consensus in the profession. The ideal historian was an objective observer, existing apart from the events that he or she observed. The construction of historical knowledge occurred in a separate world of objective inquiry.

Although Novick served the profession well by exposing historians' half-articulated assumptions, his book had the tone of an anxious lament for lost unity, with no prescription for how to restore it.[2] The heart of that anxiety is a sense that we have lost objectivity as a guiding principle and have nothing but relativism to put in its place. Confronted with a choice between objectivity and relativism, neo-objectivist historians have rushed to rehabilitate objectivity. In *Telling the Truth about History*

(1994), Joyce Appleby, Lynn Hunt, and Margaret Jacob propose a "qualified" objectivity, one that has been "refurbished" and "disentangled from the scientific model."[3] Alan Spitzer is more unequivocal in his defense of "objectivity" in *Historical Truth and Lies about the Past* (1996). He dismisses attempts by Joan Scott, Allan Megill, and others to put forward alternative standards of historical accuracy as "qualifications of historical nihilism."[4]

Novick's book appeared at a time when a sense of lost direction was already noticeable in the field of social history. The high expectations and widespread enthusiasm of the 1960s and 1970s for a new history constructed around the experience and outlook of "ordinary people" and "everyday life" seemed to run aground in the 1980s.[5] The sense of disarray that pervaded the field derived from several sources. First, the call for synthesis, so widespread among American social historians in the 1980s, reflected the desire both to reconfigure social history within a new master narrative and to contest conservative revisionists for control of the dominant story. Second, social history, particularly in Britain, was closely tied to the political fate of the Labour movement and the left and to a corresponding loss of confidence among labor and socialist historians in the face of a revitalized celebratory history of elites and elite institutions. Third, historical materialism, the reigning intellectual paradigm in much of the "new" social history of the 1960s and 1970s, lost some of its persuasive force, leaving a fragmented, directionless field that has turned, in many cases reluctantly, to language and the social construction of identity as an alternative source of analytical innovation. Fourth, in British and U.S. social history some of the most vital new work was in feminist history, a field in which historians' sense of personal engagement with their subjects lent persuasiveness to their historical accounts. "Gendered" histories decentered traditional narratives in a variety of ways and subverted the project of constructing a new master narrative. They opened new intellectual space for alternative accounts of the social relations of power, languages, and structures of domination, and subjectivity gained credibility and persuasive power.[6]

For many social historians in the early 1980s the new social history had produced what Herbert Gutman called "a heap of broken historical images" that lacked a coherent focus.[7] Eric Foner saw a portrait "of a nation constantly at war with itself, divided along lines of race, class, gender, and region" that made "the notion of unified national experience . . . almost impossible to maintain."[8] Thomas Bender offered the most sustained and compelling critique: "[The new social history] is devoted almost exclusively to the private or *gemeinschaftlich* worlds of trades, occupations, and professions; locality; sisterhood; race and ethnicity; and family. What we have gotten are the parts, all richly described. But since they are somehow assumed to be autonomous, we get no image of the whole, and no suggestions about how the parts might go together or even whether they are intended to go together."[9]

But if such calls for synthesis asked, as David Brody put it, "what does it all add up to?" or proposed to construct narrative unity, as Thomas Bender did through a new conception of politics as "public culture," they also invited criticism that questioned the whole project.[10] For Lawrence Levine, the politically focused master narrative was an "invented tradition" among historians by which "we generalize the things we study right out of their complexity." He called on social historians to continue "complicating simple pictures, finding intricacies where before we had certainties, turning unity into multiplicity, clarity into ambiguity."[11] Joan Scott saw the synthetic master narrative as "not only incomplete but impossible of completion in the terms it has been written." It is based "on the forcible exclusion of Others' stories." To reconstruct history around those stories has "the effect of fragmenting historical vision into conflicting accounts." "Partiality" and "particularity" are necessarily essential features of "all stories historians tell."

Socialist and labor historians in Britain participated in the defensiveness that characterized American social history in the late 1980s and early 1990s, but on different grounds. In Britain there has always been a franker recognition of the importance of personal commitment and individual point of view in the writing of history, in part because of the obvious political commitments of the best social historians. E. P. Thompson's *The Making of the English Working Class* was undoubtedly the most influential English-language book of the last half century for social historians. Thompson displayed rhetorical contempt for formal theory. His own personal and political commitments were never in doubt. The very high quality of Thompson's writing reflects in part his acknowledgment of the rhetorical character of social history. Thompson strove not for "objectivity" but to persuade in the interests of a specific point of view. Objectivity was the characteristic rhetorical tool of conservative historians.

Support for the tradition of politically engaged social history found expression on both sides of the Atlantic. The editors of *Radical History Review*, a journal published in the United States, interviewed an influential group of American and British radical historians who affirmed the continuing vitality of a "radical history" that challenged the "prevailing social and political arrangements." These historians also contested, in the words of the editors, conventional notions of objectivity by demonstrating "the links between personal experience and 'history' that underlie the production of all historical knowledge." [12]

In the 1980s the disarray of social history was treated less as a failure to contribute to synthesis and more as a political failure brought about by political events. Of the new journals dedicated to social history, *History Workshop* contained the most interesting and engaged writing. But a tenth-anniversary retrospective essay (1985) by two of its editors, Raphael Samuel and Gareth Stedman Jones, focused almost entirely on the journal's failures. Failure was defined as both rhetorical and political. In the conservative wave of the 1980s, social historians had failed to persuade.[13] In a series of influential articles Eric Hobsbawm reiterated this sense of a link between political defeat and the rhetorical impotence of labor and social history, a point of view echoed in Gareth Stedman Jones's influential *Languages of Class*, which included an essay titled "Why the Labour Party Is in a Mess." [14]

The loss of confidence among social historians in Britain matched in the late eighties and early nineties the publication of enthusiastic celebratory narratives of elite institutions of eighteenth- and nineteenth-century Britain. J. C. D. Clark celebrated the established church, John Brewer the ability of the eighteenth-century British state to make war around the world, Linda Colley the triumph of nationalism among the middle and upper classes, and David Cannadine the virtues of the English aristocracy.[15] These books made the place of social history problematic and the insights of E. P. Thompson and his successors largely irrelevant. With the exception of Clark, the political critique remained masked in the language of Olympian objectivity. But as Thompson put it in his own review of Colley's *Britons*, "if she is right, then I am wrong." [16]

Among social historians political commitment had long been intertwined with historical materialism. Now, in field after field of history, the relationship between ideas, institutions, and culture on the one hand, and broader underlying processes of economic and social change on the other, has become problematic. The challenge of poststructuralism has been felt with particular force by historical materialists, as Canadian labor historian Bryan Palmer's book-length salvo, *Descent into Discourse*, revealed with stunning clarity. That the challenge should have come most directly from erstwhile labor historians, Joan Scott and Gareth Stedman Jones, was particularly galling to historical materialists.[17]

The looming presence of critical theory, "Foucault, Derrida, and all that," has led to furious debates over epistemology and a number of illuminating works based on the analysis of discourse.[18] These works lead away from social history as it has been practiced, with its emphasis on historical materialism. For other social historians the linguistic turn can hardly be said to have provided more than a greater sensitivity to language and a rhetorical convention of deference to Foucault and others, typically in prefaces and opening chapters. Bryan Palmer's judgment on the work of Judith Walkowitz could serve for many others: She "in effect straddles the conceptual fence separating discourse and materialism. . . . Unable to embrace discourse theory unambiguously, Walkowitz nevertheless grasps it far more purposely in the present than she ever did in the past."[19]

In the United States, the rise of a new institutionalism, the advent of critical legal history, and the influence of political scientists calling on social historians to "bring the state back in," have revived interest in what Ira Katznelson provocatively calls "the 'bourgeois' dimension." Counseling against abandoning either "materialism" or "the post-modern turn," Katznelson would nevertheless turn states into actors and class into a secondary variable. At the heart of his story are "different kinds of states (distinguished from each other by normative visions, institutional arrangements, and policy instruments) that distinctively position groups, including the working class, in contexts that not only help shape who they are discursively and strategically but actually organize politically disparate stratification systems and pathways of transaction between states and markets and between states and civil societies."[20] Peter Mandler has identified the new emphasis on the growth of the twentieth-century state as the distinctive feature of the new three-volume *Cambridge Social History of Britain*.[21]

The decay of historical materialism is most evident in skepticism about the primacy of social class, which Gareth Stedman Jones has described as the "principal casualty" in the reorientation of social history.[22] The influential work of Patrick Joyce, a contributor to the *Cambridge Social History*, has been devoted to de-centering social class in British social history, first from a Gramscian and later from a Foucauldian theoretical stance. But such critics never openly acknowledge the political dimensions of revising highly political historians such as E. P. Thompson and

Eric Hobsbawm. Despite his engagement with linguistic and postmodern theory, Joyce remains implicitly objective and Olympian. Gazing at the entire body of nineteenth-century social history, he finds that other things are simply more important than class.[23]

The persistence of an implicit, objective point of view pervades the *Cambridge Social History*, with no acknowledgment of a corresponding political agenda. In his preface the editor, F. M. L. Thompson, does recognize the fragmentation in the field but suggests that, with a careful search, the reader might find a synthesis in these volumes. The twenty-one chapters in three volumes, he argues, "taken together . . . add up to a comprehensive and balanced account," but what the nature of that account might be is left up to the reader. "Each major feature is given critical appraisal by a leading specialist, while the landscape as a whole is left to look after itself in the expectation that an impression will form in the mind of the beholder."[24] Presumably the beholder is a dispassionate, detached observer, and the impression of the comprehensive and balanced account will resemble "the whole story," but Thompson does not describe it. Unlike socialist and labor historians, or conservative celebrators of elite institutions such as J. C. D. Clark, Thompson evades the problem with a retreat into objectivity.

Among social historians, feminists have been notably resistant to defeatism or neo-objectivist faith in objectivity. The best feminist histories in Britain and the United States display a self-confidence that reflects the authors' optimism about the fate of feminism and their ability to persuade.[25] Martha Vicinus's *Independent Women*, for instance, brilliantly combines many elements of the impersonal style of mainstream British history with a passionate admiration for the achievements of British middle-class women. A rich new vein of scholarship on the American frontier emphasizes gender and racial hierarchies and makes clear the social and environmental commitments of its authors. Patricia Nelson Limerick, a self-described "poster child for the narrative problem of multi-culturalism," argues for incorporating the "perspectives and experiences of various cultures and classes" in any account of the discoveries of America. One element of vigorous, persuasive historical writing is an explicit or implicit acknowledgment of the historian's point of view.[26]

The debate remains polarized between objectivity and a commitment to master narrative on the one hand and seemingly relativist and fragmented historical accounts on the other. Much of the anxiety among historians about the current unmasking of objectivity reflects a reasonable worry about what might take its place. Usually the only alternative that scholars can envisage is "anything goes," typically labeled relativism. In "Erasing the Holocaust," Walter Reich lists among his explanations for the persuasiveness of denials of the Holocaust "current assumptions, increasingly popular in academia, regarding the indeterminacy of truth."[27] If one story is as good as another, if there is no archimedean standpoint from which to judge all stories, then all stories are equally plausible. Such a formulation appears to leave open the possibility that the fact of the Holocaust might be cleverly argued out of existence. Furthermore, if historians acknowledge point of view, argument appears to become a question of identity with no possibility of common rules of agreement. We dispute this proposition, even as we contest the utility of inherited master narratives.

The "new objectivity" outlined in *Telling the Truth about History* provides a good description of the standards to which historians adhere when paying greater attention to the creation of a narrative. It is unfortunate that the vertigo the authors face when staring into the abyss of relativism leads them into an unnecessary grasping for the label of "objectivity" and assertions about the "knowability" of the past.[28] Their alarmist statements about the consequences of reflections on the practice of history bear little relationship to history as practiced.[29] But while in history, as in other disciplines, the dominant narratives have been subjected to growing skepticism, changes in practice point us in no single direction. Skeptics often continue to work within established traditions of scholarship. Edward Said's account of the state of postcolonial scholarship might be applied to the practice of social history in the 1990s: "Yet whereas postmodernism in one of its most famous programmatic statements (by François Lyotard) stresses the disappearance of the grand narratives of emancipation and enlightenment, the emphasis behind much of the work done by the first generation of postcolonial artists and scholars is exactly the opposite: the grand narratives remain, even though their implementation and realization are at present in abeyance, deferred, or circumvented."[30] The essays by participants in the University of Iowa Workshop on the Rhetoric of Social History in 1992 suggest that the grand narratives are not so much held in "abeyance, deferred, or circumvented" as challenged by competing alternative narratives.

In our experience, historians are motivated by personal and professional commitments to solving a problem, or telling a story, not by epistemological and ontological certitude. It is not confidence that "reality really exists" that guarantees standards of truth and falsehood but the shared practices of the profession, which the values of civil society nurture. Those values extend beyond scientific objectivity, and they deserve more confidence than the critics of relativism and historical nihilism extend to them. Attention to competing narratives is in an important sense more scientific than the search for one synthetic master narrative, the "whole story" of scientific objectivity. As the debate over secularization has shown, scholarly progress depends less on the search for one overarching story to be proved or disproved than on a willingness to compare competing stories.[31] It is impossible to tell if one story is the best story unless alternatives are reviewed.

If social historians call into question the persuasiveness of Olympian, "objective" master narratives, it is because the stories no longer approximate the world as they have come to see it, not because of epistemological doubt. As the subjects of social history proliferated, so did its audiences. Social historians faced the rhetorical task of constructing alternative narratives that persuasively described the world that its expanded, critical audience inhabited. This practice is no more, or less, than what good historians have always done.

The distinguished Indian historian Sumit Sarkar, writing in *Subaltern Studies*, acknowledged the utility of critical attention to alternative narrative strategies: "The craft does seem to require the construction of narratives of the 'as-if-true' kind, constructions which should remain open-ended and which are privileged only within the text the historian is engaged in composing at the moment."[32] The phrase "as-if" specifies an important contingent quality of historical narrative.

If, by the early 1990s, the loss of objectivity left a vacuum for some social historians, others moved to fill that vacuum by attending to rhetorically self-conscious alternative narratives, in the historical record itself and in their own scholarship. Allan Megill's ranking of the levels of narrative in historical explanation, with its useful distinction between "grand narrative" and "master narrative," helped to give names to the new practices employed by historians.[33] The notion of a single, all-encompassing story has given way to a new competitive environment of alternative narratives claiming common rhetorical space. In this environment the art of persuasion and the standards for what makes a convincing story have begun to receive new attention.

The essays in this volume reflect a new and more explicit self-consciousness about the choice of narrative strategies, along with an awareness of the importance of storytelling in shaping history. Social history plays a key role because of its focus on the multiplicity and diversity of past experience, which provides a source for alternative narratives. The essays also reflect a skeptical search for the narrative strategies embedded in our own and in other scholarly arguments, and a recognition that every historian has a point of view. The authors are not fleeing from objectivity to relativism but are searching for shared scholarly principles that guide the practice of history, including the principles of self-awareness, self-criticism, and fairness. Those values derive not from a set of universal normative principles that guide persons who make arguments about history in any imaginable context but from the shared values of the historical profession and related disciplines and the civil society within which we make our arguments.

Self-awareness begins when historians make explicit their narrative strategies. *Self-criticism* involves the open consideration and evaluation of alternative stories, which is what distinguishes scholarship from political rhetoric, many forms of forensic discourse, and propaganda. *Fairness* involves a willingness to consider the views of other scholars and alternative narrative accounts in history. (Many historians mean "fairness" when they say "objectivity.") All three assume a readiness to be persuaded by arguments. A social science historian who asks, "What evidence would you accept as disproof of your hypothesis?" is invoking the standards of laboratory science. Most historians would be happier with the question "What sort of arguments would persuade you to change your mind?" Evidence alone does not change minds, but arguments derived from evidence do. The essays in this volume shift the focus from an impoverished scientism of objectivity to a broader rhetorical approach. Rhetorical awareness can enrich history and make it more scientific, if science means searching for the most persuasive explanation among a variety of explanations that the evidence sustains rather than simply recording the results derived from scientific observation.

The present set of essays collectively asserts the importance of reading historical narratives with more explicit attention to the views of author and audience and understanding the terms by which narrators seek to persuade. By critically examining past master narratives in light of alternatives, these essays ask us to reexamine how we tell stories, within what narrative traditions they are situated, and whom they are designed to persuade. Through a history enriched by competing narratives, however fragmentary, they invite us to look beyond "objectivity" and see a wider range of rhetorical possibilities and new audiences. They do so within three broad areas of inquiry, reflecting the interests of the contributors.

The first group of essays explores the gendered character of social history rhetoric by exposing alternative, feminist traditions of social scientific and social historical writing. Sociologist Barbara Laslett scrutinizes the early twentieth-century origins of "masculine" sociology conceived as an objective science that marginalized emotion, engagement, and the female reformer/social scientists whose work represented an alternative method of inquiry. Literary critic Florence Boos uncovers a strand of feminist literary/historical writing in late Victorian Britain that operated beyond the margins of conventional scholarship and that constructed an alternative historical account of the family in which women were central actors. Literary critic Adriana Méndez Rodenas examines Frances Calderón de la Barca's travel account of mid-nineteenth-century Mexico as gendered social history. Calderón's "history" is a blend of discourses, characteristic of women travel writers in the nineteenth century. Freed from (or excluded by) conventional norms of historical argument, Calderón constructed a more complex, mediated, multivocal narrative in which genres were mixed and conventional social categories subverted. An alternative discourse centered on female concerns mingled in her writing with dominant (male) narrative forms.

The second group of essays, on alternative narrative traditions in non-European contexts, begins with historian Daud Ali's examination of the anomalous status of social history in the colonial, Orientalist histories of India and their nationalist successors. Both construct the history of India from Western categories that emphasize the state and imply that a part of the world with only a social history has no history. Consequently, a social history of India has had to be reinvented in recent times outside the nationalist framework of the state, especially in the highly influential series of *Subaltern Studies* (1982–). Historian Stephen Vlastos pursues in the Japanese context an issue raised in Eric. J. Hobsbawm and Terence Ranger's *The Invention of Tradition* (1983)— the dialectical relationship between tradition as cultural practice and modernization as cultural process. Vlastos examines the rhetorical construction of "village Japan" as an invented tradition within different strains of radical agrarian thought. Repulsed by certain features of both capitalism and socialism, one strand of that thought, embodied in the Aikyôkai, was appropriated to serve the conservative nationalism of the imperial state in the early 1930s. China historian Charles Hayford also looks at alternative narratives of rural life and finds both Marxists and American progressives depicting the Chinese "peasant" trapped in a medieval stage of development that derives from Western historical categories. The alternative story is found only in a romantic strain of twentieth-century writing on village China, notably in the works of Pearl Buck.

The third section focuses on the rhetorical uses of synthesis in social historical writing. Historian Ruth Crocker demonstrates how accounts of the history of Progressive Era settlement houses in America were shaped by a master narrative of Progressivism that remained dominant until the very recent past. Crocker's study challenges the very premises of synthesis and urges historians to draw on the "comparative and competitive storytelling" embedded in the multiple narratives of the settlement movement. Social historian Randolph Roth issues a similar call for greater tolerance of "disruptive" social history in his examination of the politics of the "call for synthesis" in American social history. The rhetoric of mediation, in his view, pervades the project of synthesis and threatens to "civilize" the discontent of the others.

These essays highlight a range of narrative possibilities available to historians who become self-conscious about the pervasive use of unexamined master narratives. They show how limited and constructed that tradition can be when compared with the diverse alternative narratives deriving from gendered traditions of nineteenth-century Latin American travel writers, or Victorian women's historical writing, or a vigorous "subaltern" tradition in Indian social history. The volume argues for neither the abandonment of historical materialism nor the elimination of all master narratives. It advocates instead a self-conscious and reflective reinvigoration of social history using alternative narratives to make rhetorical space for new and more persuasive arguments.

NOTES

1. Peter Novick, *That Noble Dream: The "Objectivity Question" and the American Historical Profession* (Cambridge: Cambridge University Press, 1988).

2. See "The Objectivity Question and the Future of the Historical Profession," AHR Forum: Peter Novick's *That Noble Dream, American Historical Review* 96, no. 3 (June 1991): 675–708.

3. Joyce Appleby, Lynn Hunt, and Margaret Jacob, *Telling the Truth about History* (New York: Norton, 1994), p. 254.

4. Alan B. Spitzer, *Historical Truth and Lies about the Past: Reflections on Dewey, Dreyfus, de Man, and Reagan* (Chapel Hill: University of North Carolina Press, 1996), p. 5. The "historical nihilists" that Spitzer identifies include Peter Novick, Dominick LaCapra, Joan Scott, Allan Megill, Frank Ankersmit, and Richard Rorty.

5. The declining optimism for the prospects of a new social history can be traced through a series of anthologies published in the 1960s, 1970s, and 1980s. See Stephan Thernstrom, ed., *Nineteenth-Century Cities: Essays in the New Urban History* (New Haven: Yale University Press, 1969); Michael Kammen, ed., *The Past before Us: Contemporary Historical Writing in the United States* (Ithaca: Cornell University Press, 1980); James Gardner, ed., *Ordinary People and Everyday Life: Perspectives on the New Social History* (Nashville: American Association for State and Local History, 1983); Olivier Zunz, ed., *Reliving the Past: The Worlds of Social History* (Chapel Hill: University of North Carolina Press, 1985); and Eric Foner, ed., *The New American History* (Philadelphia: Temple University Press, 1990). In *Telling the Truth about History*, chapters 4 and 5, Appleby, Hunt, and Jacobs place great stress on the diversification of American higher education and the demystification of scientific heroes as underlying causes for the loss of certainty in the profession.

6. Joan Scott broke important new ground with her essays gathered in *Gender and the Politics of History* (New York, 1988). But see also Joan Kelly, "The Doubled Vision of Feminist History," in *Women, History, and Theory: The Essays of Joan Kelly* (Chicago: University of Chicago Press, 1984); Linda K. Kerber, "Separate Spheres, Female Worlds, Woman's Place: The Rhetoric of Women's History," *Journal of American History* 75, no. 1 (June 1988): 9–39; Nancy Cott, "What's in a Name? The Limits of 'Social Feminism'; or Expanding the Vocabulary of Women's History," *Journal of American History* 76 (December 1989): 809–29; and Alice Kessler-Harris, "Treating the Male as Other: Redefining the Parameters of Labor History," *Labor History* 34 (Spring–Summer 1993): 190–204.

7. Herbert G. Gutman, "Whatever Happened to History? The Missing Synthesis," *Nation* (November 21, 1981): 553–54.

8. Eric Foner, "History in Crisis: The Fragmentation of Scholarship," *Commonweal* 18 (December 1981): 726.

9. Thomas Bender, "Wholes and Parts: The Need for Synthesis in American History," *Journal of American History* 73, no. 1 (June 1986): 127.

10. David Brody, "The Old Labor History and the New: In Search of an American Working Class," *Labor History* 20 (Winter 1979): 111–26.

11. Lawrence Levine, "The Unpredictable Past: Reflections on Recent American Historiography," AHR Forum: The Old History and the New, *American Historical Review* 94, no. 3 (1989): 674, 679.

12. MARHO, Henry Abelove et al., eds., *Visions of History* (New York, 1984), pp. ix, xi.

13. "It was not the Workshop nor the Left which showed the potency of history for contemporary politics, but Mrs. Thatcher, with her invocation of 'Victorian Values,' a cornerstone of her 1983 election campaign and a leitmotif of her rhetoric from the time she assumed leadership of the Conservative party"; Raphael Samuel

and Gareth Stedman Jones, "Editorial: Ten Years After," *History Workshop: A Journal of Socialist and Feminist Historians*, no. 20 (Autumn 1985): 2, 3.

14. See Eric Hobsbawm, Martin Jacques, and Francis Mulhern, eds., *The Forward March of Labour Halted?* (London: NLB in association with *Marxism Today*, 1981); Gareth Stedman Jones, *Languages of Class: Studies in English Working Class History, 1832–1982* (Cambridge: Cambridge University Press, 1983); cf. Jeffrey Cox, "Labor History and the Labor Movement," *Journal of British Studies* 25, no. 2 (April 1986): 233–41.

15. J. C. D. Clark, *English Society, 1688–1832: Ideology, Social Structure, and Political Practice during the Ancien Regime* (Cambridge: Cambridge University Press, 1985); John Brewer, *The Sinews of Power: War, Money, and the English State, 1688–1783* (London: Unwin Hyman, 1989); Linda Colley, *Britons: Forging the Nation, 1707–1837* (New Haven: Yale University Press, 1992); David Cannadine, *Aspects of Aristocracy: Grandeur and Decline in Modern Britain* (New Haven: Yale University Press, 1994).

16. *Dissent* (Summer 93): 377–81.

17. Bryan Palmer, *Descent into Discourse: The Reification of Language and the Writing of Social History* (Philadelphia: Temple University Press, 1990). See also the exchange between Palmer and Joan Scott in *International Labor and Working-Class History* 31 (1987): 1–13 and 32 (1987): 39–45; Gareth Stedman Jones's *Languages of Class* and Patrick Joyce's *Visions of the People: Industrial England and the Question of Class, 1848–1914* (Cambridge: Cambridge University Press, 1991) have set off an extensive debate with historical materialists on both sides of the Atlantic.

18. Mary Poovey, *Uneven Developments: The Ideological Work of Gender in Mid-Victorian England* (Chicago: University of Chicago Press, 1988); Lynn Hunt, *The Family Romance of the French Revolution* (Berkeley: University of California Press, 1992); Judith Walkowitz, *City of Dreadful Delight: Narratives of Sexual Danger in Late-Victorian London* (Chicago: University of Chicago Press, 1992); Lenard Berlanstein, ed., *Rethinking Labor History: Essays on Discourse and Class Analysis* (Urbana: University of Illinois Press, 1993); Antoinette Burton, *Burdens of History: British Feminists, Indian Women, and Imperial Culture, 1865–1915* (Chapel Hill: University of North Carolina Press, 1994).

19. Palmer, *Descent into Discourse*, p. 164.

20. Ira Katznelson, "The 'Bourgeois' Dimension: A Provocation about Institutions, Politics, and the Future of Labor History," ILWCH Roundtable: What Next for Labor and Working Class History? With responses by Lizabeth Cohen et al., *International Labor and Working-Class History* 46 (Fall 1994): 7–92 (Katznelson quote, p. 28); cf. the parallel views of Theda Skocpol in Peter Evans, Dietrich Rueschemeyer, and Theda Skocpol, eds., *Bringing the State Back In* (Cambridge: Cambridge University Press, 1993); and Skocpol, *Protecting Soldiers and Mothers: The Political Origins of Social Policy in the United States* (Cambridge: Harvard University Press, 1992).

21. Peter Mandler, "Taking the State Out Again: The Social History of Modern Britain," *Journal of Interdisciplinary History* 22, no. 3 (Winter 1992): 465–76.

22. *Economic History Review* 64, no. 4 (November 1991): 731, review of *The Cambridge Social History of Britain, 1750–1950*.

23. See especially Patrick Joyce, *Visions of the People: Industrial England and the Question of Class, 1848–1914* (Cambridge: Cambridge University Press, 1991).

24. F. M. L. Thompson, ed., *The Cambridge Social History of Britain, 1750–1950* (Cambridge: Cambridge University Press, 1990), 1:xiv, xii.

25. See, for instance, Martha Vicinus, *Independent Women: Work and Community for Single Women, 1850–1920* (Chicago: University of Chicago Press, 1985); Deborah Valenze, *Prophetic Sons and Daughters: Female Preaching and Popular Religion in Industrial England* (Princeton: Princeton University Press, 1985); Leonore Davidoff and Catherine Hall, *Family Fortunes: Men and Women of the English Middle Class 1780–1850* (London: Hutchinson, 1987). Similar tendencies are evident among feminist historians of the United States. See, for instance, Nancy Cott, *The Grounding of Modern Feminism* (New Haven: Yale University Press, 1987); Mary P. Ryan, *Women in Public: Between Banners and Ballots, 1825–1880* (Baltimore: Johns Hopkins University Press, 1990); Jean Boydston, *Home and Work: Housework, Wages, and the Ideology of Labor in the Early Republic* (New York: Oxford University Press, 1990); and Linda Gordon, *Heroes of Their Own Lives: The Politics and History of Family Violence, Boston, 1880–1960* (New York: Viking, 1988); and *Pitied But Not Entitled: Single Mothers and the History of Welfare* (New York: Free Press, 1994).

26. On point of view, see Jeffrey Cox, "Audience and Exclusion at the Margins of Imperial History," *Women's History Review* 3, no. 4 (1994): 501–14; Patricia Nelson Limerick, "Disorientation and Reorientation: The American Landscape Discovered from the West," *Journal of American History* 79, no. 3 (December 1992): 1021–49, especially 1023.

27. *New York Times Book Review*, July 11, 1993, p. 34.

28. The vertigo allusion is taken from *Telling the Truth about History*, p. 243, where the authors quote Clifford Geertz's comment on the "vertigo of relativism," from "The Impact of the Concept of Culture on the Concept of Man," in *The Interpretation of Cultures* (New York: Basic Books, 1973), p. 44.

29. For example, on the knowability of the past, see Appleby et al., *Telling the Truth about History*: "The archives in Lyon, France, are housed in an old convent on a hill overlooking the city. It is reached by walking up some three hundred stone steps. For the practical realist — even one equipped with a laptop computer — the climb is worth the effort; the relativist might not bother. . . . Historians carry their laptop computers up the three hundred stone steps in Lyon because records from the past are there. From that conviction of their knowability, knowledge grows" (pp. 269–70).

30. Edward W. Said, "Orientalism: An Afterword," *Raritan* 14 (Winter 1995): 32–59, 56.

31. On secularization and its alternatives, see Callum Brown, "A Revisionist Approach to Religious Change," in Steve Bruce, ed., *Religion and Modernization: Sociologists and Historians Debate the Secularization Thesis* (Oxford: Clarendon Press, 1992), pp. 31–58; Jeffrey Cox, "Master Narratives of Long Term Religious Change," in Hugh McLeod and Werner Ustorf, eds., *The Decline of Christendom in Western Europe, c. 1750–2000* (Maryknoll, N.Y.: Orbis Books, forthcoming).

32. *Subaltern Studies* 6 (1989): 4. In his rhetorical analysis of *Subaltern Studies*, Jim Masselos correctly observes: "The underlying conceptual contradictions — between the not-knowing of past realities and the timebound contemporary producers of history — are not resolved in the Subaltern Series volumes nor do they affect the various papers by lack of resolution"; "The Dis/appearance of Subalterns: A Reading of a Decade of *Subaltern Studies*," *South Asia* 15, no. 1 (1992): 105–25, 113.

33. His arguments were presented to the Workshop on the Rhetoric of Social History, Summer 1992, Iowa City, and later published as "Grand Narrative and the Discipline of History," in Frank Ankersmit and Hans Kellner, eds., *A New Philosophy of History* (Chicago: University of Chicago Press, 1995), pp. 151–73. In his formulation, a master narrative is a big story that makes smaller stories intelligible. Because it is a master narrative, it is often partly hidden, lying in the background, to be deployed selectively by the historian. For Megill, a master narrative is more limited than a "grand narrative," which is the "whole story" as told by the objective scientist, or by God. Dorothy Ross uses the phrase "grand narrative" in much the same sense that Megill uses "master narrative" in her "Grand Narrative in American Historical Writing: From Romance to Uncertainty," *American Historical Review* 100, no. 3 (1995): 651–77; Appleby, Hunt, and Jacob use the term "meta-narrative" in *Telling the Truth about History*, pp. 232–35. On the explanatory function of narrative, see Allan Megill, "Recounting the Past: 'Description,' Explanation, and Narrative in Historiography," *American Historical Review* 94, no. 3 (June 1989): 627–53.

Gender

BARBARA LASLETT

GENDER AND THE RHETORIC OF SOCIAL
SCIENCE: WILLIAM FIELDING OGBURN AND
EARLY TWENTIETH-CENTURY SOCIOLOGY
IN THE UNITED STATES

Recent debates in social history have pitted linguistic and rhe-torical analyses against political and class analyses (Scott 1987, 1988; Tilly, 1989). Yet it is of course the case that literary prac-tices involve more than language and rhetoric and that political and class analyses involve them both. These practices and analyses, however, do not take place in abstract time or space; they have a history that is both social and intellectual. They occur in particular historical settings under particular historical conditions. And some ways of doing history (or so-ciology or any other intellectual activity) — some ideas, presuppositions, assumptions, analytic techniques, and categories of thought — are more effectively reproduced than others because they are institutionalized in colleges, universities, and graduate training programs where new gener-ations of scholars learn their craft. Professional associations, peer review panels, funding agencies, prize committees, and academic publishers are also part of the institutional infrastructure that enhances the power of certain rhetorics, certain ways of doing research, certain ideas of what constitutes evidence, certain conceptual frameworks, to shape a field of inquiry. And these institutionalized habits help construct a canon that has rhetorical as well as substantive and methodological standards for professional behavior and professional rewards.[1]

Institutional standards, however, are not sustained without vigilance, without the efforts of social actors to maintain or change accepted in-tellectual practices within their fields. There is a question, then, about power and about action — about how institutional practices are con-structed and about the human agency that such constructions require. How does it happen, we can ask, that certain rhetorical forms and certain intellectual practices become the standards for other scholars to emulate and contest? How and why do certain methodologies come in and out of favor? How are the historically situated meanings of theoretical concepts, such as class, gender, and race, maintained or changed? How do meanings get canonized? And how is canonization contested? More succinctly, what are the fields of power relations that shape our intellectual practices? And what motivates the social actors whose actions produce those fields?[2]

This essay presents a partial answer to some of those questions for a particular discipline, time, and place — for American sociology in the first half of the twentieth century. It is also an effort at contestation, an effort to challenge the stories that have been told of the histories of the social sciences in the United States (see, for instance, Novick 1988 and Ross 1991). My story is about gender as well as class and politics, about sexuality as well as social interests. And the device I am using for this purpose is the life story of one white male sociologist who was particularly prominent during the 1920s, 1930s, and 1940s in the United States: William Fielding Ogburn, born in Butler, Georgia, in 1886.[3]

In presenting this argument, I have a theoretical as well as a historical goal: I want to use this occasion not simply to tell a new, or another, or even a better story about one person's life, nor is it to excavate some previously hidden elements of the historical record alone. I am using this occasion also to present some of the general ideas that have emerged for me in the course of investigating and writing about Ogburn's life and work. This propensity toward generality is more characteristic of sociologists than social historians. Indeed, as a sociologist, I would be uncomfortable if I were not "doing theory."[4] Historians, by contrast, are often uncomfortable if they are. Yet, of course, and despite disciplinary differences, we all "do theory" — although with different degress of explicitness, with different degress of self-consciousness, and with different expectations that we are (or are not) defying or complying with the intellectual norms of our fields. It is important to recognize, however, that just as empirical work is never done independently of some theoretical preconception, however implicit, theoretical work is never done independently of the historical case and context from which one's theorizing emerges. The argument that follows reflects my research on William Fielding Ogburn and the ideas about gender that have been highlighted to me in the course of doing it.

In his presidential address to the American Statistical Association in 1931, William Fielding Ogburn took as his theme the difference between statistics and art. His argument, articulated here and in a wide range of writings throughout his career, was that "statistics has been developed to give an exact picture of reality, while the picture that the artist draws is a distortion of reality" (Ogburn 1932, 1). He then went on to argue that emotion leads to distortion in our observations. "It is this distorting influence of emotion and wishes," he said, "that is more responsible for bad thinking than any lack of logic" (Ogburn 1932, 4). But statistics, he believed, could ameliorate the distorting effects of emotion on our empirical observations. There was a problem, however, because "the artist in us wants understanding rather than statistics. But understanding is hardly knowledge; . . . The tests of knowledge are reliability and accuracy, not understanding" (Ogburn 1932, 5).

This practice of creating categories of knowledge and behavior through differentiation, by drawing distinctions, by creating differences and distances, rather than, for instance, examining connections and commonalities, infused many of Ogburn's beliefs about the proper conduct of sociology and sociologists. In his presidential address to the American Sociology Society in 1929, he said, "Sociology as a science is not interested in making the world a better place in which to live, in encouraging beliefs, in spreading information, in dispensing news, in setting forth impressions of life, in leading the multitudes, or in guiding the ship of state. Science is interested directly in one thing only, to wit, discovering new knowledge." Scientific work involved careful and rigorous methods to establish proof and "in the scientific work of proof," he said, "of establishing real enduring knowledge, thinking must be free from the bias of emotion." Thus it was "necessary to crush out emotion and to discipline the mind so strongly that the fanciful pleasures of intellectuality will have to be eschewed in the verification process" (Ogburn 1930, 300–301, 302, 306).

These beliefs also extended to Ogburn's ideas about writing: in his view, scientific writing should be different from other writing. One of the new habits that would develop as sociology became more scientific, he believed, was "the writing of wholly colorless articles and the abandonment of the present habit of trying to make the results of science into literature. . . . Clarity and accuracy will be the only virtues of exposition. The expression of emotion will be bad form. The audience for these articles will be the scientific guild; and no attempt will be made to make these articles readable for shop girls or the high-school youth." But "this specialization in the exposition of science," he went on, "does not mean that there will be any diminution in the popularization of science." Indeed, "the scientist himself may engage in such types of writing; but if so it will be in the capacity of another self, not as the functioning of his scientific self" (Ogburn 1930, 301).

Ogburn took his wish to be one person when authoring a scientific article and another when writing for a more popular audience to considerable lengths: he tried to publish what he defined as different types of texts under different names. Only once, however, was he successful in this regard. In 1948 he published an article, "Long Trail Winding," under a pseudonym (Wynne 1948). In his private journal, however, he admitted that with this one exception, his efforts to use different names for different authorial purposes were unsuccessful and that the only reason he had been able to publish something under a pseudonym in this instance was because he knew the journal editor (Ogburn 1948b).

In this same journal entry, he wrote that his *Georgia Review* article was "a bit personal, and being a reserved person, I did not like to spread out my life for anyone to read" (Ogburn 1948b). Yet, in practice, the categories and concepts that William Wynne used to write about the South in which he had grown up were very similar to those William Fielding Ogburn used in his more "scientific" articles (see, for instance, Ogburn 1943, 1945). Although Ogburn wanted to differentiate types of knowledge and ways of knowing from each other, even he, it seems, with all his conscious commitment to such an enterprise, found it difficult to put his ideas into practice.

Ogburn's beliefs about science and emotion also shaped his standards for proper professional behavior. In his journal, he articulated again and again his disappointment with colleagues for their display of emotion, for insufficient control of their feelings. He approvingly described a meeting of the Census Committee on Demography in 1948 in the following way:

> One of the most enjoyable meetings I have ever attended. . . . curiously there was no emotion discernible on the surface or underneath. . . . I hate discussions . . . which are supposed to be scientific, that become emotional. For emotion and science do not go together, to my way of thinking. . . . Emotion is alright in its place, which is

often to move people. But good thinking is not to move people. (Ogburn 1948a)

Ogburn was engaged in a range of activities in which he tried to shape standards for the practice of sociology. In his academic work, he was particularly interested in the study of social change and was an advocate of the use of quantitative techniques in sociological research. He was also an adviser to the federal government, particularly during the presidencies of Herbert Hoover (1929–33) and Franklin Delano Roosevelt (1933–44). He explained the problem that maintaining the dichotomy between emotion and science posed for him, and his solution to it, in his retirement address at the University of Chicago in 1951. He said, "In many trips to Washington, around the White House, the Department of the Interior, or the Department of Commerce, I never considered my advice was scientific. Though I made use of what scientific knowledge I possessed, I could see that science was not the same as wisdom, nor as understanding" (Ogburn 1951).

Ogburn recognized that maintaining these distinctions in writing, in research, in professional demeanor, was not automatic. "There was still," he said, "a problem for me personally . . . I [did not] want to have the 'integrated mind' where science and intellect are mixed together like scrambled eggs. . . . The key to the solution I worked out for myself . . . I turned with admiration to the schizophrene!" (Ogburn 1951). For William Fielding Ogburn, schizophrenia was not an illness but a strategy that made it possible for him to meet his self-defined standards for proper professional behavior and proper scientific detachment.[5]

Ogburn's use of a psychological rhetoric to explain his behavior reflected his knowledge of and interest in psychoanalytic theory. He lectured on Freud to his students as early as 1915, and in 1919, while in Washington, D.C., he underwent psychoanalysis. He was, nevertheless, troubled by ulcers all his life. Perhaps his efforts to keep parts of his life separate from each other were no easier than his efforts to keep his writing styles distinct. But throughout his career he acted on the conviction that they should be. Given his institutional locations and professional prominence, his standards for the proper conduct of scientific sociology contributed to the development of a new type of professional culture and a new type of scientific rhetoric — one in which science was distanced from politics and from emotion. In the discussion that follows, I argue that these changes had both gendered causes and gendering consequences for the social sciences in twentieth-century America[6] and that gender as a theoretical concept, one that is attentive to historically variable material — political, cultural, psychological, and sexual relationships, not just demographic ones — can contribute to our understanding of general historical processes.

To some — especially, perhaps, a readership attuned to a rhetorical analysis of social history and social science — Ogburn's beliefs about emotion and science will appear familiar, if dated. The use of statistics to control emotional "bias," defining reliability and generalizability in ways that erase the historical constructedness of their meanings, seeing objectivity in essentially technical terms, are all examples of the Ogburnian vision.[7] It is important to note, however, that these criteria reflect as well as create power relations within and beyond intellectual institutions. In many quarters — in my field at least — they represent a still-dominant view of what constitutes good social scientific practice. And the continued persuasiveness of this approach to social inquiry reflects the power of institutions — graduate programs, professional journals, peer review boards, granting agencies, and so on — and the people who run them to perpetuate often unconscious rhetorical styles and often unexamined philosophies of knowledge. Yet the hegemony of a given approach is always fragile. Indeed, this process can be observed in my own professional history and in my choice of William Fielding Ogburn as a subject for research.

Although I never met him, I was socialized into the discipline of sociology at the University of Chicago, where Ogburn spent many years of his career and left his imprint on the faculty and graduate program. My thesis supervisor, the late Robert W. Hodge, was trained by one of Ogburn's most famous and faithful students, Otis Dudley Duncan. Hodge was, therefore, an Ogburn "grandchild" and I was a "great-grandchild"; the language of kinship was actually used to describe relations between the generations of students that each man worked with. It was, perhaps, because I was an attentive student that when I began to question the positivist tenets with which I had been raised, Ogburn should come to mind as one of the most ardent proponents of those tenets in the history of American sociology. As his ideas about sociology suggest, however, my choice was based on more than personal history.

The question with which I began my research was how to understand the development of an objectivist, scientistic, quantitative sociology in the interwar period in the United States. Frankly, I don't remember why I decided to use a biographical research design to answer this question. It is a rather unusual undertaking for a sociologist. It took me a long time to realize that my attraction to an individual life story reflected my wish to understand how people construct their own life stories within the constraints of particular social locations.[8] For reasons that reflect my own life history (Laslett 1997), I articulated these concerns in political terms and have had a long-standing commitment to learning how human action could construct a more equitable society. The legitimacy of my political commitments as part of my attraction to sociology came under attack in the course of a professional socialization shaped by Ogburnian standards. It was only with the political movements of the 1960s and 1970s, especially the civil rights, antiwar, and women's movements, and the intellectual developments that grew out of them, that I began to question the Ogburnian "schizophrenia" that had shaped my scholarship.

It is doubtful, however, that my attention to the significance of gender would have developed as it has were it not for the feminist scholarship that emerged out of the women's movement in the United States and elsewhere over the past thirty years. Thus, just as an audience receptive to scientism in the social sciences was consequential for institutionalizing the professional practices and rhetorical style that Ogburn espoused, and an audience for analyses of the rhetoric of inquiry is consequential for the fortunes of this volume, so feminism in academia and the scholarship it has fostered is consequential for the argument I am developing here. It helped me to see new dynamics and new dimensions of social science discourse that had not previously been discussed to any large extent.

The answer I expected when I began my research about why scientism emerged in American sociology when and how it did focused on the expanded demand for social scientists by government agencies, especially from World War I through the New Deal, and on the actions of social scientists who might have benefited from these opportunities. These were the social interests, I believed, that shaped how and what sociological knowledge was pursued. And they could be seen in Ogburn's life history. Having moved from Reed College, where he had his first regular academic appointment (1912–17) to the University of Washington, he left Seattle early in 1918 to accept a position as examiner and head of the

Cost-of-Living Department of the War Labor Board and then, briefly, at the Bureau of Labor Statistics, in Washington, D.C., where he remained until 1919. Ogburn's time in Washington was highly productive and brought him considerable professional rewards. Mrs. Ogburn described that time in their lives to her sons: "He [WFO] wrote in the year and a half he was in Washington seventeen articles which were published. These articles brought him recognition which led to his being offered professorships in the East" (R. R. Ogburn 1955, 38). In 1919, W. F. Ogburn joined the faculty of Barnard College/Columbia University, a move that had major consequences for his career trajectory.[9]

Central to the growth of government interest in the social sciences was a faith that such knowledge could solve social problems, a faith that had grown out of the mid-nineteenth century in the United States (Haskell 1977, 1984), with an increasing emphasis on planning in the twentieth century (Karl 1969, 1983). But meeting the increased demand for social scientists in government also reflected the changing structure of the occupational opportunities available to American men as the economy moved away from its agrarian past and into a more industrial, urban, and capitalist future.

For men aspiring to middle-class status, the occupations and professions that had traditionally undergirded their social position — farming, small business, law, medicine, the clergy — were in flux. Salaried work was increasingly replacing self-employment, and some professions, such as the clergy, were declining in status while others, such as medicine, were raising standards and limiting entry (Starr 1982, ch. 3; Morantz-Sanchez 1985). The expansion of state activities and political institutions after the Civil War, but particularly after World War I, opened new occupational opportunities for social scientists within state and federal government in the growing array of data-gathering bodies, such as the Bureau of Labor Statistics and the Census Bureau. And these developments have been central to the economic and political interpretations in recent histories of the social sciences (Ross 1991; Turner and Turner 1990), to recent work in the sociology of scientific knowledge,[10] and to recent interpretations of social scientists' involvement in the rise of state welfare provisions in the United States and elsewhere (Amenta and Carruthers 1988; Orloff 1992; Weir, Orloff, and Skocpol 1988; Skocpol 1992).

While the expanded demand for social scientists in government reflected changes in the political arena, the demand alone did not determine how knowledge was to be gathered or what form it would take. Although inheriting certain intellectual traditions and rhetorics about science from earlier discourses, the mostly white, male social scientists of the post–World War I period were key actors in defining the demand that they were then able to fill. But while I continue to believe that class and political explanations of social science history are centrally important, I now see them as incomplete.

The conclusion I drew about why scientism in American sociology emerged how and when it did was this: however much political developments, professional aspirations, and material interests had affected the history of sociological ideas and practices, gender relations, sexuality, and personal life were also key dimensions of that history. In my study of Ogburn's life story I came to see that the development of scientism in the social sciences in the early decades of the twentieth century was connected to the gendered character of social organization in the nineteenth. Of particular importance was the organization of family, economic, and political life around the rhetoric and practice of separate spheres during the earlier time period and its reorganization early in the twentieth century.

Much has been written about the doctrine of separate spheres in nineteenth-century America that created a social distinction between personal and private life on the one hand and public life on the other. Especially important in this organization was the gendering of these newly dichotomized domains — with the family coded as female and commerce and public life coded as male.[11] Yet in practice, both women and men were active in nineteenth-century social reform and social science (Leach 1989; Sklar 1991; Gordon 1994). Under these conditions, to construct the modern social sciences in objectivist terms was to gender them in ways that fostered and reflected new definitions of middle-class white masculinity, ones that emphasized emotional distance and control.

At the same time, new definitions of middle-class white femininity were also being constructed — ones that on the one hand recognized the increasing participation of these women in wage work and public life and on the other created new beliefs about their sexuality. "New womanhood," for the twentieth century, in contrast to "true womanhood" of the nineteenth, was being constructed by women searching for ways to participate in the modern world.[12] Rather than arguing that their domestic and moral virtues were appropriately attached to the home, they stressed the importance of women's involvement in the public world of wage work and public life — in women's clubs, mothers' groups, and political reform organizations. Rather than an emphasis on women's passionlessness (Cott 1979), as had been characteristic of the mid-nineteenth-century ideal of womanhood, in the early twentieth century, women's sexual desire was increasingly viewed as central to intimacy within heterosexual, monogamous, and more egalitarian marriage (Seidman 1991). Once women's sexuality was socially recognized, however, it could not be as successfully controlled or as successfully limited to heterosexuality.

John D'Emilio (1983) has argued that the development of male homosexuality as a social identity was associated with the rise of capitalism and the growth of an impersonal labor market. He contends that the increasing access to material resources outside the heterosexual, patriarchal family made it possible for some men to create institutions that constructed their sexual preferences for other men as a social category. A similar dynamic can be seen for women, particularly in the scholarship on the involvement of white middle-class women in social reform and the settlement house movement at the turn of the century (Faderman 1991, ch. 1).

Considerable debate exists about whether the "romantic friendships" between many middle-class white women in the nineteenth century were actually erotic. A less-contested issue is whether the changing educational and occupational opportunities for white working- and middle-class women at this point in time — the expansion of coeducational secondary education and the opening of women's colleges, the expansion of white-collar jobs that middle-class women could fill and to which working-class women could aspire — made it possible for women to live personal lives relatively more free from patriarchal control and authority than had been the case for earlier generations of women. In general, as the nineteenth century turned into the twentieth, women, through either inheritance, higher education, or their own labor, had more access to the resources necessary to create alternatives to heterosexual marriage and the patriarchal family. And their choices — choices that found institutional support in women's colleges, in settlement houses, and in the emerging professional associations among, for instance, teachers and home economists, as well as in women's clubs and reform groups[13] — could (and did) include intimate relationships built on homosocial and homosexual intimacies (Cott 1987; Faderman 1981, 1991; Smith-Rosenberg 1985; D'Emilio and Freedman 1988).

Not all women were drawn to the emerging social sciences for the same reasons, however. In particular, not all of them were drawn to the maternalism and social reform or to the communities of women on which much of this work depended.[14] The life and work of sociologist-turned-anthropologist Elsie Clews Parsons, who received a Ph.D. in sociology (from Columbia) in 1899, provides an example of a different personal as well as professional trajectory, one that also reflects the changing norms and attitudes about the family and sexuality (Deacon 1992, 1997a, 1997b). In Parsons's case, anthropology — particularly field-work—made it possible for her to detach herself from the conventional social world in which she normally lived. As an anthropologist, she was able to explore both intellectually and experientially alternatives to socially acceptable views of marriage and sexuality for women of her race and class, although her own relationships remained heterosexual. One dimension, then, of women's participation in the professionalizing social sciences was as part of a search for alternatives to the accepted norms of separate spheres and passionlessness that had shaped the lives of white middle-class women. Women's search for a new kind of inti-macy — sexual and emotional — was thus also part of the turn-of-the-century reorganization of American society.

At the same time, institutional supports for nineteenth-century defi-nitions of masculinity were also being eroded. The nineteenth-century doctrine of separate spheres articulated the normative basis of white middle-class gender relations for both sexes — men were to be family breadwinners first and foremost, while women were to be homemakers, rearers of children, and the moral force within the family and the soci-ety. But putting this doctrine into practice, even among white middle-class families, where it might be possible to maintain a separation — normative and spatial — between private and public lives, raised new problems, especially for the men. In the family economy and through apprenticeships, it was the fathers, neighbors, employers who had, in the course of their daily lives, been responsible for teaching boys how to be men. But adult men were increasingly pursuing their occupational and professional lives away from the home while childrearing, now defined as the responsibility of women, was increasingly taking place within it. Under these circumstances, how was an appropriate gender identity to be achieved by white middle-class young men who were expected to take their place as leaders in the social order of nineteenth-century America? How were American boys to learn how to be men if their mothers and female teachers were their primary sources of instruction? Models for achieving a socially approved gender identity were no longer as directly available to American boys. Rather, the process was increasingly mediated through gender relations, gender norms, and gender possibilities, all of which were in the process of transformation.

As the earlier discussion has already suggested, being the family breadwinner became problematic for middle-class American men over the course of the nineteenth century. The changing occupational opportunities — the decline of small businesses and family farms, the expansion of salaried and bureaucratic occupations such as clerks and salespersons — meant that the value of a son's status inheritance from his father was less secure. This was especially the case for the sons of small businessmen — as Ogburn was — and for sons of previously high-status professionals — such as clergymen — whose social standing was also in jeopardy.[15] In this context, becoming a professor was a good choice — the job paid relatively high salaries (for historians, see Novick 1988, 50, 170) and was believed to confer high social status (Novick 1988, 22–24; Ross 1978). Given a new definition of manhood that emphasized employment and breadwinning rather than, for instance, moral leadership, as had been the case earlier (Demos 1986), occupations took on a new meaning, one that was infused with the problematic of achieving a positive masculine identity under changing historical conditions. The new forms of gender relations as well as economic conditions within which men like William Fielding Ogburn were growing up were, I believe, crucial to the growth of scientism in American sociology, to when and why it emerged as it did (see Bederman 1995 also in relation to race).

In addition to his academic work and his activities as a government adviser, Ogburn was also active in psychoanalytic circles in Chicago after he joined the faculty at the university in 1927. He was a member of the original board of trustees of the Institute for Psychoanalysis in Chicago, founded by Franz Alexander in 1932, and he was president of the board of trustees of the institute from 1942 to 1947. Perhaps Ogburn's commitment to psychoanalytic categories was part of what led him to explain his dedication to objectivity in the following terms: "My father, planter and merchant, died in 1890 when I was four. Then began my long struggle to resist a dear mother's beautiful but excessive love. To the successful outcome, I attribute my strong devotion to objective reality,

[and] an antipathy to the distorting influence of emotion." [16] Family relations, Ogburn tells us, were connected to his intellectual commitments — whether in precisely the way he analyzes them or not. [17]

Through Ogburn's own insights, I came to view his analysis of his intellectual interests, and the energy with which he pursued them, as having general implications for understanding the history of the social sciences and the rhetoric through which that history has been expressed.
First, I began to understand the individual characteristics used to define
an actor's social location — most often occupation, education, profession, and status — as unnecessarily limited to socioeconomic attributes.
Occupational success was becoming more central to a man's gender
identity, while the opportunities for achieving such success were being
reorganized. At the same time, women were becoming increasingly involved in both political activity and wage work outside the domestic
sphere — previously the primary domain of men — and the social definition of femininity was also being recast. Yet these changes in gender relations have gone largely unnoticed in most recent histories of the social
sciences as they became professionalized early in the twentieth century
(Novick 1988; Ross 1991).

Second, the same, limited, components of social location — social
class and social status — have also been used to identify the interests
that motivate individual action. Gender interests — the interests of male
social scientists as men — have not been recognized as pertinent to explaining their behavior nor have changing gender relations been seen as
relevant to the meanings of class and status that were developing. Given
the differences between men and women social scientists of the time,
however (Bannister 1987; Deegan 1988; Fitzpatrick 1990; Gordon 1992),
being inattentive to gender relations misses an important component of
social science history in the United States.

And, third, the psychological and cultural dynamics that shape the
definition and recognition of "interests" have received little or no examination in the social science literature. How are the motivations and
intentions of social actors formed and fueled? How do the emotional
and psychosexual dimensions of human development, historically variable though they are, become attached to institutional activism and intellectual advocacy? As a result of inattention to questions such as these,
the development and relevance of a gendered subjectivity and/or identity have not been thought germane to an explanation of intellectual

changes in the construction of social science knowledge. My Ogburn research provided me with an important theoretical insight that, I believe,
helps answer such questions.

There was a gender dimension to the rise of scientism in American sociology for the mostly middle-class white men who were key social actors in its history. Women's construction of new forms of intimacy and
new types of relationships, public and private, emotional and erotic, and
men's construction of a new culture of heterosexual masculinity within
academia were both part of the gendered history of the social sciences in
the United States. Despite Ogburn's personal efforts to separate emotion
from science, and despite the rhetoric he fostered insisting that such a
separation was both possible and desirable, his own biography demonstrates the contrary. Emotion not only fueled Ogburn's advocacy but can
also help explain it.

There are, I think, at least two sociological reasons for Ogburn's commitments to the differentiation of science and emotion that he espoused.
Constructing different affective norms for work and family — for it must
be recognized that the coolness Ogburn preferred for his work environment is as much an emotional tone as are the more passionate emotions
that he criticized — might help to protect private life and the private self
from the rationalization that increasingly defined the culture and organization of American society. Thus, his relations with wife and children,
with extended family members, with his southern personal history,
about which he felt strongly, could be shielded from public scrutiny and
the demands for consistency that might accompany it. At the same time,
coolness as an emotional quality could help to create a work environment that supported the newly emerging definitions of masculinity and
professional success.

These conclusions suggest that sex, gender, and emotion as theoretical concepts have to be conceptualized in more complex, nuanced, and
historically variable terms. First, the gendered division of labor has
been a basic dimension of social structure, and the social assignment of
some tasks to women and others to men is one determinant of how and
why people do what they do. Under such social conditions, action is
likely to be gendered — that is, to be culturally and demographically defined as female or male, feminine or masculine. But both sexuality and
gender relations are social categories that have historically variable meanings and referents. Changes, and continuities under changed conditions,

in gendered activities and relationships from the nineteenth and into the twentieth century affected what women and men did, what they thought, and how they related to each other. This is part, I believe, of what led the Ogburnian generation to institutionalize particular discourses, practices, and rhetorics that have shaped intellectual practices. They have also encoded a set of dichotomized categories of thought that simplify social relationships and social possibilities.

Efforts to professionalize and institutionalize the study of society in the research universities after World War I in the United States led to the construction of a masculine rhetoric. I would argue that this did not necessarily happen because rationality and coolness are essentially masculine traits — indeed, perhaps it is precisely because they are not that the search for social supports for such traits was particularly strong. The rhetoric was "masculine" because its construction reflected the efforts by some male social scientists to construct a professional sphere that would buttress their identities as men. It is important to note, however, that defining scientific sociology as Ogburn (and others like him) did was neither automatic nor uncontested (see Laslett 1990; Bulmer 1984; Bannister 1987). Successful institutionalization of the rhetoric was also a matter of power — of the capacity of some men to impose their definitions of knowledge upon others. For the first generation of professionalizing social scientists in the United States, university administrators — usually white, usually male, working to establish the legitimacy of their newly established institutions — were willing allies.

Second, sex and gender are related to personal life in particular ways. Family relationships, sexual meanings, and sexuality itself can provide powerful motives for human actions, and gender relations are central to understanding those motives. Furthermore, sexual energy and emotional meaning can be attached to social phenomena in ways that are not obviously related to sexuality or gender. And the sexual nature of that energy gives some actions, but not others, a particular charge, a particular emotional power. For instance, while an occupational activity has no intrinsic connection to masculinity or femininity, it can take on such meaning under given historical circumstances — a dynamic that can be widely seen historically (Davidoff and Hall 1987; Rose 1991; Baron 1991) and in the contemporary world (Cohn 1996).

Third, gendered meanings — particularly, I think, in modern times the task of achieving gender identity, of achieving a satisfactory sense of masculinity or femininity — are often part of, if not central to, social institutions, cultural forms, and intellectual categories (see, for instance, Cohn 1996; Martin 1996; Sperling 1996). But the historical conditions under which these meanings and identities are constructed change. Economic and political transformations as well as the reorganization of sexuality and the family in late nineteenth- and early twentieth-century America — not the least of which were the continuing efforts of some middle-class women to reduce patriarchal control over their lives — may have created particularly ambiguous conditions for men. This was, indeed, one of the conclusions I drew from my research on William Fielding Ogburn.

Histories of higher education (Vesey 1965) and of the policy sciences during this period — economics, political science, sociology — in late nineteenth- and early twentieth-century America (Ross 1991; Bannister 1987; Furner 1975; Haskell 1984) make it clear that to achieve legitimacy as university subjects, the newly academic social sciences had to be separated from the social reform and political issues that had motivated the earlier interest in them. Ogburn's life story illustrates this process.

An early interest in social problems with which Ogburn entered graduate school was sustained by institutional pressure to be active in social reform while he was a faculty member at Reed College in Portland, Oregon, between 1912 and 1917. But by the time he assumed his position at Barnard College/Columbia University in 1919, he had rejected that involvement in favor of building professionalism and scientism in sociology (Laslett 1990). In connection with the efforts by men like Ogburn to separate social science from social reform, women's interest in the social sciences created a problem.

Middle-class American women had become active in social reform and social science, first through traditions of charity work, religion, and abolition (see, among others, Leach 1989, ch. 11; Ryan 1981). Legitimacy for their public involvements was often sought in the nineteenth-century doctrine about women's special capacities for morality and nurturance (Laslett and Brenner 1989). Under such conditions, it is unlikely that women would have abandoned their interests in social reform and social science as readily as men did; social reform activities were quite consistent with one reading of the womanly virtues emphasized in the ideology of separate spheres, making it possible for women to become public figures, to participate in the great social changes that were occurring around them (Sklar 1991). In this sense, women's gender interests were served by their social reform activities. This was not the case for men, however. For white male social scientists to continue their involvement in social reform was contrary to their interest in developing academic careers. Again, Ogburn's case is instructive.

At his University of Chicago retirement dinner, Ogburn talked about the reasons for moving away from the reform activities in which he had been engaged while on the faculty of Reed College. Thinking back to his civic involvements while in Oregon, he said,

> I realized that my activities off campus were not those of a scientist. I was using such science as I knew . . . but I was behaving merely as a citizen. A scientist *qua* scientist must necessarily be ineffective in social action. . . . Then, I was never sure that it was fair to my employer, the university, to be active in social movements. . . . Sooner to later . . . this activity in social movements is likely to get the university in disfavor with a substantial portion of the public, with the trustees, with potential donors or with some of the faculty unless the activity is for universally approved goals. . . . Most issues and movements are controversial.[18] (Ogburn 1951)

He spoke about his hesitancy further in a 1959 letter written to the historian of Reed College:

> My irritation at Reed mainly centered upon two points. One was the tremendous pressure I felt on me to teach, to see students, to take part in city affairs. The second irritation turned on the fact that . . . I had very little time for research or for keeping up with the scientific literature in my field. . . . I was also young, but with a growing family and family expenses and trying to live on a meager salary. I didn't like the fear that I might get pocketed at Reed and receive no calls from other colleges or universities. (Ogburn 1959)

Under these conditions — social, political, and personal — professionalizing the social sciences in late nineteenth- and early twentieth-century America had a gendered meaning as well as a political one: it was connected to the gendered subjectivity of the mostly white male social scientists who were its supporters.[19] Ogburn's advocacy of a professional culture and scientific practice characterized by cool rationality and "unfeeling knowledge" — a knowledge separate from emotion, from politics, from social action — was part of that project.

Linda Gordon's (1992) work on U.S. welfare history between 1890 and 1935 provides further evidence for the gendered nature of social science discourse at this point in time. While insisting that this discourse was not dichotomized between women and men — that there were similarities as well as differences, class and race differences being particularly important[20] — she argues that reformers had recognizably gendered visions of welfare in the United States. Women were demonstrably more concerned with poverty and with individual needs, while men were more concerned with rights and social insurance. And the rhetoric of each group reflected these differences. The social work approach to poverty, found primarily among women,

> used narrative and cited actual cases far more often than the social insurance advocates did. . . . By contrast, the social insurance rhetoric was more often abstract. . . . Writers spoke the language of actuarial computation and administration and argued from a logic that assumed profit motives as the only motives. . . . Altruism was not only absent but was implicitly denied force as a social motive. (Gordon 1992, 30–31)

But altruism was one of the justifications for women's involvement in social reform, and it was women who most often brought needs talk into political debate.

Dorothy Smith (1987, 1990) provides a useful theoretical framework for understanding these gender differences in discourses and rhetorics.[21] She emphasizes women's location in the everyday/everynight worlds of family, neighborhood, and community. That location, she argues, provides a different experiential basis for knowledge of the social world than was available to the mostly middle-class white male social scientists active during the time period under consideration here. Their actions and identities, in contrast to those of women, were embedded in bureaucratic hierarchies and in a scientific culture that encouraged aloofness and distance. As a consequence, social science rhetoric and social science knowledge became relentlessly abstract, and that abstraction has been claimed as one hallmark of its scientific credentials. Gordon's historical research (1992) and Smith's theoretical framework (1987, 1990) also suggest that the capacity of professional men to define abstraction as part of scientific practice reflects their position and power at the top of two hierarchies of labor performed by others — one at work, the other at home.

It should be noted that advocacy of scientism in sociology or objectivism in history by such men as Ogburn — and he was certainly not alone in espousing such ideas — was not the unique invention of those men. New ideas about science — establishing its meaning and practice in terms of a set of dichotomous categories that counterposed fact and value, objectivity and subjectivity, rigor and intuition, male and female (McCloskey 1985, 42) — had been in place in some form or other since at least the eighteenth century. Just as women social reformers used the rhetoric of the special responsibilities and moral qualities of women to buttress their claims to a rightful place in the public world of late nineteenth- and early twentieth-century America, the concrete response of men like Ogburn to the historical changes surrounding them was not to invent distinctions but rather to use already existing ideas to break the connection between social science and social reform and to institutionalize this separation in professional and academic life. And their power to do so had distinctly gendered causes and distinctly gendering consequences.

As my understanding of the theoretical implications of Ogburn's biography grew, I came to see not only how the organization and culture of gender relations during his lifetime were related to the development of scientism in American sociology but also how they were related to a theory of human agency. The development of scientism in sociology can be seen, in part, as a construction by men of a cultural domain in their professional lives to which they could aspire without threat to their masculinity; it also provided a basis for gatekeeping, for limiting the entry of women into the profession. Given beliefs about women's special empathetic, maternal, and moral qualities and responsibilities, a scientific culture that emphasized "unfeeling knowledge" and "cool rationality" — such as Ogburn advocated — was less likely to attract or welcome women participants. It reflected men's gendered subjectivity — their *feelings* about themselves as men — and, perhaps, their interest in reducing competition from women, as well. The creation of this masculinist culture can reasonably be seen, I believe, as a reaction to the challenge — emotional, economic, and cultural — that the increasing public involvement of middle-class women in the worlds of social reform, wage work, and higher education posed to the concept of public sphere as men's domain. It reflected the "fears of feminization" that were widespread in schools and colleges in late nineteenth- and early twentieth-century

America. It was also connected to the status- and institution-building concerns of male educators in the new universities.

By the beginning of the twentieth century, middle-class women were increasingly flocking to institutions of higher learning. At the University of Chicago, women were present in especially large numbers, and there were fears that the seeming "feminization" of the university would undermine its search for authority and legitimacy as a new institution in the field of higher education (Rosenberg 1982, esp. ch. 2; Fitzpatrick 1990, 84). There was particular contention over the issue of sex-segregated education, resulting in institutional differentiation between academic sociology, practiced primarily by men, and reform-oriented sociology (or social work), practiced particularly by women, a separation that limited the social science work in which women could engage (Deegan 1988).

The social sciences were becoming gendered in ways that affected the opportunities open to women and men. But it was a two-sided development. While some professional activities were coded as masculine, others — social work and home economics, for instance — were defined as acceptable professions for women. As limiting as these constraints may have been, they also opened up new possibilities for women in their personal as well as their professional lives. They made it possible for highly educated women to use their educational and occupational opportunities to build intimate relationships outside of the control of the patriarchal, heterosexual family. For highly trained and engaged professional women, whose work provided a salary and connected them to the feminized world of social reform and settlement houses, the most significant emotional relationships and attachments were more likely to be with same-sex partners. This was not true for men.[22]

As this interpretation suggests, I do not believe that the emergence of a scientistic culture among American social scientists at this point in time can be adequately explained by economic or political factors — or by "rational" actors' "interests" — alone. While the impact of changes in political and professional life have been widely recognized in research on this topic, the impact of gender relations and sexuality has not been acknowledged. Yet constructing scientific practice in the social sciences in terms of hard fact and cool rationality was a response to changing gender relations as well as changing occupational opportunities and political forces at the turn of the century in the United States.

The realization that gender and family relationships might help explain intellectual developments in the social sciences in ways that have been relatively unexplored had another implication for me as well. My research on William Fielding Ogburn left me convinced that an analysis that includes the study of gender relations can contribute to an understanding of the process of "structuring"— a concept developed by the historical sociologist Philip Abrams. According to Abrams, "structuring" involves the recognition that "history and society are made by constant and more or less purposeful individual actions *and* that individual action, however purposeful, is made by history and society" (Abrams 1982, xiii).

In my view, gender as a theoretical concept has an important contribution to make to our analysis of structuring. First, the idea that sexuality, gender, and a gendered identity are accomplishments — something that people construct over their life course rather than some inborn essence that unfolds with age — allows for an examination of historical variability in all three and thus has the potential for explaining social change as well as reflecting it.

Second, while a gendered division of labor has been a basic dimension of social structure and is one determinant of how and why people act as they do, it has also been historically variable. Women's increasing responsibility for childrearing and the family's increasing responsibility for social morality in nineteenth-century America gave women both reasons and legitimacy to move beyond the domestic sphere. Women's and men's positions in the social division of labor also affected their conceptions of social problems — in terms of needs versus rights — and the rhetorics through which they were expressed. And for some women, dependence on the male wage and the patriarchal family changed as they increasingly had access to higher education and places in the paid labor force. In addition, for some of the women involved in social science and social reform, the new opportunities for autonomy made it possible to create erotic and emotional intimacies outside of the heterosexual, patriarchal family.

And third, gendered meanings are often attached to institutional cultures — to the emotional qualities of professional life and professional relationships. But these cultures do not emerge accidentally, nor do they follow from some inner logic of intellectual goals or institutional structures. They are the result of conscious action that fosters their growth, and they require an investment of time and energy to accomplish. Ogburn's life story is replete with his efforts to keep his immediately professional environment "cool," the emotional quality that he found most comfortable (Laslett 1990, 1991b). But his efforts also met resistance, and some of them were more successful than others.[23]

Convinced though I am that my interpretation of Ogburn's life makes sense for the time and place in which he lived, the general theoretical approach has much broader implications. We need to problematize the separation between the public and private domains that has been central to so many professional and personal histories. Yet this has been extremely rare in historical accounts of social science history. Peter Novick's work (1988) on the American historical profession suggests one possible explanation. Novick examines, among other topics, the controversy among historians over interpretations of who was responsible for World War I. In the heat of the debate, personalities were invoked and name-calling indulged — Anglophilia, Germanophobia, career opportunism — a practice that was severely criticized by other historians. One commentator on this dispute put his criticism this way:

> If we indulge in personalities it will not only create an unpleasant atmosphere but will damage cool and scientific research. . . . I esteem the question of . . . complexes and motivations of very slight importance and irrelevant to the question of war guilt. Provide the truth of your assertions objectively without going into the problem of what warps . . . judgment of the facts. . . . The truth or falsity of a historical thesis can be and should be settled by appeal to evidence alone. (Novick 1988, 218)

In some ways this emphasis on evidence, objectivity, and coolness is worthy and has afforded some protection for disdained groups and oppositional positions. Unpopular positions, when supported by such evidence, have a better chance of being heard than do ones without such support. But Ogburnian standards of social science inquiry also have potentially limiting consequences for understanding how social actors construct, advocate, and criticize what is called "evidence." The call for more systematic, more "objective," evidence needs to be recognized as a rhetorical strategy used in the process of professional and intellectual contestation *as well as* a reflection of different techniques of inquiry and different qualities of scholarly performance. Furthermore, this rhetoric is more than strategic, it often reflects the strong feelings of participants in academic debate. It is ill-advised, in my view, for social historians (or sociologists) to ignore the affective dimensions of social action — whether in relation to their own scholarship or in relation to their criticism of others. Perhaps more germane is to ask why and when this dictum to eschew the personal and the emotional is successful and when it is not. The irony of efforts to exclude emotion and personal intentions from the analysis of professional practices among scholars is that the commitment to that exclusion has to be explained. But the power to insist that such an explanation is relevant is not only "scientific," it is also political.

There is an emotional component — what German sociologist and historian of sociology in Western Europe Wolf Lepenies (1988) has called a "culture of feeling" — to our professional norms and practices. The "coolness" of tone, the very definition of attention to individual intentions and personal motives as "unprofessional," the insistence that we eschew emotion, all limit our ability to see how (and whether) the organization and culture of personal life affects intellectual work and scientific discourse. And to the extent that sexual identity and a gendered subjectivity are linked to strong feelings, such limitations also inhibit attention to the gendered character of that discourse. To the extent that emotion, sexuality, and intimacy are defined as *merely personal*, historians of the social sciences are limited in their ability to understand the phenomenon that they study.

Ogburn's strategy for meeting the demands of science as he defined them, his preference for "unfeeling knowledge," "cool rationality," even for "totally colorless articles," and his efforts to institutionalize them as criteria for social science discourse in twentieth-century America are part of the legacy within which we work. And it is a gendered legacy, with criteria created out of the political, economic, and *gender* interests, preferences, and feelings of the mostly white middle-class men who constructed them in the early part of the twentieth century in America.

Contestation is part of the very nature of scholarship. But the rhetoric through which that contest is expressed often masks how and why it is organized as it is. Part of that mask, I have been arguing, is a set of practices that limit our ability to see how gender relations have shaped the discourses in which we are all engaged. Ogburn's life story suggests one set of silences that those masks impose — silences about emotion, about sexuality, about gender relations. While the feminist movement, and the scholarship that it fostered, have made it possible for me to "think gender" where it had not previously been thought, the power to go beyond the individual insight, or the margins of academic discourse, to become a central player in the politics of knowledge involves more than a good idea. It also involves advocacy, organization, and institutionalization.

The personal is political. So is the intellectual!

NOTES

An earlier version of this essay was delivered, in abridged form, as my presidential address to the Social Science History Association in 1991; a published version appears in *Social Science History* 16, no. 2 (Summer 1992). My thanks to participants in the Workshop on the Rhetoric of Social History and the Project on the Rhetoric of Inquiry at the University of Iowa in June 1992 and to the University of Iowa and NEH for support.

1. My formulation of these ideas was influenced by, among others, Shils 1980, on institutionalization; Scott 1988 and 1991, on language; and McCloskey 1985, on rhetoric.

2. Theoretical works that influenced my asking these questions include Bourdieu 1975 and 1977; Foucault 1980; and Keller 1985.

3. William Fielding Ogburn (1886–1959) was a major figure in the history of American sociology, especially from 1919, when he joined the faculty of Barnard College/Columbia University, through the beginning of the 1950s, when he retired from the University of Chicago, having completed careers at arguably the two most important institutions in the early history of American sociology as an academic discipline. Ogburn was also well known during his lifetime through his professional and popular writings and through his work with the Social Science Research Council between 1924 and 1941; he was its chairman from 1933 to 1936. For further details of Ogburn's life, see Laslett 1990. See also Tobin 1995.

4. By "doing theory" I mean being attentive in an explicit way to general models, ideas, or interpretations that go beyond the particular case pursued in a given piece of empirical work — in this case, Ogburn's ideas about science and emotion. Doing theoretical work also involves thinking through the diverse and complex meanings of such concepts as gender and the explanations for links between them — for instance, gender and human action — each of which will be taken up in the text.

5. Contemporary scholars, feminists in particular, have very different sensibilities about the strategies of separation that Ogburn held dear. See, for instance, Keller 1994 and Lugones 1996.

6. Although a similar pattern can be seen in Europe (Lepenies 1988), the Ogburnian vision and version of scientism in sociology may have been peculiarly American.

7. See Bannister 1987 for an extended discussion of the various meanings of "objectivity" in American sociology. Feminist sociologists and philosophers of knowledge have also been much concerned with this issue. See Smith 1987, 1990; Harding 1986 and 1991.

8. This interest has led to the project I am working on with two colleagues at the

University of Minnesota, M. J. Maynes (Department of History) and Jennifer Pierce (Department of Sociology), on the uses of personal narratives in the social sciences.

9. For more details on Ogburn's experiences in Washington, see Laslett 1990.

10. The sociology of scientific knowledge distinguishes itself from an older tradition in the sociology of knowledge and the sociology of science. The older fields claim to explain sociologically the social organization of science, the scientific questions that get asked, the standards for acceptance of answers, the patterns of influence among scientists, and so on, but they have little to say about the content of scientific knowledge itself. The newer field claims to be able to explain the content of scientific knowledge sociologically. I review some of this material in Laslett 1990. For more work from this perspective, see Pickering 1992, 1995. Unfortunately, this literature rarely considers the social sciences.

11. Kerber (1988) and Davidoff (1990) suggest that the separate spheres concept, as metaphor and as ideology, has been associated with the development of women's history in the twentieth century and with efforts to understand society scientifically in the nineteenth.

12. For a review of the literature on separate spheres and "true womanhood," see Kerber 1988. For "new womanhood," see Cott 1987; Smith-Rosenberg 1985; Laslett 1991a. For men and masculinity, in a way that is attentive to race as well as gender and class, see Bederman 1995.

13. It should be noted that these new professional associations often lent support to the emerging standards of scientism that were being articulated by such social scientists as Ogburn.

14. A revisionist literature on the settlement house and social reforms movements is now beginning to appear. See, for instance, Crocker 1992 and the essays in this volume.

15. Coser 1978 shows that clergymen and their sons were overrepresented among the early American sociologists.

16. This quotation comes from an undated typescript given to me by Ogburn's son, Fielding. For further discussion, see Laslett 1990.

17. One might ask whether or not Ogburn's absent father was not as significant an element of his psychological development as his "overfond" mother — or, indeed, the fact that the social standing of Ogburn's family plummeted after his father's death (see Laslett 1990).

18. Historically, the pressures on universities in the United States not to be politically engaged, particularly on behalf of left-wing political positions, provided clear grounds for Ogburn's arguments (Furner 1975). And it can be seen in his own life story as well. The Federal Bureau of Investigation kept a secret file on Ogburn's activities from approximately 1950 until his death in 1959; I obtained a copy of this material through the Freedom of Information Act. It confirms the mildness of Ogburn's political activities and affiliations and at the same time verifies that they were nevertheless considered important enough to warrant some level of surveillance.

19. For African American male social scientists, the situation would likely have been quite different, although also shaped by issues of masculinity, a subject that

could usefully be examined further. The relationship of whiteness to white masculinity also needs further exploration. For examples of some of the existing literature, see Stanfield 1985; Gordon 1991; Young 1993; Lemert 1995, esp. chs. 6 and 8; Roediger 1991; Bederman 1995.

20. See also Gordon 1991 on contemporaneous African American reform efforts.

21. There is a large feminist literature that addresses this issue under the label of "standpoint theory." See, in addition to Smith, particularly, Harding 1986, 1990, 1991. For a series of more recent essays on standpoint theory, see *Signs* 1997 : 366 – 402.

22. Of course it is not the case that all professional women were unmarried. See, for instance, the biography of Lucy Sprague Mitchell (Antler 1987). But numerous studies have shown that in the early part of the century highly educated women, especially those with independent professional careers, were substantially more likely than men to be unmarried. See also Ware 1987 on Molly Dewson. See also Gordon 1992.

23. While in the text I emphasize the success of the Ogburnian vision for social science, his efforts had varying outcomes. A few examples will have to suffice. Ogburn once proposed that the Department of Sociology at the University of Chicago change its requirements for the Ph.D. so that three published scientific articles could substitute for a dissertation. He was unsuccessful in that effort. In his 1951 retirement address he spoke of the battles he had faced at Chicago over his advocacy of statistics. His correspondence also speaks about failures in shaping the collection of census data, on which much social science research of the time was dependent. For a specific contestation over the Ogburnian vision, see Sorokin 1933 and Ogburn's 1933 response.

REFERENCES

Abrams, Philip. 1982. *Historical Sociology*. Ithaca: Cornell University Press.

Amenta, Edwin, and Bruce G. Carruthers. 1988. "The Formative Years of U.S. Social Spending Policies." *American Sociological Review* 53 : 661–78.

Antler, Joyce. 1987. *Lucy Sprague Mitchell: The Making of a Modern Woman*. New Haven: Yale University Press.

Bannister, Robert. 1987. *Sociology and Scientism: The American Quest for Objectivity, 1880 –1940*. Chapel Hill: University of North Carolina Press.

Baron, Ava, ed. 1991. *Work Engendered: Toward a New History of American Labor*. Ithaca: Cornell University Press.

Bederman, Gail. 1995. *Manliness and Civilization: A Cultural History of Gender and Race in the United States, 1880 –1917*. Chicago: University of Chicago Press.

Bordo, Susan. 1986. "The Cartesian Masculinization of Thought." *Signs* 11 : 439–56.

Bourdieu, Pierre. 1975. "The Specificity of the Scientific Field and the Social Conditions of the Progress of Reason." *Social Science Information* 14 : 19 – 47.

———. 1977. *Outline of a Theory of Practice*. Cambridge: Cambridge University Press.

Bulmer, Martin. 1984. *The Chicago School of Sociology: Institutionalization,*

Diversity, and the Rise of Sociological Research. Chicago: University of Chicago Press.

Cohn, Carol. 1996. "Sex and Death in the Rational World of Defense Intellectuals." In Barbara Laslett, Sally Gregory Kolhstedt, Helen Longino, and Evelynn Hammonds, eds., *Gender and Scientific Authority*, pp. 183–214. Chicago: University of Chicago Press.

Coser, Lewis A. 1978. "American Trends." In Tom Bottomore and Robert Nisbet, eds., *A History of Sociological Analysis*, pp. 287–320. New York: Basic Books.

Cott, Nancy. 1979. "Passionlessness: An Interpretation of Victorian Sexual Ideology, 1790–1850." *Signs* 4:219–36.

———. 1987. *The Grounding of Modern Feminism.* New Haven: Yale University Press.

Crocker, Ruth H. 1992. *Social Work and Social Order: The Settlement Movement in Two Industrial Cities, 1889–1930.* Urbana: University of Illinois Press.

Davidoff, Leonore. 1990. "'Adam spoke first and named the order of the world': Masculine and Feminine Domains in History and Sociology." In Helen Corr and Lynn Jamieson, eds., *Politics of Everyday Life: Continuity and Change in World and the Family*, pp. 229–55. New York: St. Martin's Press.

Davidoff, Leonore, and Catherine Hall. 1987. *Family Fortunes.* Chicago: University of Chicago Press.

Deacon, Desley. 1992. "The Republic of the Spirit: Fieldwork in Elsie Clews Parsons's Turn to Anthropology." *Frontiers: A Journal of Women's Studies* 12, no. 3:13–38.

———. 1997a. "Brave New Sociology? Elsie Clews Parsons and Me." In Barbara Laslett and Barrie Thorne, eds., *Feminist Sociology: Life Histories of a Movement*, pp. 165–93. New Brunswick, N.J.: Rutgers University Press.

———. 1997b. *Elsie Clews Parsons: Inventing Modern Life.* Chicago: University of Chicago Press.

Deegan, Mary Jo. 1988. *Jane Addams and the Men of the Chicago School, 1982–1918.* New Brunswick, N.J.: Transaction Books.

D'Emilio, John. 1983. "Capitalism and Gay Identity." In Ann Snitow, Christine Stansell, and Sharon Thompson, eds., *Powers of Desire: The Politics of Sexuality*, pp. 100–116. New York: Monthly Review Press.

D'Emilio, John, and Estelle B. Freedman. 1988. *Intimate Matters: A History of Sexuality in America.* New York: Harper and Row.

Demos, John. 1986. *Past, Present, and Personal: The Family and the Life Course in American History.* New York: Oxford University Press.

Faderman, Lillian. 1981. *Surpassing the Love of Men: Romantic Friendship and Love between Women from the Renaissance to the Present.* New York: William Morrow.

———. 1991. *Odd Girls and Twilight Lovers: A History of Lesbian Life in Twentieth-Century America.* New York: Columbia University Press.

Fitzpatrick, Ellen. 1990. *Endless Crusade: Women Social Scientists and Progressive Reform.* New York: Oxford University Press.

Foucault, Michel. 1980. *Power/Knowledge: Selected Interviews and Other Writings, 1972–1977*. New York: Pantheon.

Furner, Mary O. 1975. *Advocacy and Objectivity: A Crisis in the Professionalization of American Social Science, 1865–1904*. Lexington: University Press of Kentucky.

Gordon, Linda. 1991. "Black and White Visions of Welfare: Women's Welfare Activism, 1890–1945." *Journal of American History* 78:559–90.

———. 1992. "Social Insurance and Public Assistance: The Influence of Gender in Welfare Thought in the U.S., 1890–1935." *American Historical Review* 97:19–54.

———. 1994. *Pitied But Not Entitled: Single Mothers and the History of Welfare, 1890–1935*. New York: Free Press.

Harding, Sandra. 1986. *The Science Question in Feminism*. Ithaca: Cornell University Press.

———. 1990. "Feminism, Science, and the Anti-Enlightenment Critiques." In Linda J. Nicholson, ed., *Feminism/Postmodernism*, pp. 83–106. New York: Routledge.

———. 1991. *Whose Science? Whose Knowledge?: Thinking from Women's Lives*. Ithaca: Cornell University Press.

Haskell, Thomas L. 1977. *The Emergence of Professional Social Science: The American Social Science Association and the Nineteenth-Century Crisis of Authority*. Urbana: University of Illinois Press.

———. 1984. *The Authority of Experts: Studies in History and Theory*. Bloomington: Indiana University Press.

Karl, Barry. 1969. "Presidential Planning and Social Science Research: Mr. Hoover's Experts." *Perspectives in American History* 3:347–409.

———. 1983. "In Search of National Planning: The Case for a Third New Deal." Paper presented at the meetings of the Organization of American Historians.

Keller, Evelyn Fox. 1985. *Reflections on Gender and Science*. New Haven: Yale University Press.

———. 1994. "The Paradox of Scientific Subjectivity." In Allan Megill, ed., *Rethinking Objectivity*. Durham: Duke University Press.

Kerber, Linda K. 1988. "Separate Sphere, Female Worlds, Women's Place: The Rhetoric of Women's History." *Journal of American History* 75:9–39.

Laslett, Barbara. 1990. "Unfeeling Knowledge: Emotion and Objectivity in the History of Sociology." *Sociological Forum* 5:413–33.

———. 1991a. "Women's Work in Late-Nineteenth-Century Los Angeles: Class, Gender, and the Culture of New Womanhood." *Continuity and Change* 5:417–41.

———. 1991b. "Biography as Historical Sociology: The Case of William Fielding Ogburn." *Theory and Society* 20:511–38.

———. 1992. "Gender in/and Social Science History." *Social Science History* 16:177–95.

———. 1997. "On Finding a Feminist Voice: Emotion in a Sociological Life Story." In Barbara Laslett and Barrie Thorne, eds., *Feminist Sociology: Life Histories of a Movement*, pp. 48–72. New Brunswick, N.J.: Rutgers University Press.

Laslett, Barbara, and Johanna Brenner. 1989. "Gender and Social Reproduction: Historical Perspectives." *Annual Review of Sociology* 15:381–404.

Leach, William. 1989. *True Love and Perfect Union: The Feminist Reform of Sex and Society.* 2d ed. Middletown, Conn.: Wesleyan University Press.

Lemert, Charles. 1995. *Sociology after the Crisis.* Boulder: Westview Press.

Lepenies, Wolf. 1988. *Between Literature and Science: The Rise of Sociology.* New York: Cambridge University Press.

Lugones, Maria. 1996. "Purity, Impurity, and Separation." In Barbara Laslett, Sally Gregory Kolhstedt, Helen Longino, and Evelynn Hammonds, eds., *Gender and Scientific Authority*, pp. 275–96. Chicago: University of Chicago Press.

Martin, Emily. 1996. "The Egg and the Sperm: How Science Has Constructed a Romance Based on Stereotypical Male-Female Roles." In Barbara Laslett, Sally Gregory Kolhstedt, Helen Longino, and Evelynn Hammonds, eds., *Gender and Scientific Authority*, pp. 323–39. Chicago: University of Chicago Press.

McCloskey, Donald N. 1985. *The Rhetoric of Economics.* Madison: University of Wisconsin Press.

Morantz-Sanchez, R. M. 1985. *Sympathy and Science: Women Physicians in American Medicine.* New York: Oxford University Press.

Novick, Peter. 1988. *That Noble Dream: The "Objectivity Question" and the American Historical Profession.* New York: Cambridge University Press.

Ogburn, R. R. 1955. Letters to My Son. Private publication.

Ogburn, William Fielding. 1930. "The Folkways of a Scientific Sociology." *Scientific Monthly* 30:300–306.

———. 1932. "Statistics and Art." *Journal of the American Statistical Association* 27:1–8.

———. 1933. "A Reply" [response to Sorokin]. *Journal of Political Economy* 41:210–21.

———. 1943. "Southern Regional Folkways Regarding Money." *Social Forces* 21:298–301.

———. 1945. "Ideologies of the South in Transition." *Social Forces* 23:334–42.

———. 1948a. Journals of William Fielding Ogburn, 6.3.48. Ogburn Collection, Regenstein Library, University of Chicago.

———. 1948b. Journals of William Fielding Ogburn, 14.10.48. Ogburn Collection, Regenstein Library, University of Chicago.

———. 1951. "A Few Words by Professor Ogburn." Address presented at the annual institute and banquet of the Society for Social Research, June 8–9. Typescript.

———. 1959. Letter to Dorothy O. Johansen, March 10. Reed College Archive.

Orloff, Ann. 1992. *The Politics of Pensions: A Comparative Analysis of Britain, Canada and the United States, 1880–1940.* Madison: University of Wisconsin Press.

Pickering, Andrew. 1995. *The Mangle of Practice: Time, Agency, and Science.* Chicago: University of Chicago Press.

———, ed. 1992. *Science as Culture and Practice.* Chicago: University of Chicago Press.

Roediger, David R. 1991. *The Wages of Whiteness: Race and the Making of the American Working Class*. New York: Verso.

Rose, Sonya. 1991. *Limited Livelihoods: Gender and Class in Nineteenth-Century England*. Berkeley and Los Angeles: University of California Press.

Rosenberg, Rosalind. 1982. *Beyond Separate Spheres: Intellectual Roots of Modern Feminism*. New Haven: Yale University Press.

Ross, Dorothy. 1978. "Socialism and American Liberalism: Academic Thought in the 1880s." *Perspectives in American History* 11:7–79.

———. 1991. *The Origins of American Social Science*. New York: Cambridge University Press.

Ryan, Mary P. 1981. *Cradle of the Middle Class: The Family in Oneida County, New York, 1790–1865*. New York: Cambridge University Press.

Scott, Joan W. 1987. "On Language, Gender, and Working-Class History." *International Labor and Working Class History* 31:1–13. See also replies.

———. 1988. *Gender and the Politics of History*. New York: Columbia University Press.

———. 1991. "The Evidence of Experience." *Critical Inquiry* 17:773–97.

Seidman, Steven. 1991. *Romantic Longings: Love in America, 1830–1980*. New York: Routledge.

Shils, Edward. 1980. "Tradition, Ecology, and Institution in the History of Sociology." In *The Calling of Sociology and Other Essays on the Pursuit of Learning*, pp. 165–256. Chicago: University of Chicago Press.

Sklar, Kathryn Kish. 1991. "Hull-House Maps and Papers: Social Science as Women's Work in the 1890s." In Martin Bulmer, Kevin Bales, and Kathryn Kish Sklar, eds., *The Social Survey in Historical Perspective, 1880–1940*, pp. 111–47. New York: Cambridge University Press.

Skocpol, Theda. 1992. *Protecting Soldiers and Mothers: The Political Origins of Social Policy in the United States*. Cambridge: Harvard University Press.

Smith, Dorothy E. 1987. *The Everyday World as Problematic: A Feminist Sociology*. Boston: Northeastern University Press.

———. 1990. *The Conceptual Practices of Power: A Feminist Sociology of Knowledge*. Boston: Northeastern University Press.

Smith-Rosenberg, Carol. 1985. *Disorderly Conduct: Visions of Gender in Victorian America*. New York: Oxford University Press.

Sorokin, Pitirim A. 1933. "Recent Social Trends: A Criticism." *Journal of Political Economy* 41:194–210.

Sperling, Susan. 1996. "Baboons with Briefcases: Feminism, Functionalism, and Sociobiology in the Evolution of Primate Gender." In Barbara Laslett, Sally Gregory Kohlstedt, Helen Longino, and Evelynn Hammonds, eds., *Gender and Scientific Authority*. Chicago: University of Chicago Press.

Stanfield, John H. 1985. *Philanthropy and Jim Crow in American Social Science*. Westport, Conn.: Greenwood Press.

Starr, Paul. 1982. *The Social Transformation of American Medicine*. New York: Basic Books.

Tilly, Louise. 1989. "Gender, Women's History, and Social History." *Social Science History* 13:439–63.

Tobin, William A. 1995. "Studying Society: The Making of *Recent Social Trends in the United States, 1929–1933*." *Theory and Society* 24:537–65.

Turner, Stephen Park, and Jonathan H. Turner. 1990. *The Impossible Science: An Institutional Analysis of American Sociology*. Newbury Park, Calif.: Sage Publications.

Vesey, Lawrence R. 1965. *The Emergence of the American University*. Chicago: University of Chicago Press.

Ware, Susan. 1987. *Partner and I: Molly Dewson, Feminism, and New Deal Politics*. New Haven: Yale University Press.

Weir, Margaret, Ann Orloff, and Theda Skocpol. 1988. *The Politics of Social Policy in the United States*. Princeton: Princeton University Press.

Wynne, William. [William Fielding Ogburn.] 1948. "Long Trail Winding." *Georgia Review* 2, no. 3:306–14.

Young, Alford A., Jr. 1993. "The 'Negro Problem' and the Character of the Black Community: Charles S. Johnson, E. Franklin Frazier, and the Constitution of a Black Sociological Tradition, 1920–1935." *National Journal of Sociology* 7: 95–133.

ADRIANA MÉNDEZ RODENAS

"THE CANNON ARE ROARING":
CALDERÓN DE LA BARCA'S *LIFE IN*
MEXICO AS GENDERED HISTORY

O n the morning of July 15, 1840, Frances Calderón de la Barca recorded in her diary the first in a series of violent outbreaks caused by the federalist/centralist split in nineteenth-century Mexico. She detailed Valentín Gómez Farias's uprising against President Anastasio Bustamante, who was furtively taken captive in the night: "The storm, which has for some time been brewing, has burst forth at last. Don Valentín Gómez Farias and the banished General Urrea have 'pronounced' for federalism. At two this morning, joined by the fifth batallion and the regiment of *comercio*, they took up arms, set off for the palace, surprised the President in his bed, and took him prisoner."[1] As news leaked out the next morning that the president had managed to escape, Frances Inglis attempted to record the ensuing political chaos, only to be interrupted by "the cannon are roaring . . . and the sound is anything but agreeable" (300).

Hailed by historians as "the best Latin American travel account,"[2] Frances Erskine Inglis's *Life in Mexico*, first published in 1843, contains her recorded impressions of Mexican life and mores during the two-year period when her husband, Don Angel Calderón de la Barca, served as the first Spanish ambassador to an independent Mexico (late 1839 to early 1842). While in Mexico, Madame Calderón (as she is known in Spanish American literary history) was witness to a series of revolutions and counterrevolutions that shook the political life of the Mexican republic shortly after independence. Hugh Thomas explains with his usual dry humor that "having been born in Edinburgh of a wholly Scottish family, she was well prepared to survive the many hair-raising experiences which she and her husband encountered on their extensive travels. She survived a revolution in Mexico City, escaped bandits, crossed swollen rivers in remote gorges, and even received a visit from the entire Mexican Cabinet who came to beg her not to wear a certain, as they supposed [,] indelicate gown at a fancy-dress ball."[3]

These scenes, depicting the Calderóns' journey from the port city of Veracruz to the capital, makes of *Life in Mexico* an intimate record of a European woman's encounter with the New World. Moreover, Calderón's sustained contact with "the still vibrant viceregal aristocracy of Mexico City" as well as her acute observations of the diverse social strata — Indian women in the marketplace, clergy, nuns, domestic servants, the customs and manners of upper-class Mexicans — form a social history of nineteenth-century Mexico.[4] She writes "a little history of Mexico" in print (286), through which we glean an ironic glimpse of Mexican politics and the shaping events of Mexican nationalism. In her role as historical witness, Calderón de la Barca not only offers valuable insights into a turbulent period of Mexican history but also marks her travelogue with a gender difference.

If for her observations of Mexican society Frances Calderón relied on her own intuitive understanding, for interpretations of current events she drew heavily on contemporary histories such as Lorenzo de Zavala's *Ensayo histórico de las revoluciones de Mégico* [*sic*] (1831), a book that figured in her husband's library as an authoritative source of Mexican history.[5] This knowledge is revealed in her famed character snapshots of political figures, such as her amusing portrait of General Santa Anna after he asumed power again with much pomp and circumstance in 1841. Calderón de la Barca's dependence on and departure from previous historical sources, such as Alexander von Humboldt's *Political Essay on the Kingdom of New Spain* (English translation, 1814) or Francisco Javier Clavijero's *Historia antigua de México* (1826), along with her reliance on the texts of other foreign travelers,[6] result in a hybrid history of revolution in Mexico as well as in a gendered vision of Mexican social history. The institutionalized subtext of the scientific voyage — represented by Alexander von Humboldt's *Political Essay* — is effectively mixed with a more intimate perspective conditioned by the author's own female experience. The narrative of travel is thus effectively hybridized by combining factual documentation with lived experience, keen observation with perceived insight, at times grafting the historical subtext onto the autobiography, at times reversing this movement.

In comparison with other nineteenth-century histories, *Life in Mexico* debunks the "grand narrative" of Latin American historiography designed to forge a nation after the crucial transition of the wars of independence. The period of nation-building created a separatist discourse, primarily of male political actors who used the autobiographical memoir as a means to document their exemplary lives as well as to justify their own political program.[7] Domingo Sarmiento's *Recuerdos de provincia* (1850) reads as "a text endowed with historical and moral significance, an example for posterity and a national testimony."[8] In Sarmiento, the male autobiographical narrator adopts a heroic stance in which self becomes synonymous with homeland, leading to a paternalistic conception of nationhood in which he proudly figures as "father of the country."[9] Following this paradigm, nineteenth-century Latin American history is mostly written "as a pantheon of heroic, exemplary figures."[10]

This rhetoric of self-aggrandizement characterizes the bulk of nineteenth-century historical prose, a discourse responsible for articulating the bases of Latin American cultural identity and its sense of "historical uniqueness."[11] The equation of Self and Nation prolongs another, more pervasive literary convention, which founds the genre of autobiography itself. According to Sidonie Smith, this is "the naive conflation of male subjectivity and human identity," so that "male experience is identified as the normative human paradigm."[12]

Calderón de la Barca's *Life in Mexico* consciously en(gender)s "an alternative women's history,"[13] a different reading of the discourse of Spanish American nationalism than that provided by official or canonized accounts. In reading *Life in Mexico* as gendered history, I want to show how women's travel narrative, though written from an autobiographical perspective, nevertheless fulfills an important historiographical function: to demystify the heroic, proto-nationalist plot fabricated by educated Creoles such as Sarmiento. My reading thus resists the classification of European women travelers within the category of "exploratrices sociales" (social explorers) who contributed to the post-independence capitalist boom;[14] on the contrary, I argue that it was precisely their foreignness and gender identity that allowed European women travelers like Madame Calderón both a more empathic view of the Other than that provided by their male counterparts and their own distinctive critical view of an emerging Spanish American nationalism. Since women have for the most part been excluded from the terrain of (male) monumental history, their contribution to the field, at least in the Latin American tradition, has been largely through "private" genres like the letter, the intimate portrait, the memoir, or the travel account.

The difference lies, however, in the reception of women's histories, which are, at best, relegated to the margins or, at worst, excluded from most accounts of Latin American nationalism. In this light, it is interesting to note that *Life in Mexico* reached the public eye only by the inspiration of Sir Walter Prescott, a longtime friend of the Calderóns' who encouraged Frances to publish her letters, as stated in his preface to the original edition.[15] And it is ironic indeed that Prescott then "made appreciative use . . . of [Calderón's] descriptions of the country he himself never saw" (*Life in Mexico*, xxii) in his own *History of the Conquest of Mexico* (1843), a classic text of Romantic historiography.[16] Hence, while Prescott achieved instant notoriety (his book was widely circulated in Mexico and was even the source of vigorous polemics), Calderón de la Barca's memoirs not only raised suspicion but nearly provoked a diplomatic breach between France and Mexico.[17] The resistance against Calderón's frank treatment of national affairs came both from the Mexican press and from Spaniards living in Mexico. Whereas the first simply discarded the book as "a collection of despicable trivia," the second saw it as "a poisonous satire against Mexicans" that seriously compromised the person of the ambassador and the Spanish government. The press also claimed that Frances Calderón had "betrayed the generous hospitality which she and her husband had been shown by Mexicans."[18]

Despite these attacks, which fortunately never reached the author herself,[19] Calderón de la Barca maintains a tone of detached objectivity in her descriptions of the many political intrigues, plots, and counterplots hatched in the Palace of Government during her two-year stay in Mexico. Since the start of her journey, Frances Calderón had shown a vivid interest in Mexican politics, sprinkling her account with character sketches of generals and presidents, such as her contrast of General Santa Anna, Anastasio Bustamante, and General Victoria in terms of political personalities, strategies, and motivations.[20] Given her public role as wife of the Spanish ambassador, Calderón de la Barca carefully avoids giving any possible cause for rumor as she repeatedly underlines in her memoirs the assumed position of detached observer, best represented in the crytic declaration "I [am] not interfering in Mexican politics" (284).

Yet in spite of these protestations, *Life in Mexico* documents a portion of the civil strife between centralists and federalists (liberals and conservatives) that riddled the first twenty-five years of the Mexican republic.[21] More specifically, Frances Calderón details the 1841 federalist uprising against President Anastasio Bustamante after much "roaring of cannon," an event that eventually led to the reinstatement of General Santa Anna as provisional president in October 1841.[22] These events, documented in consecutive letters of Life in Mexico, are interpersed with travels to the sugar country and news of the end of Calderón's mission.[23]

In analyzing the author's reenactment of the 1841 revolt, I want to show Life in Mexico as constructing a gendered or alternative history that debunks the elevated "grand narrative" of nineteenth-century heroic autobiographical prose in Latin America. This claim is based on Calderón's rhetorical strategies for depicting a complex historical event; mainly, the refiguration of the event itself, the questioning of the truth claims of historiography, and the demystification of male historical actors, with a consequent focus on female agency. These various strategies are ultimately subsumed in the author's persistent and subversive ironic stance. In my reading of this episode, I contrast the ironic account of the 1841 revolt and its aftermath with Calderón's later analysis of Mexican politics and her consequent appraisal of the post-independence nation, what in traditional historiography constitutes a final "synoptic judgment."[24] Although the discourse of history in Life in Mexico proceeds from the particular to the general, from concrete documentation to a synthesizing statement (Mink's "synoptic judgment"), the abstractions and generalizations proper to the historian's task are reached by a more circuitous route. In this text, rational thinking and the historian's "ingredient conclusions" (Mink's term) are complemented by the elusive trait of feminine intuition and by subjective impressions deriving from the subject's lived experience.[25] In short, in the passages pertaining to civil strife in Mexico, Frances Calderón effectively hybridizes what can be classified as "male" and "female" discourses, thus constructing a historical text that reads more as a continuum or discursive blend than as an outright "clash" of contesting discourses.[26]

The historical event is dramatically represented in Life in Mexico with the initial statement at the head of letter 24, dated July 15, 1840: "Revolution in Mexico!— or pronunciamiento, as they call it" (295).[27] Assuming a tone of factual reporting, Calderón supplies the reader with both background information and an update of current events. However, the focus of her account rapidly shifts to an assessment of the effects of ensuing political chaos both on the population at large and on her own immediate, more privileged, circle — diplomats, foreign visitors, and aristocratic acquaintances. Clustered around phrases like "The firing has begun!" and "The cannon are roaring now" (295) are vivid images of Mexicans either scrambling to safety ("The Indians are hurrying back to their villages in double-quick trot") or standing eagerly in expectation of what is to come ("All along the street people are standing on the balconies, looking anxiously in the direction of the palace") (296). By representing the 1841 revolt as an event or rupture in the Mexican social fabric, Calderón de la Barca acquiesces to what Michel de Certeau calls the "*topos* of intelligibility" of historical discourse, a radical discontinuity in the temporal and social order that beckons interpretation (historiographical writing).[28] By interpersing factual statements pertaining to the sequence of events with more personal observations, however, she leans towards a more contemporary notion of history as a relational series rather than as a set of facts or a single event.[29]

The counterpoint between documentation and intuitive understanding is rhetorically marked, in that the narrative unfolding of the crucial episodes of the revolt is depicted as an interruption to the writing of the diary itself. This technique is particularly effective in the scene recounting President Bustamante's mysterious flight from captivity: "A roar of cannon from the palace . . . made the house shake and the windows rattle, and caused me to throw a blot over the President's good name" (297). Whether her irony here was a direct response to discordant versions of the president's fate remains unknown.[30] By drawing attention to the writing of the memoirs, however, Frances Calderón debunks one of the founding assumptions of historiographical writing — that fact and record are never simultaneous, that a gap is needed between past and present in order for the historian to fill in the void with *his* reconstruction of events and particular form of knowledge.[31] Rather than adopting the historian's pose, she introduces her own "particular form of knowledge" by drawing upon the conventions of the travel book, which strives to represent a traveler faithfully transcribing experiences at the same time that he or she is gasping at the sights. When imposed upon the narrative of political actions, this rhetorical tactic has the effect of diffusing the representation of the plot and highlighting in turn the tenuous link between record and event. If the root paradigm of historiographical writing is the implicit connection "between two antinomic terms — the real and discourse," Calderón de la Barca works in a different direction, showing up the inadequacies of this convention when confronted with the "real": the effect of "the roaring of cannon" upon the general populace and the frightful hour-by-hour experience of the 1841 revolt.[32]

Historical discourse in *Life in Mexico* adapts the convention of the "*laminated* text," in which the ongoing, referential narrative grafts onto itself either another text — in the form of "chronicle, archive document" — or a tissue of *citation[s]*.[33] Adapting the convention of objectivity typical of historiography to her purposes, Calderón interperses documents from the two opposing camps amid the heightened narration of events in order to exemplify the contesting political positions.[34] For the representation of the 1841 revolt alternates between official government bulletins signed by President Bustamente and Valentin Gómez Farias's counteracting claims, including the latter's accusations that the former was guilty of "breaking his solemnly pledged word" to the Mexican nation (297–99). By incorporating sources and quotations into the body of her text, Calderón de la Barca effectively accredits her account as a factual one, thereby sustaining the "verisimilitude of narrative" and asserting herself as "a locus of authority."[35]

Once she determined the reliability and truth claim of her account, Calderón de la Barca adopted a gendered stance in her ironic commentary on the rebels' political rhetoric, whose grandiose claims far exceed reality. In commenting on a particularly overdramatic passage, Calderón de la Barca mocks the inflated tone used by male political actors: "We see anarchy raising his rascally head above the water (most likely adorned with a liberty cap), and the brave soldiers instantly driving it down again. We behold Gómez Farias and Urrea rushing up a ladder of dead bodies. And then the Lucrezia Borgia kind of scene that follows! — alluring their victims with bitter fruit (or perhaps with sour grapes), drinking blood, and singing horridly out of tune . . . ! The teeth of humanity are set on edge only by reading it" (307). Although by representing "two sides to every story" (298) Calderón effectively dons the mask of the historian in apparent submission to the convention of objectivity, she simultaneously undermines this position by adopting the stance of literary critic.

The questioning of official government rhetoric is further bolstered by the fact that Calderón seems to privilege oral sources over written records, thus contesting the primacy of archival interpretations of history:[36] "As a clever Mexican, the Marquis of Apartado, says: 'Some years ago we gave forth cries (*gritos*)— *that* was the infancy of our independence. Now we begin to pronounce (*pronunciamos*). Heaven knows when we shall be old enough to speak plain, so that people may know what we mean!'" (304) By humorously questioning the concept of *pronunciamiento* itself, *Life in Mexico* deflates the "I, the state" rhetoric of nineteenth-century Latin American political prose as the dominant discourse of power.[37]

Despite her boldness, Frances Calderón exhibits the nineteenth-century female author's characteristic ambivalence when confronted with the need to justify her daring incursion into the masculine domain of historiography. At the end of chapter 24, which detailed the first phase of the revolt, she consciously adopts the "discourses of femininity," thus resorting to the traditional apology used by women who dare to write themselves into history: "I shall close this long letter, merely observing in apology— as Madame de Stael said in answer to the remark that 'women have nothing to do with politics'— That may be, but when a woman's head is about to be cut off, it is natural she should ask: '*Why?*'" So it appears to me that when bullets are whizzing about our ears, and shells falling within a few yards of us, it ought to be considered extremely natural, and quite feminine, to inquire into the cause of such phenomena" (315).[38]

Later, when recounting the sequel to the 1841 uprising in a subsequent chapter, Calderón overturns this traditional feminine apology for entry into the historiographical terrain. The letters included in the section "Revolution Again: Santa Anna Returns" detail a second *pronunciamiento*, led by General Valencia in late August 1841 against President Bustamante, which provoked General Santa Anna to usurp the presidency in October of that same year.[39] As the political plot thickened with the rambunctious entry of General Santa Anna on the scene, Calderón describes the movements of the four principal actors— Santa Anna, Paredes, Valencia, and Bustamante— as "a game of chess, in which kings, castles, knights, and bishops are making different moves, while the pawns are looking on or taking no part whatever" (497), a metaphor that effectively mocks the notion of male military might. Soon after this, the Calderóns are forced to leave Mexico City, since the government confiscated their house, intending it as a gathering place for arms (503). When personally affected by the turn of events, Calderón de la Barca is quick to abandon the feminine discourse of apology in favor of this energetic assertion: "I make no further excuses for talking about politics. We talk and think of little else" (508).

From her hideaway at the country hacienda of San Xavier, she keeps careful watch on the developing drama by directly documenting events. As the principal actors pass by Tlanepantla, Frances again alternates "the discourses of femininity" with the discourse of history, solving the apparent conflict in favor of the latter yet maintaining her genuine gender concerns. While her husband, the auspicious Calderón, goes out to greet President Bustamante, who was on his way to agree with General Paredes, thus privileging male historical actors, Frances Calderón deviates from the official script of history to witness the arrival of Paredes and his troops. Her attention is not on the "world-historical individual"[40] but rather on ordinary men forced into combat as fodder for a political plot beyond their individual concerns: "Cavalry, infantry, carriages, cannons, &c., are all passing through the village. These are the *pronunciados*, with General Paredes, following to Mexico. Feminine curiosity induces me to stop here, and to join the party who are going down to the village to see them pass" (511).

From this point on in the narrative, Calderón records the heightening of the political drama with the same straightforward journalistic style tinged with characteristic irony that she used earlier. She carefully documents Santa Anna's march into Mexico City, Bustamante's strategy of allowing the three opposing generals to meet, the resolutions reached at Tacubaya, and, finally, Bustamante's surprising *counter-pronunciamiento*[41] in favor of federalism, the event that provided a catalyst for Santa Anna's rise to power (511–17). The climax of the narrative, marked by Bustamante's resignation and uncertainty as to Santa Anna's true motives, combines the documentary script — ciphered by the sentence "Everything is in a state of perfect anarchy and confusion" (515)— with more-conclusive statements that reveal Calderón's gendered stance.

In these passages, the image of the roaring cannon is expanded rhetorically to reflect on erratic political ambitions and the abuse of power:

> The sound is horrible! There is something appalling, yet humbling, in these manifestations of man's wrath and man's power, when he seems to usurp his Maker's attributes, and to mimick His thunder. The divine spark kindled within him has taught him how to draw these materials from earth's bosom; how to combine these simple materials, so

as to produce with them an effect as terrible as the thunderbolts of heaven. His earthly passions have prompted him so to wield these instruments of destruction as to deface God's image in his fellow men. The power is so divine — the causes that impel him to use that power are so paltry! The intellect that creates these messengers of death is so near akin to divinity — the motives that put them in action are so poor, so degrading even to humanity! (515)

In this manner Calderón subverts the discourse of power and of military might that characterized the centralist counterrevolution of 1841, thus critiquing as well the course of Mexican nationalism as a constant bickering of factions.[42] By equating "the roaring of cannon" with "man's power" and "man's wrath," and by consequently showing up the illusion of power as originating from One Indivisible Subject (the subject of history), Calderón effectively undermines the assumptions of masculine historical discourse as well as the notion of historical event. The presumptuousness of power is represented, with all pomp and circumstance, in the person of General Santa Anna and his new cabinet (517).[43] However, Calderón prefers the ousted President Bustamante for "his constant and earnest desire to spare human life," thus deflating once again the myth of the male hero.

Rather than affirming the political ploys engaged in by Santa Anna and the other leaders (517), Calderón de la Barca's account of the 1841 revolt focuses on examples of female heroism. The Mexican underclass, along with women, are depicted as victims of their country's never-ending political strife. *Life in Mexico* casts women in the double role of wives and mothers, thus drawing on the traditional "discourses of femininity": one Señora Marran, concerned for her husband's safety in the midst of the roaring cannon, and an archetypical Señora Barbachano, who rushed to shelter at the Calderóns' only when her baby was at risk (300). In the chapter assessing the aftermath of the revolution, Calderón de la Barca praises women for using wits instead of bullets, thus validating their role as marginal witnesses and/or fugitives from the scene of the firing: "Ladies and children escaped, in many instances, by the *azoteas*, going along the street from one roof to another, not being able to pass where the cannon was planted. The Señora ———, with her six beautiful boys, escaped in that way to her brother's house, in the evening and in the very thick of the firing" (321). These fleeting episodes nevertheless construct an image of women as historical subjects, an image that counters the one deployed in the documentary sources, where women figure only as pawns for the political struggle. Contrast Calderón's representations with the poignant example included in Gómez Farias's bulletin of a pregnant woman who had been "killed as she was passing the palace gates under the belief that . . . the firing would be suspended, as in fact it was on our side" (299).[44]

Indeed, the presence of women amid the roaring cannon puts into question the methods and motives of the warring factions, thus casting a shadow of skepticism on the entire event. Calderón's gendered perspective allows her to ironize the bizarre strategies of the Mexican military: "It seems also a novel plan to keep up a continual cannonading by night and to rest during a great part of the day" (300), an observation followed by a healthy dose of female logic: "One would think that were the guns brought closer to the palace, the whole affair would be sooner over" (300). Though women are represented as subjects on the fringes of the historical spectacle, they paradoxically play a vital role in it, serving to underscore the futility of violence and, ultimately, of the entire political wrangle.

Signs of an alternative historiography go beyond the focus on female heroism, for in these passages on civil war Calderón writes herself as an empathic witness to the plight of the poor, a position that duplicates her own stance as historical witness. Rather than abstracting a principle from the events described, as a male historian would, Calderón de la Barca ends the account of the 1841 revolt with the following observation:

> The tranquillity of the sovereign people during all this period is astonishing. In what other city in the world would they not have taken part with one or other side? Shops shut, workmen out of employment, thousands of idle people subsisting heaven knows how — yet no riot, no confusion, apparently no impatience. Groups of people collect on the streets, or stand talking before their doors, and speculate upon probabilities — but await the decision of their military chiefs as if it were a judgment from heaven from which it were useless and impious to appeal. (314)

By identifying in this manner with the silent masses of Mexicans, Calderón de la Barca subverts the detached stance of the male historian in favor of a more empathic position, hence reversing the fundamental "historiographical operation," which posits distance from the past as a prerequisite of historical writing. Rather than reenact the implied connection between historiography and the ghosts of the past,[45] Calderón de la Barca's gendered stance focuses on the living, not "so [they] can exist elsewhere" but rather so they may be able to inhabit (inherit) their own social space and time.[46]

As a result of these diverse modes of representation, *Life in Mexico* debunks many of the founding premises of the "grand narrative" of nineteenth-century Latin American historiography. To begin with, the historical event itself is minimized in favor of the mundane and concrete details of everyday life. The conclusion of the August 1841 revolt is signaled in the text by an official bulletin announcing the restitution of order and centralist rule.[47] Drawing again on the conventions of travel narrative to subtly modify the "high seriousness" of historiographical prose, Calderón de la Barca informs an invisible interlocutor that "the arrival of the English packet, which brings all these *nouveautés*, is about the most interesting event that occurs here" (323), thus diminishing the importance of "the roaring of cannon."

The use of humor to subvert the stature of the historical text is especially evident in the following passage to the same unknown interlocutor: "I write more to occupy my thoughts than in hopes of interesting you, for I am afraid that you will almost be tired of this *revolutionary* letter" (304). By conflating the function of addressee of the letters (or narratee of the published diary) with the implied reader, Calderón relegates the task of imparting a final "synoptic judgment" to the reader of the memoirs, reversing once again the "historiographical operation," in which this task was the historian's absolute domain.[48] As the ironic highlight on the word "revolutionary" suggests, the 1841 federalist revolt is depicted not as an event with far-reaching consequences for Mexico's future but as a farcical and repeated "tale of two parties" contending for power,[49] the only perceptible outcome of which was "a change in ministry" (321).[50]

Consequently, in her final passage, Calderón de la Barca is skeptical of any hope for change — whether based on constitutional reform or on more violent means:

> [The Mexicans] have seen the revolution of Dolores of 1810, with continuations and variations by Morelos, and paralyzation of 1819; the revolution of Iturbide in 1821; the Cry of Liberty (*Grito de Libertad*) given by those generals, *"beneméritos de la patria,"* Santa Anna and Victoria in 1822; the establishment of the federal system in 1824; the

horrible revolution of the Acordada, in which Mexico was pillaged, in 1828; the adoption of the central system in 1836; and the last revolution of the federalists in 1840. Another is predicted for next month, as if it were an eclipse of the sun. (423)

This ironic assessment of the 1841 revolt results, then, in its eventual "erosion" from the historical field or its fading into the margins.[51] The many repetitions and reversals of the event itself along with the set of (re)writings suggest a virtual "disappearance" of the concept of revolution or *pronunciamiento*, a mainstay in Mexican historiography. Hence, Calderón de la Barca's *Life in Mexico* moves away from a totalizing concept of history and toward a sense of history written as/with a difference.[52]

Typical of the balance between "male" and "female" discourses operative in *Life in Mexico* is the scene in which Calderón de la Barca herself later assumes the task of casting a final judgment on Mexican politics, which is included in chapter 36, "Distinguished Men of Mexico" (418–24). Presumably addressed to her brother, Henry Inglis (762 n. 1), this letter reads as a capitulation of sorts, as a past review of Calderón's own involvement with the key actors in Mexican public life and as a sobering reflection on the country's destinies. She begins with a classification of historical actors — "soldiers, statesmen and literary men" (418) — all of which exemplify Lukács's ideal of a "historical type" who embodies the underlying forces and tensions of a particular era.[53] In her words, "there is not one amongst those I have mentioned who, if he were to write merely his personal history, would not by so doing write the history of these civil wars" (418), a statement in line with the established tradition of male autobiographers/leaders who equate their own selves with the state.[54] Calderón de la Barca further identifies the characters who best fit these types: "Bustamante as an honest man and brave soldier; Santa Anna as an acute general, active and aspiring . . . ; General Victoria, a plain, uneducated, well-intentioned man, brave and enduring" (418). Yet her subversive move away from the "grand narrative" of Latin American history surfaces here, for the men who occupy her continuing reflections are not the chosen three but other statesmen and literary figures who played a less dramatic role in forging Mexican nationalism. Indeed, many of these figures were either personal friends of the couple (such as Don Francisco Tagle [423]) or relatives of their close acquaintances (Señor Fagoaga, presumably the brother of the marquis of Apartado).[55] Not only is Calderón de la Barca's gendered vision evident in her highly subjective choice of statesmen, but also her descriptions underscore salient features of these "famous lives" not usually recorded in traditional histories — most noticeably, their "good fortune" in choosing "women who are either their equals or superiors — if not in education, [then] in goodness, elevation of sentiment and natural talent" (423). Furthermore, what Calderón de la Barca singles out in her brief overview of Mexican statesmen is their chosen retreat from public life in order to calmly pursue "domestic retirement and literary occupation" (422).[56] Hence, by privileging female-connoted values over the male drive for mastery, Calderón de la Barca transfers a gendered vision onto the liberal/conservative split in post-independence Mexico. Despite her earlier criticism of their extravagant actions, she values the ability of Mexican statesmen to cancel out their hostilities in the private realm,[57] thus suggesting, once again, a valorization of the feminine drive for harmony over military might.

As gendered history, *Life in Mexico* not only contributes to the field of women's history — the "her/story" approach signaled by American historian Joan Scott as the first phase of feminist inquiry — but also points the way to a hybrid genre of historical writing proper to European women's travelogues.[58] In this light, Frances Calderón's account fulfills a similar function in helping to shape Mexican identity and nationality as canonical autobiographies like Sarmiento's *Facundo* (1842) did for the definition of Argentine and Latin American identity, but in a different mode.[59] It was for this reason that the noted twentieth-century Mexican writer and early feminist Rosario Castellanos aptly dubbed Calderón de la Barca *"partera de almas"* — midwife of the soul — a term that captures her ability to represent the "underside" of gender difference that has, until very recently, gone unheeded in most accounts of Spanish American nationalism.[60]

NOTES

I am indebted to Shelton Stromquist for the notion of gendered history and to Charles A. Hale and Josefina Z. Vázquez for bibliographic references on Mexican history. I am grateful to Alejandro Cortazar for his valuable assistance in locating sources and articles on travel narrative to Mexico. This essay was written at the University of Iowa's Obermann Center for Advanced Studies under the generous support of a Howard Foundation grant.

1. *Life in Mexico: The Letters of Fanny Calderón de la Barca, with New Material from the Author's Private Journals*, ed. Howard T. Fisher and Marion Hall Fisher

(New York: Doubleday, 1966), p. 295. Future references will be to this edition and will appear in the text.

2. Charles A. Hale, review of 1966 edition of *Life in Mexico, Hispanic American Historical Review* #48 (November 1967): 582. Hale rightly points out that the value of this edition is in incorporating additional material that did not get into print.

3. Hugh Thomas, "Visits to Mexico," *Encounter* 73, no. 5 (1989): 34. The "indelicate gown" was a folkloric dress typical of the *china poblana* or Indian women from Puebla, who traditionally wore colorful, wide-skirted costumes. Though Calderón de la Barca had gone to great lengths to acquire an authentic "native" costume, hoping to please her Mexican hosts, she soon discovered that the *china poblana* dress had quite the opposite effect. In fact, the president himself, along with his entire cast of politicians, made a surprise visit to the Spanish ambassador's home to inform them that Frances's appearance at the ball would be sure to cause a scandal, because "all Poblanas were *femmes de rien*." Frances Calderón dutifully gave up the *china poblana* costume in favor of a more discreet Roman toga, but she subtly ironized the attitudes of the Mexicans. This amusing yet culturally revealing episode is told in *Life in Mexico*, pp. 125–26.

4. Hale, review.

5. "Fanny [*sic*] quotes or paraphrases from it [Zavala's *Ensayo histórico*] on several occasions — particularly from Chapter VIII of the first volume, rich in characterizations of important Mexicans" (editors' note, ibid., p. 678).

6. The editors identify these authors and their works as likely sources in certain key passages of *Life in Mexico*. Calderón makes constant references to Henry George Ward's *Mexico in 1827*, a book that she admired mainly on account of Mrs. Ward's sketches of Mexican life, which she considered the pictorial equivalent of her own narrative descriptions. See *Life in Mexico*, n. 7, p. 678.

7. Sylvia Molloy, *At Face Value: Autobiographical Writing in Spanish America* (Cambridge: Cambridge University Press, 1991), pp. 146–47.

8. *Life in Mexico*, n. 5, p. 678.

9. "It is not merely that Sarmiento pictures himself as an exemplary Argentine: he *is* Argentina, forming with his country one, inseparable body" (ibid., p. 148).

10. Ibid., p. 8.

11. Roberto González Echevarría, *Myth and Archive: A Theory of Latin American Narrative* (Cambridge: Cambridge University Press, 1990), pp. 7–9.

12. Sidonie Smith, *A Poetics of Women's Autobiography: Marginality and the Fictions of Self-Representation* (Bloomington: Indiana University Press, 1987), pp. 17, 12. Thus woman is relegated to "the margins of critical discourse," outside the Symbolic realm. This dominant paradigm presents greater obstacles for the female autobiographer as she attempts to re-present (forge) herself in her own words. See particularly pp. 12–15.

13. In her study of British women travelers to India, Tibet, and Africa, Sara Mills warns against what she considers to be the pitfalls of feminist criticism: to read women's travel writing either as strictly autobiographical or as an example of a "protofeminist" genre. Thus she questions inserting travel narrative within "the larger project concerned with the construction of an alternative women's history."

See Sara Mills, *Discourses of Difference: An Analysis of Women's Travel Writing and Colonialism* (London and New York: Routledge, 1991), pp. 28–29. In this paper I affirm precisely the opposite, since in the Latin American tradition the "lost continent" of women's writing has just begun to be unearthed by historians and literary critics, thus proving the value of this alternative project.

14. Mary Louise Pratt, *Imperial Eyes: Travel Writing and Transculturation* (London and New York: Routledge, 1992), pp. 144–71.

15. Editors' introduction, *Life in Mexico*, p. xxii. Michael P. Costeloe claims, however, that "[Sra. Calderón] began the process of seeking a publisher and . . . turned to Prescott for help," at which point Prescott procured a publisher for the American edition and actively sought out a British edition. See Michael P. Costeloe, "Prescott's *History of the Conquest* and Calderón de la Barca's *Life in Mexico*: Mexican Reaction, 1843–1844," *The Americas* 47, no. 3 (January 1991): 343.

16. Thomas (p. 30) documents the amazing fact that Prescott was blind and could never have seen the famed sights described in his *History*.

17. Costeloe describes how the Mexican press compared her unfavorably with an unwelcome French diplomat ("Prescott's *History*," p. 344). Though this author explains the different reactions to Prescott and Calderón in terms of the Mexicans' need to bolster a positive national image (p. 347), I believe that it was also the result of gender difference and the prevailing resistance to women authors.

18. Ibid., pp. 344–45.

19. According to Costeloe, "Sra. Calderón appears to have been quite unaware of the controversy [her book] aroused in Mexico and of the bitter criticism of herself and her husband" (ibid., 345–46).

20. This is included in the chapter that the Fishers title "Distinguished Men of Mexico" (p. 418).

21. For an account of Mexican history, I have drawn on Jan Bazant, "Mexico, from Independence to 1867," in *Cambridge History of Latin America* (Cambridge: Cambridge University Press, 1985): 3:423–70.

22. Ibid., 3:438–39.

23. The federalist revolt led by Gómez Farias is narrated in letter 24, dated Wednesday, July 15, 1840, and letter 25, Tuesday, July 28, 1840, respectively (*Life in Mexico*, pp. 295–323). The chapter headings included by the Fishers read, for the first letter, "The President Seized in His Bed" and for the second, "Quiet after the Cannonading." Titles like these suggest that the editors, despite their avowed reliance on Calderón's manuscripts, also fictionalized the account.

24. Louis Mink, *Historical Understanding*, ed. Brian Fay, Eugene O. Galob, and Richard T. Vann (Ithaca: Cornell University Press, 1987), pp. 77–79, 81–82. Further references to Mink are drawn from these same pages.

25. I use the term "feminine intuition" consciously, both as a means to affirm gender difference and to underline the fact that women apprehend historical phenomena in a different way.

26. I follow here Sara Mills's thesis that women's travel writing effectively shows a tension between the "discourses of femininity," which have molded women into traditional roles, and the discourse of colonialism, inherited from the predomi-

nantly male paradigm of the European travel book. This tension is manifested not in terms of a "simple binary opposition" but rather as an expanding and contracting textual circuit (Mills, *Discourses of Difference*, pp. 18, 44–45). Since Mills bases her thesis primarily on British women's travelogues, I am adjusting it for my own purposes.

27. The Fishers highlight the historical episode by using this phrase as subtitle to a section of the travelogue (p. 293).

28. "[D]epending upon the periods of historiography, it is the event, or it is the continuous series, which is the point of departure and the definition of the intelligible"; Michel de Certeau, *The Writing of History*, trans. Tom Conley (New York: Columbia University Press, 1988), p. 48.

29. Ibid., p. 81.

30. "The revolutionaries or pronunciados insisted that the President had not escaped, but had been allowed to depart from the palace with the understanding that he bore definite terms of peace from the insurgents and would work for agreement between factions" (editors' note, 734, n. 7).

31. Tom Conley, "Translation's Introduction: For a Literary Historiography," in de Certeau, *The Writing of History*, p. viii. See also discussion at pp. 36–37.

32. "Historiography bears within its own name a paradox — almost an oxymoron — of the relationship between two antinomic terms — between the real and discourse. Its task is connecting them (or) working *as* if two were being joined" (ibid., p. xxvii).

33. Ibid., p. 94; author's italics.

34. The Fishers provide the following apt summary of the contending forces that culminated in the 1841 uprising: "In theory the basic issue involved in this revolution was federalism versus centralism — Mexican names for the opposing viewpoints between liberals and conservatives. . . . The more liberal federalists, dominant for a while after the overthrow of Emperor Iturbide and at other periods since, were out of power at this time. In general they wanted as the embodiment of national policy a document similar to the supplanted constitution of 1824, under which Mexican state governments wielded strong influence. . . . The more conservative centralists, whose principles were embodied in the constitution of 1836, believed in a more authoritarian and centralized national government. Their constitution at this time was the law of the land, and Mexico was administered under departments rather than states, with each department headed by a military governor" (*Life in Mexico*, p. 733, n. 1).

35. De Certeau, *The Writing of History*, p. 94.

36. Cf. de Certeau's notion that "archival endeavors are always fragmentary" (ibid., p. ix). This demystifying move reverses the trend in Latin American literature toward representation of a grand Archive of Books as depository of (forbidden) knowledge. Roberto González Echevarría develops this notion in *Myth and Archive: A Theory of Latin American Narrative* (Cambridge: Cambridge University Press, 1990).

37. In the twentieth century, this grandiose rhetoric developed into a full-fledged

genre. As exemplified in Augusto Roa Bastos's *Yo, el supremo* (I, the Supreme One) (1974), the novel of the dictatorship manifests the discourses of power as an act of transcription between a powerful "I" and a more humble (and humbled) scribe. It also results from a collage of historical and biographical works and from an editing or process(ing) of texts. See Roberto González Echevarría, "The Dictatorship of Rhetoric/The Rhetoric of Dictatorship," in *The Voice of the Masters: Writing and Authority in Modern Latin American Literature* (Austin: University of Texas Press, 1985), pp. 77–79.

38. On p. 736, n. 34, the editors note that "it was not Mme de Staël, but an un-named lady whom she cited (in 1797, after the Reign of Terror). Napoleon said: 'Madame, I don't like women to mix in politics.' The lady retorted: 'You are right, general, but in a country where heads are cut off, it is natural that women should like to know why' (*Considérations sur les principaux événements de la révolution françoise*, II, 201 — edition of 1818)."

39. Though the Fishers include in this section a final chapter titled "The Warmth of Mexican Charity," which recounts Calderón de la Barca's visit to hospitals and foundling homes (pp. 528–43), the historical narrative is displayed only in the first three chapters. See "Manifestoes and the Roaring of Cannon," "Refuge in the Country," and "Back to the Capital" (*Life in Mexico*, 495–527). Historian Jan Bazant describes how the Mexican Congress was forced to draft a new constitution to moderate Santa Anna's near despotic rule. Finally, "when Santa Anna's fiscal extortions became unbearable, General Paredes, known for his honesty in financial matters, rebelled in Guadalajara. . . . Santa Anna was overthrown at the end of 1844, imprisoned and then exiled for life" ("Mexico from Independence to 1867," pp. 440–41).

40. The term is used by Georg Lukács in *The Historical Novel* (Boston: Beacon Press, 1963).

41. The Fishers use this term to describe Bustamante's retreat (p. 783, n. 18).

42. The alliance formed between Generals Valencia, Paredes, and the ubiquitous Santa Anna is described as "a centralist revolt against centralism" (Bazant, "Mexico from Independence to 1867," p. 439).

43. "Santa Anna's government became increasingly reactionary and autocratic. He loved the pageantry and pomp of office but despised the daily work of administration" (ibid., p. 451).

44. The story goes on as follows: "This government, informed of the misfortune, sent for the husband of the deceased, and ordered twenty-five dollars to be given him; but the unfortunate man, though plunged in grief, declared that twelve were sufficient to supply his wants" (p. 299).

45. "Historiography . . . represents the dead along a narrative itinerary" (de Certeau, *The Writing of History*, p. 100). The author discusses historiography as "a burial rite" that simultaneously exorcises and honors the dead from previous historical periods (pp. 99–102).

46. In de Certeau's formulation, the gap between past and present, marked by historical writing in terms of the divide of death, allows the living to fully participate in or fulfill the present time (p. 101).

47. Cf. Bazant, "Mexico from Independence to 1867," p. 438.

48. Contrast Mink's *Historical Understanding* with de Certeau's claims that "the reader [is placed] in the position of what is quoted" (*The Writing of History*, p. 95).

49. The Fishers make a similar point: "In practice, *pronunciamientos* often lacked the simplicity of a struggle based on clear-cut principles. What complicated them, and sometimes rendered them intellectually and economically meaningless, was the cynical opportunism of some of the high-ranking military figures of the day" (p. 733, n. 1).

50. The editors gave chapter 25 the title "Quiet after the Cannonading" (pp. 316–23) and express a more cynical view of the whole affair when they state that "nothing was accomplished" (p. 736, n. 1).

51. De Certeau, *The Writing of History*, p. 99.

52. "The historian is no longer a person who shapes an empire. He or she no longer envisages the paradise of a global history. The historian comes to circulate *around* acquired rationalizations. He or she works in the margins" (ibid., p. 79; author's italics). The difference between nineteenth- and twentieth-century historiography is explained as a shift from "the totalizing function" of history to "a critical experimentation" (p. 80).

53. Lukács, *The Historical Novel*.

54. Cf. Molloy, *At Face Value*.

55. It must be noted that in both of these cases, the "distinguished men" had also been the Calderóns' hosts. During the September 1841 episode, the couple had taken refuge at the Fagoagas' country estate of San Xavier (p. 766, n. 1; p. 506); they had previously visited the Tagles' hacienda in San Angel and "will shortly return to it again" (p. 767, n. 23). Hence the gesture of including them among Mexico's luminaries could be interpreted more as an appreciative token of respect than as a "truth claim" on Mexican nationalism.

56. The passage is worth quoting in full: "It is very much the case, in Mexico at present, that the most distinguished men are those who live most retired — those who have played their part on the arena of public life, have seen the inutility of their efforts in favor of their country, and *have now retreated into the bosom of their families*, where they endeavor to forget public evils in domestic retirement and literary occupation" (pp. 421–22; emphasis mine).

57. In speaking about Santa Anna and Bustamante, Calderón states that "if they met by chance in a drawing room, they would give each other as cordial an *abrazo* (embrace), Mexican fashion, as if nothing had happened" (p. 522).

58. Joan W. Scott, *Gender and the Politics of History* (New York: Columbia University Press, 1988), pp. 19–20.

59. "Historical discourse makes a *social identity* explicit, not so much in the way it is 'given' or held as stable, as in the ways it is *differentiated* from a former period or another society" (de Certeau, *The Writing of History*, p. 45; author's italics).

60. Rosario Castellanos, "La mujer mexicana en el siglo XIX," *Mujer que sabe latin* (Mexico City: SepDiana, 1979), p. 160.

FLORENCE S. BOOS

A HISTORY OF THEIR OWN:

MONA CAIRD, FRANCES SWINEY,

AND FIN DE SIÈCLE FEMINIST

FAMILY HISTORY

In *The Creation of Patriarchy*, Gerda Lerner argues that the exclusion of women from formal history has always been one of the chief instruments of their subordination: "Women are essential and central to creating society; they are and always have been actors and agents in history. Women have 'made history,' yet they have been kept from knowing their History and from interpreting history, either their own or that of men. . . . The existence of women's history has been obscured and neglected by patriarchal thought, a fact which has significantly affected the psychology of men and women."[1] In this essay, I will try to show that a similar sense of historical marginality troubled Victorian women and that several late nineteenth-century women writers attempted to extend the inadequate and distortive historical record they found.

These few women were disenfranchised and un-"empowered," their intended audience was relatively small, and many male reformers and socialists ignored their efforts or dismissed them with polite incomprehension and faint praise.[2] Even "revolutionaries," who accepted as a matter of course that wives should not be "subject to their husbands," continued to assume that women were "relative creatures," defined "naturally" through subordinate familial and sexual ties.[3]

Against this double gradient of virulent resistance and polite indifference, some women of the late nineteenth century began to construct an alternative history of women's experience. As they worked, they tended quite naturally to focus on the glaring injustices of contemporary marriage laws, whose historical antecedents and "social construction" they had critically begun to explore.

Marriage was an iron necessity for most Victorian women, who remained under British law in "coverture," subject to their husbands' rule, legally unable to sign contracts, and deprived of all property rights (including the rights to their own earnings). The Matrimonial Causes Act of 1857, moreover, had loosened the straitjacket of marriage for *men*— who could now divorce on grounds of adultery — but permitted divorce to *women* only when witnesses attested to bestiality, bigamy, or gross cruelty. A woman who left her husband under any circumstances was guilty of desertion and forfeited any minimal claims she might otherwise have had to common property and financial support. She also lost all right of access to her children, a provision that especially embittered those Victorian feminists and reformists who considered women's primary role to be that of mother and rearer of children. "Wives were dependent upon their husbands to keep their children near them, for wifely insubordination might be punished by a child's being dispatched to live with relatives, apprenticed out to work, or sent away to a school abhorrent to the mother." [4]

None of these sanctions, of course, applied to men. In effect, the "reforms" of the Matrimonial Causes Act permitted men to "put away" women, but not conversely. In this sense, they legalized a sexual double standard and reconfirmed marriage as a form of de facto chattel slavery.

In the latter half of the nineteenth century, parliamentary reformers introduced several modest efforts to redress this situation. Property Acts of 1870 and 1882 permitted married women limited rights to separate earnings and to property, and another Matrimonial Causes Act in 1878 gave women the right to appeal for separation on the grounds of repeated assault, though this act continued to deny them any right to divorce. A husband's "conjugal rights," by contrast — his "right" to sexual consent — remained inviolate in all circumstances, even when he carried one or another venereal disease. Only in 1895, after a major court decision in 1891, did the Summary Jurisdiction Act extend the right of appeal for legal separation to wives who had been deserted or physically abused, and "conjugal rights" survived as a category in British law until 1970.

Toward the end of the nineteenth century, then, middle-class married women and their male allies in Parliament eked out a few partial rights to escape the most blatant forms of physical and sexual abuse, but women had not yet secured the right to divorce, to remarry, or to retain custody of their children. Moreover, paternalism, not incipient egalitarianism, provided many of the rhetorical pleas for these bills. Two generations had passed since the "reform" of 1857, and the tortuous course of piecemeal efforts to redress its inequities had long since claimed the minds and efforts of feminists, who were convinced that deep forms of systemic oppression had prevented more substantive forms of social change. Most readers of the scattered essays and reviews that Eleanor Marx, Mona Caird, and Frances Swiney managed to place in *Commonweal*, the *Westminster Review*, and other progressive journals, were well aware of this recent history, and a few at least must have found ample reason to attend to more radical political and historiographical arguments.

Nineteenth-century reformers of every sort typically sought underlying systematic explanations for current social conditions in economics or in history (sometimes both), and "sages" of every persuasion — the authors of *Past and Present*, *Culture and Anarchy*, *Modern Painters*, *The Stones of Venice*, and *The Renaissance*, for example — had rewritten social institutions' "historical" origins to point out various reformist, conservative, or reactionary morals. So it was natural and appropriate for Victorian feminists to seek historical perspectives for their polemical analyses of the situation of contemporary women. Most of the period's standard histories, however — Henry Hallam's *History of the Middle Ages*, John Neale's *History of the Christian Church*, Thomas Macaulay's *Essays*, Thomas Arnold's *History of Rome*, J. R. Greene's *History of the English People*, and even William Prescott's *Histories* of Mexico and Peru, and socialist writings such as Henry Hyndman's *The Historical Basis of Socialism* — focused almost exclusively on the actions of white male rulers, warriors, scholars, artists, and artisans from central and southern Europe. Those unrecognized in the associated political and cultural debates, accordingly, were excluded ("erased") from the period's cultural histories. A historical anthropologist from another planetary system might study these works scrupulously, or the works of many of their twentieth-century successors, for that matter, and find in their pages little evidence that the human species included roughly equal numbers of men and women, and even less evidence that each of the two groups had made comparable contributions to human culture.

Against this orthodoxy, the small but vigorous conventicle of late-Victorian feminist reformers and scholars whom I wish to recall strove to reclaim and redefine women's roles in the creation of a common human past and to locate substantial aspects of a shared cultural and social history in "woman-identified" terms. In the process, they broadened contemporary history and historiography to include studies of family re-

lationships, material conditions, social life, and cultural assumptions —
and they anticipated, therefore, more recent historical practice in significant ways that are themselves now part of women's history.

Some of these late nineteenth-century feminists, such as Agnes and
Elizabeth Strickland, were historians of England; others, such as Anna
Jameson, were critics of art. Still others, such as Mary Kingsley or Barbara Freire-Marreco, wrote as travelers or anthropologists, in defense of
"primitive" or superficially alien modes of thought. A few, such as Vernon Lee, moved gracefully across several genres — in her case, biographical appreciation, essay, historical interpretation, travel narrative, and art
criticism. Basic to all their attempts to re-create women's history, however, were the concomitant efforts of a few reformers to present a revisionist history of marriage laws and women's subordination within the
family.

The near-exclusion of women from academic establishments, of
course, gave feminist reformers less access to the information needed to
prepare and mount their "historical" case. But reformist historians of
women's common past also faced a further dilemma as they prepared
their arguments. On the one hand, they felt an urgent strategic need to
argue for changes in self-evidently reasonable and inoffensive terms, a
task that might be best served by the presentation of reformist and progressive histories in basically meliorist terms. On the other, only "strong
interpretations" and indictments of the evils of women's past repression
could even begin to overcome the biases of the existing record and explain their present situation.

Still another problem, related to those mentioned already, was posed
by the difficulty of clarifying in firm evidentiary terms *which* of the historical sequences that they wished to retrace *were* "progressive," "static,"
or "regressive." By convention, Victorian histories often recorded uniformly "progressive" evolutionary patterns or pointed to (allegedly) un-
controversial and originary sources of ancestral pride. However Darwin
himself saw his account of biological origins, for example, assorted
Darwinian social historians found in it a mighty fortress of orderly
progression, dictated by rational laws and manifested in naturally or-
dained distinctions between sexes and races. Similarly, Westermarck's
patriarchal *History of Human Marriage* imposed on history the development of a pan-European pattern of male family governance and identified this pattern with the progression of morality and social order.[5]

Feminist historians thus had to decide whether to impugn the conclusions of such a metanarrative, its premises, or its methodological lines of putative inference. The works of revisionist male historiographies offered partial prototypes for all three.

ANTECEDENT MALE FEMINIST HISTORICISM

Several reformist historicists had evoked aspects of an alternatively idealized past as precursors of desirable future conditions. In fact, the two great godfathers of nineteenth-century feminism — J. J. Bachofen, in *Das Mutterrecht* (1861), and Friedrich Engels, in *Der Ursprung des Familie, des Privateigenthums, und der Staates* (*The origin of the family, private property, and the state*) (1871) — both imagined an archaic, prepatriarchal state, in which women enjoyed more determining influence (Bachofen) and greater sexual freedom (Engels). Bachofen believed the evolution from an earlier, more-inclusive matriarchal *Mutterrecht* to its present patriarchal and individualist successor was regrettable but inevitable, but he also believed that an ideal society to come would restore the lost cultural benignity of the earlier matriarchal epoch:

> At the lowest, darkest stage of human existence [mother-child love was] the only light in the moral darkness. . . . Raising her young, the woman learns earlier than the man to extend her loving care beyond the limits of the ego to another creature. . . . Woman at this stage is the repository of all culture, of all benevolence, of all devotion, of all concern for the living and grief for the dead. . . . We find the matriarchal peoples distinguished by rectitude, piety, and culture; we see women serving as conscientious guardians of the mystery, of justice and peace. . . . Seen in this light, matriarchy becomes a sign of cultural progress, a source and guarantee of its benefits, and a necessary period in the education of mankind, and hence the fulfillment of a natural law which governs peoples as well as individuals.[6]

Bachofen's notions of women's essential contributions to the earliest periods of human history of religion and culture focused primarily on woman-as-mother, unlike those of Engels and Eleanor Marx, who viewed women primarily as sexual and companionate partners, respectively. Bachofen also offered some original insights — that different relationships between children and parents might emerge in families organized by mothers, for example, rather than by legally dominant fathers, and that maternally organized communal societies might foster a different and more inclusive ethic: "Whereas the paternal principle is inherently

restrictive, the maternal principle is universal; the paternal principle implies limitation to definite groups, but the maternal principle, like the
life of nature, knows no barriers. *The idea of motherhood produces a sense
of universal fraternity among all men, which dies with the development of
paternity*" (80) (emphasis added).

Bachofen's accounts merit further interest for their strong association
of women with the origins of human culture, their recognition that al-
ternate family structures may foster less-competitive modes of behavior,
and their avowals of a need to achieve (or recover) a "religion of humanity." Against the background of Bachofen's insights, finally, Engels's
"matriarchy" can be seen for what it is: not a matriarchy at all but rather
a matrilinear patriarchal agricultural society, whose vaguely adumbrated
ethos included few norms for organization or decision making beyond
general appeals to "community."

Engels's *Origin* myth, similarly, offered an ostensibly historicist argument that women's oppression lay rooted in an allegedly reversible sequence of past events. In one now-famous formulation, for example, he
asserted that the transition from matriarchal communal tribalism to
bourgeois patriarchy marked "the world-historical defeat of the female
sex," and he considered the basic forms of class oppression to be iso-
morphic in certain respects with those of women by men. Only a society no longer based on capitalist oppression, he claimed, would free men
and women to experience the happiness of sexual choice. The motive
force of women's emancipation, however, would be a communist revolution, to be led principally by proletarian and bourgeois men.[7]

Essentially, Engels presented in *The Origin of the Family, Private Property, and the State* an impassioned defense of *sexual* freedom for both
sexes, marred by a notable lack of interest in the central role of child-
raising by "the Family" and by a certain irrealism about the consequences
and preconditions of such freedom — for example, when he remarked
that group marriage is "the form of family in which whole groups of men
and whole groups of women mutually possess one another, and which
leaves little room for jealousy" (31). Nor did Engels pause to ask what life
in his hypothetical matrilinear society might really have been like, above
all, for women as well as for men. There is no mention of women's conduct of tribal government, for example, or their contributions to religion
or art, or their shared responsibility for war, or their relationships with
their partners, or — of manifest importance within a matriarchy, after
all—their children and each other (little literal or metaphorical "sister-

hood" here). Since Engels — like Karl Marx, August Bebel, Eleanor Marx, and almost all other nineteenth-century socialists — professed to find all forms of homosexuality utterly abhorrent, gay and lesbian ties in the new/old order of "sexual freedom" are also nonexistent.

Other simplistic aspects of Engels's analyses remained to haunt the history of feminism and socialist theory. His historically inaccurate assumptions that male domination occurred only in capitalist and bourgeois civil societies wrongly suggested that the abolition of certain narrowly defined industrial hierarchies would liberate women from sexist subordination, in itself and as a matter of course. Such assumptions ignored hidden patterns of persistent violence against women — domestic abuse and rape, for example — and other patterns of behavior that lack simple economic motivation, whatever their underlying causes. What analysis of economic exploitation, for example, could explain why men of all classes attacked their wives and children, but their wives and children seldom attacked them? Why, moreover, on Engels's account, were industrial working women paid half or less of the wages earned by their male counterparts? Why did male workers often justify these inequities?

In summary, few nineteenth-century male theorists of family origins, with the partial exception of Bachofen, whatever their ostensible ideology, discerned any connection between rigid gender divisions and (for example) recurrent forms of individual and communal violence. Given these precedents, it is noticeable how few of the late nineteenth-century women who attempted to review women's history — even Eleanor Marx, whose *The Woman Question* (1887) was directly indebted to Engels — chose to appeal to a more sexually egalitarian idealized past. Perhaps, like many later historians and anthropologists, these women reformers doubted the evidence for its existence. Unlike the male socialist-feminists, these writers were not centrally concerned with extensions of women's (hetero)sexual freedom (Eleanor Marx here is an exception). Rather, one might compare their approach with that of the contemporary feminist Catharine MacKinnon, in her 1989 polemic, *Toward a Feminist Theory of the State*.[8] They sought liberation in the forms that seemed most immediately relevant to them and therefore concentrated most of their force in sustained attacks against the legal systems that bound women and against reinforced forms of systemic and systematic violence — coerced marriage, prostitution, assault, rape, and murder — inflicted on women with relative impunity throughout history. Despite many political differences, these feminists also agreed that traditional

European marriage, "bourgeois" and otherwise, was a cross-cultural, cross-temporal disaster, largely invariant under the stages or economic bases of the social order that sanctioned and defined it.

ANTECEDENT WOMEN'S HISTORIES: SYDNEY OWENSON, ANNIE BESANT, AND ELEANOR MARX

For these writers' aggrieved histories of the continuing economic and legal oppression of women, several partial earlier Victorian precedents would have been available. The first of these texts was Sydney Owenson/Lady Morgan's 1840 *Woman and Her Master*, a fiery work that deserves to be better known. Owenson/Morgan is now remembered chiefly as the author of a much earlier work, *The Wild Irish Girl* (1806), and her growing blindness delayed completion of *Woman and Her Master* for many years, so that it seems a work displaced from its original radical late Enlightenment context.

In essence, Owenson found in history a sustained conspiracy to limit women's social influence: "To limit and pervert this agency has been the great object of the social and legal institutions of imperfect civilisation; to give a full development to the design of nature, by better arrangements, will be the crowning labour of man's earthly warfare, his triumph over himself." [9] Her response to this conspiracy was to record women's achievements in the face of male social hegemony and personal domination, and her narrative focuses primarily on the accomplishments of distinguished women (Esther, Aspasia, Zenobia, Paulina). Owenson had no further agenda to unite women in resistance to their generic subordination, but she (unlike Engels) did present some women as exceptional historical agents, not merely as passive victims. She also anticipated the pride of such later feminists as Mona Caird and Frances Swiney in a traduced history of women's accomplishment: "Alluded to, rather as an incident than a principal in the chronicles of nations, [woman's] influence, which cannot be denied, has been turned into a reproach; her genius, which could not be concealed, has been treated as a phenomenon, when not considered as monstrosity!" . . . [Yet] wherever woman has been, there has she left the track of her humanity, to mark her passage." [10]

Other dissident antecedents for reformist historians of the 1890s included Annie Besant, author of *Marriage As It Was, As It Is, and As It Should Be* (1879), and Eleanor Marx, whose work *The Woman Question* appeared in 1887.[11] Both attacked the gross inequities of women's employment, denounced the repression of women's sexuality and right to raise their own children, and examined the psychological consequences of the denial of sexual autonomy.

Besant's bitter review of the injustices of marriage law anticipated Mona Caird's later indictment of women's legally enforced subordination and brought into sharp relief origins of marital "traditions" in religious and legal brutality. She dryly summarized a few such traditions, for example, as follows:

> Among some barbarous nations the winning of a bride is still harsher: the bridegroom rushes into the father's house, knocks the maiden down, picks up her senseless body, flings it over his shoulder, and runs for his life; he is pursued by the youth of the village, pelted with stones, sticks, &c., and has to win his wife by sheer strength and swiftness. In some tribes this is a mere marriage ceremony, a survival from the time when the fight was a real one, and amongst ourselves the slipper thrown after the departing bridgroom and bride is a direct descendant of the heavier missiles thrown with deadly intent thousands of years ago by our remote ancestors. (6)

In anticipation that some contemporary readers might reply that Judeo-Christian doctrine had significantly tempered such abuses, Besant briefly reviewed the relevant Old and New Testament precedents and precepts:

> After the destruction of Benjamin, as related in Judges xxi, it was arranged that the survivors should possess themselves of women as wives by force and fraud: "Lie in wait in the vineyards, and see and behold if the daughters of Shiloh come out to dance in dances, then come ye out of the vineyards, and catch you every man his wife. . . . And the children of Benjamin did so, and took their wives according to their number, of them that danced, whom they caught." (Judges xxi. 20, 21, 23, 6)
> . . . both the New Testament and the Church have insisted on the inferiority of the female sex: "the husband is the head of the wife" (Eph. v. 23); "wives, submit yourselves unto your own husbands" (Col. iii. 18); "your women . . . are commanded to be under obedience" (I Cor. xiv. 34); "ye wives, be in subjection to your own husbands . . . even as Sara obeyed Abraham, calling him lord, whose daughters ye are as long as ye do well." (I Pet. iii. 1, 6)

Besant concluded that redress could come only from open opposition to such institutionalized forms of domestic oppression — that is, the complete rejection of marriage in any form:

> I take leave to think that women have a fairer chance of happiness and comfort in an unlegalised than in a legal marriage. . . . If all the men and women who disapprove of the present immoral laws would sturdily *and openly* oppose them; if those who desire to unite their lives, but are determined not to submit to the English marriage laws, would publicly join hands, making such a declaration as is here suggested, the unlegalized marriage would be recognized as a dignified and civilized substitute for the old brutal and savage traditions. (36)

The only woman-authored socialist-feminist treatise of the period was Eleanor Marx's *The Woman Question* (1887), nominally coauthored with her husband, Edward Aveling. Revised and expanded from an earlier review for *Commonweal* of August Bebel's *Woman and Socialism*, *The Woman Question* showed markedly greater interest in and sympathy for contemporary literature by and about women than earlier socialist-feminist treatises by male authors, and partially exempted two major forms of female solidarity from the usual charges of mere "bourgeois reformism": the campaign for the repeal of the Contagious Diseases Act and the movement to extend wider educational opportunities to women.[12]

Also absent from male-authored feminist treatises was *The Woman Question*'s critique of the psychological harm inflicted by several of women's subordinate roles, including their mandated passivity in courting and sexual behavior: "We suggest as another wrong to women the rigorous social rule that from man only must come the first proffer of affection, the proposal for marriage" (18). More significantly, Marx argued even more pointedly than Besant that women must organize themselves to change their collective future: "Both the oppressed classes, women and the immediate producers, must understand that their emancipation will come from themselves. Women will find allies in the better sort of men, as the labourers are finding allies among the philosophers, artists, and poets. But the one has nothing to hope from man as a whole, and the other has nothing to hope from the middle class as a whole" (15).

In another passage, Marx denounces the pervasive effects of ordinary women's double drudgery: "The man, worn out as he may be by labour, has the evening in which to do nothing. The woman is occupied until bedtime comes. Often with young children her toil goes far into, or all through the night" (19).

Most impassioned, however, are *The Woman Question*'s attacks on prudery, and pointed demands for (hetero)sexual education. There must be free discussion of "the sexual question in all its bearing," by men and women "looking frankly into each other's faces" (23). "There can never be a time when falsehood should be taught about any function of the body" (21), for "with the false shame and false secrecy, against which we protest, goes the unhealthy separation of the sexes that begins as children quit the nursery, and only ends when the dead men and women are laid in the common earth" (22). Such remarks have the sting of felt observation and immediate response; they go beyond Engels's and Bachofen's judicious generalities.

Like Besant's *Marriage*, *The Woman Question* also advocates female independence, a full range of creative occupations, and an ideal of intellectual companionship in heterosexual unions. In one remark, which recalls several passages from John Stuart Mill and Harriet Taylor's *The Subjection of Woman* (1869), Marx invokes an ideal of mental as well as emotional fellowship between the sexes:

> The highest ideal seems to be the complete, harmonious, lasting blending of two human lives. Such an ideal . . . needs at least four things. These are love, respect, intellectual likeness, and command of the necessities of life. . . . Intellectual likeness. The same education for men and women; the bringing up of these twain side by side, until they join hands at last, will ensure a greater degree of this. That objectionable product of capitalism, Tennyson's "In Memoriam" young woman, with her "I cannot understand, I love," will be a myth. Every one will have learnt that there can be no love without understanding. (27–28)

The passage's wistful tone marks its visionary counterfactuality, and it bears observation that the period's only woman-authored socialist-feminist treatise pointedly idealized mental and sexual companionship in marriage, rather than the parenting of children. Besant, by contrast, firmly advocated children's rights to freedom from violence and coercion, and Besant and Mona Caird, both mothers, were more attentive to the social implications of family life.

MONA CAIRD'S *THE MORALITY OF MARRIAGE*:
FEMINIST EGALITARIANISM AND THE "NEW WOMAN"

Two of the period's more comprehensive attempts to rewrite women's history were Mona Caird's *The Morality of Marriage and Other Essays on the Status and Destiny of Woman* (1897), which advocated a strong form of feminist egalitarianism, and Frances Swiney's *The Awakening of Women* (1897), which mingled a fierce sense of women's potential contributions to society with an occasionally rather bizarre assortment of evolutionary scientism, mystical and anti-erotic Protestant Christianity, and preachments of female and Anglo-Saxon supremacy. To her credit, Swiney also attempted to provide a cross-cultural narrative of women's past achievements, and succeeded, in fact, in providing one of the earliest comparative accounts in English of women's lives in Europe, Asia, and India.

Caird's *The Morality of Marriage* devotes five chapters to a historical account of women's position in the family. She draws freely on other nineteenth-century historians and anthropologists (Tylor, Westermark, Reclus) to cite vastly divergent systems of (alleged) tribal regulation, inheritance, and family structure, and she advocates skeptical suspension of judgment about any one among them. Like Owenson, she was also attracted to evidence that women may have been honored in past societies and that their actual contributions throughout history may well have been equal to or superior to those of men. With pleasure, for example, she records the anarchist ethnologist Elie Reclus's description of the society of Indian Nairs, in which "proud and haughty warrior though he be, the Nair cheerfully obeys his mother. . . . Formerly, in grand ceremonials, the reigning prince himself yielded precedence to his eldest daughter, and of course recognized still more humbly the priority of his mother, before whom he did not venture to seat himself until she had given him permission." [13]

Following lines of argument pioneered by Owenson, August Bebel, and Reclus, Caird also set forth her claim that women were the originators and preservers of early civilizations:

Researches of recent years have brought to light the remarkable fact that woman, as the first agriculturalist, the first herbalist, the initiator of the art of medicine, the discoverer of the most ancient of human lore, is, as Karl Pearson says, "the pioneer of all civilisation." So far from being the receptive and adaptive creature of popular imagination, she, in fact, holds the position of leader and originator in all the arts of industry: the prophetess and teacher of humanity from the beginning of its upward career. (70)

A major component of her argument, however, remains her sustained appeal to cultural plurality as a source of enlightened — we might say "deconstructive" — skepticism. A radical relativist, Caird adduced with evident delight customs that contravened a wide range of Victorian assumptions about "natural" behavior: societies in which family ties are based on the bond between nephew and uncle, for example; or in which the families of women buy them husbands, who then are granted a status somewhere between that of kinspeople and chattel. The more eccentric and improbable these examples were, of course, the more readily they supported Caird's thesis that "there is, perhaps, no set of ideas so fundamental that human beings have not somewhere, at some period of the world, lived in direct contradiction to them" (23).

History thus became for Caird in part a pastiche of "socially constructed" oddities, but it also provided a nearly blank tablet of human desires, on which the living may write a better future:

> In short, we are forced either to ignore all that is now known about the primitive habits and ideas of mankind, or to resign ourselves to surrender any pet theory about "human nature" which we may happen to cherish. And having submitted to that painful sacrifice, we are rewarded by finding another belief in the place of the former one, which is, after all, more inspiring. We discover that "human nature" need not be a perpetual obstacle to change, to hope, and to progress, as we have hitherto persistently made it; but that it is the very instrument or material through which that change, that hope, and that progress may be achieved. (40)

Several of Caird's most persuasive arguments, however, were *not* relativist. She clearly appealed to an implicit and underlying sense of personal and distributive justice — which she presumably hoped would, after all, be an "essential" part of protean "human nature" — in her bitter account of the ways in which English marriage laws have systematically and historically kept women in economic bondage. In these pages of the work, history suddenly ceased for her to be a random collection of inconsistent curiosa, as she reviews the systematic rapine of women's labor by legal institutions, which effected monopolies of male power. Here Caird's feminist history, like that of Besant, expressed pure anger that such clear and pervasive forms of injustice have endured for so long, cloaked by customs that sanctify desire for domination and naked greed.

She traced the familiar patriarchal notion that a woman is her husband's property, for example, to the prerogatives of the Roman *pater-familias*, who "handed her over to the power of her husband, who then had the same rights of punishment — nay, of life and death, which the father had previously enjoyed. He might even sell her into slavery" (41). . . . "In ancient history the woman has been under the power of the father; modern history shows her under that of the husband" (47). Following Mary Wollstonecraft and Harriet Taylor, Caird denounced the historical antecedents of patriarchy in the "right of capture": "The point to be made clear is that paternal rights take their rise in the ownership of the mother, and not in the relationship to the children or the support which the father may afford them. These latter circumstances are now merely employed as a justification of the anomaly that she who bears the children is deprived of full rights regarding them" (50). . . . "Woman originally became the property of man by right of capture; now the wife is his by right of law" (72).[14]

Interestingly, the Scottish Caird considered the medieval Roman Catholic Church somewhat more favorably inclined to women than its puritanical Protestant successors. Along with many other Victorian progressives, such as John Stuart Mill and Harriet Taylor, Walter Pater, and Vernon Lee, she also considered chivalric ideals a relatively benign mitigation of the "law of the stronger" and found little of value in the dour clericalism of the Protestant Reformation. Especially offensive to her was what she believed to have been Luther's view that marriage is a necessary concession to "evil" desires: "Indeed, it is difficult to see how the Father of Evil himself, in his most inspired moments[,] could have devised a means of placing marriage on a more degrading basis than that on which it was placed, of malice aforethought, by the great reformer" (79). She cited with particular disgust Melanchthon's grim injunction to women, to bear children until they drop: "If a woman becomes weary of bearing children, that matters not: let her only die from bearing, she is there to do it" (85).

Caird also reacted skeptically to claims that the Reformation had a softening effect on family relations: "The woman's position, as established at this epoch, was one of great degradation. . . . A man might indeed be a tyrant in his own home, in the devout belief that he was doing no more than exercising his just rights, nay, performing his bounden duties as ruler of the household" (81).

More significantly, Caird also examined two other issues that have continued to preoccupy feminists in the succeeding century: the social origins of prostitution and the rigid enforcement of double standards in sexual behavior. In the Renaissance, for example, arose "that professional class of women, who were at once imperiously demanded and sternly punished by the community, their offence being their response to the demand. . . . The arrangement was more than convenient. It secured from a friendless class enormous services (or at least it secured that which society demanded); it afforded the woman who had become the legal property of one man, the satisfaction of looking down on a position which she was able to consider more despicable than her own — wherefore, has never yet been explained — and thus helped to reconcile her to a social arrangement which told so heavily against her. . . . Anyone who realises the conditions of life at that time, cannot fail to understand what must have been the fate of such unfriended women" (82–83).

Caird's parenthetical remark ("wherefore, has never yet been explained") makes it clear that she also shared one radical view of late nineteenth-century socialist-feminists: marriage is legally sanctioned and regulated *prostitution* (and not, say, legally regulated reproduction of human capital): "A religious rite or a legal form is, for a woman, to mark the whole difference between irredeemable sin and absolute duty. From this significant fact it is easy to infer the nature of the married woman's position, and to see that — unless human laws have some supernatural power of sanctification — her position is, *per se*, degrading" (87).

In a bold, if somewhat mixed, metaphorical leap, Caird also reclaimed for women the historical significance of their unrecorded labor: "And thus, while women were ignored in the obvious course of human affairs, and history soared above their bowed heads, the material of that very history was forming under their hands. In those shrouded homes, where the minds of children received their life-long stamp from the mothers of the race, all the determining elements of human sentiment were initiated and fashioned" (85). Some aspects of her assertion are familiar, of course ("The hand that rocks the cradle . . ."). But it also anticipates later theoretical claims that "the early modern subject" was modeled in the lives of women and that, in Gerda Lerner's formulation, "it is inconceivable for anything ever to have taken place in the world in which women were not involved, except if they were prevented from participation through coercion and repression" (228).

Caird's final summary briefly reviews several aspects of her indictment: "The result of such a bird's-eye view is not cheering . . . :— strict marriage, prostitution, . . . commercialism and competition in the most exaggerated forms, the subjection of women, . . . their . . . purchase by men, under differing names and conditions through society; and finally, the (. . . consequent) dual moral standard for the two sexes" (91). Her analysis is not without its middle-class liberal limitations, of course — a lingering problem for her intellectual descendants, us included. Her text gives little attention, for example, to the routine physical drudgery performed by poor women, and she makes no explicit mention of the extent to which sexual "purchase" included the right to inflict venereal disease — both omissions were addressed by Swiney. In contrast to Bachofen and Owenson, however, this "new woman" of the 1890s *did* envision a looser form of (heterosexual) social bonding than that of the nuclear family: "In a still distant condition of society, it is probable that unions may exist outside the law but inside society; men and women caring only for the real bond between them, and treating as of quite minor importance the artificial or legal tie" (125).

One final feature also separates Caird's discussion from most of its antecedents, with the clear exception of Besant: her explicit concern for "the children of the future." In the chapter which bears this title, however, she argues that only competent, eager, and presumably at-times-paid child-minders should take over the job: "Some day a mother's affection will show itself, not in industrious self-sacrifice, which reduces her to a pulpy nonentity, feeble in body and mind, and generally ends in bringing her child to a similar condition; but in a resolve to take the full advantage of all that science is busily providing, for those who will accept her bounties" (156).

Caird's class standing may have prevented her from considering the possibility of collective child care here, and some personal distaste for the job may be reflected by her apparent failure to consider alternative constructive models for childrearing by adults of both sexes. Her evasion of this issue is shared by other Victorian advocates of divorce reform, however, who were less than eager to confront the genuinely vexing moral issues involved for children as well as parents. Also, like other Victorian reformers of both sexes, she was simply unable to envision a world in which fathers might willingly rear children. I only find it disappointing that someone who understood so clearly the degrading effects of legally enforced subordination and abuse on *women* should have side-stepped the implications of *patria potestas* for the development of much more dependent and physically vulnerable *children*.

FRANCES SWINEY'S *THE AWAKENING OF WOMEN*: SEPARATISM AND FEMALE SUPERIORITY

Frances Swiney's *The Awakening of Women: Or, Women's Part in Evolution* was more simplistic and less consistent than Besant's stringent treatise or Caird's polemical tour de force, but it also offered a more extended overview and valuation of women's underreported contributions to several cultures and pioneered some lines of thought that have reappeared in the work of later feminists.[15] Swiney prefaced her account of women's history with some bold claims about women's putative physiology and psychology: "[The] testimony of women's 'superhuman' powers is exceedingly valuable in conjunction with the advanced scientific opinion, that the child and the woman approximate nearest to the higher line of evolution; they foreshadow, as it were, the future development of the race" (38); "it is remarkable that European women are much more susceptible to occult influences than men" (37); "the progress of the human race is dependent on the development of . . . woman to be the embodiment of that love which compassed the universe, and is the ultimate goal of all creation in the cosmic plan" (48).

In radical contrast to Besant, Caird, and Eleanor Marx, Swiney saw no reason for women to demand more sexual freedom, for "they have not to battle with fierce and almost uncontrollable passions; they can, serenely and unmoved, go on their appointed way, undisturbed by the lower instincts of human nature" (67); "marriage is necessary to woman only as it affects the reproduction of the species — her organism is not dependent on it; and it is probable that as woman develops more and more her intellectual faculties . . . , she will evince an ever-increasing repugnance to marriage, as a mere outlet of animal passion, and only enter on so holy and mysterious a bond under certain well-defined restrictions and conditions" (105).

Despite Swiney's apparent separatism, the commentator Ignota characterized *The Awakening of Women* in the *Westminster Review* as a book "written by a woman for women . . . [which] may none the less be read with great profit by every earnest-minded man desirous of comprehending the inner meaning of the 'woman movement.' Every such person, however much he may differ on special points, will find ample material for searching thought in each of its 300 suggestive pages."[16] A more-critical writer for the *Englishwoman's Review* noted some several of the work's apparent inconsistencies and remarked that the reader might be tempted

> to close the book in despair, though, after all, that would be doing it an injustice. . . . It inclines too much to the very questionable practice of regarding men and women as two distinct species, losing sight of the fact that they are both primarily human beings, with a good stock of qualities in common, and able to supplement each other out of those wherein they differ. . . . Mrs. Swiney is the first writer we have met with who has seriously maintained that woman is complete by herself and has no need of man, while he cannot get on without her.[17]

More useful than *The Awakening*'s potpourri of mysticism, scientism, transcendentalism, and anti-eroticism is its attempt to provide a survey of women's historical roles in chapters titled "Woman as the Wife," "Woman as the Mother," "Woman as the Sister," "Woman as the Worker in the Past," and "Woman's Work in the Present and the Future." Swiney's loosely organized account of women's labor throughout the centuries follows Reclus, Caird, and American anthropologist Otis Mason's ascriptions of a high degree of creativity to early women:

> Primitive woman was always practical; . . . but usefulness of aim did not deter her from exercising her sense of the beautiful, or dull her powers of observation. As a close student of nature, in touch with all the treasures of earth, and wood, and field, she instinctively imitated natural forms, curves, colours, and combinations; and thus toiling for duty's sake, she produced beauty. It says also much for primitive woman's intuitive love of the beautiful, her artistic perception of colour and form, that geometric designs, emanating from her fertile brain thousands of years ago, are still copied, . . . and her early decorative efforts are in the present day of priceless value, as exemplars for reproduction. (204–5)

Swiney's account also reviews issues of sexuality: the high incidence of prostitution, sexually transmitted diseases, and the implicit legal sanction of rape. Some of Swiney's beliefs were less reformist than Caird's (she opposed the liberalization of divorce laws, for example), but her summary of Victorian laws and social behavior is marked by caustic attention to detail. She notes, for example, the limited information on venereal diseases available to women, the imprisonment of adolescent girls for acts that carry no penalty for their adult partners, and the absence in England and Ireland of a legal proscription against incest. Of the parliamentary opposition to women's suffrage on the part of members who refuse to consider the social origins of prostitution, she remarks that such Honourable Members are "willing rather to drive a thousand more women on the streets, victims to men's passions, than see one woman efficiently and intelligently filling a public office, taking upon herself the responsibilities of citizenship, or earning a competency in any trade or profession" (257).

Swiney's cross-cultural interests, similarly, are undercut by her belief that "Anglo-Saxon women" have been "the pioneers bearing the banner of progress into the Land of Promise" (221), but her volume does devote considerable attention to the past and present situation of female workers in many regions of the world: Belgium, Scandinavia, Austria, Hungary, Italy, Germany, Russia, Turkey, New Zealand, the United States, India, China, and Japan. Swiney is also unusual — at least among non-Marxists — in her assumption that a history of women should view them primarily as workers and consider their labor in cross-cultural ways.

Swiney's appeals to women's alleged pacific nature and "spirituality" offer a somewhat "essentialist" early prototype of what might be called the Greenham-Common view of social progress. She mounts a genteel but sustained attack on the psychological origins of war, and her appeals to women's suffrage as a means toward the abolition of conscription and militarism echo ironically against the fact that Parliament finally granted women the vote in 1918 in part as a reward for their support of "the war-effort":

> Women will plead for arbitration between nations; they will be the universal peacemakers: they will bring into public adminstration that element of stability, of sterling moral worth, of justice and equality, upon which alone depends a nation's true progress. . . . The matriarchal rule will be re-established, not on the crude and primitive lines of the pre-historic races, but in accordance with the unconscious evolution, physical, mental, and spiritual, of mankind in general.
>
> The time will come when men will be considered too valuable and essential to the well-being of the industrial community to be offered as targets for marksmen. (301)

In partial solidarity here with the male socialist feminists Engels and Bebel, Swiney thus equated the freedom of women with abstractly formulated advances in egalitarianism and international social justice.

It is also interesting to contrast the works of Besant, Eleanor Marx, Caird, and Swiney with those of contemporary male historians of the family. These male writers were noticeably more concerned with exhibiting the family as an alleged microcosm of the (hierarchically organized) state, for better or for worse. They took pains, therefore, to assimilate the putatively parallel bases of these two "governments" in law and authoritative modes for the establishment of paternity, ownership, and transmission of property. Understandably, woman polemicists were little attracted to such forms of "legitimacy." It was clear to them that the traditional family's basis lay more in naked violence and institutionally sanctioned forms of gender oppression, repression of female sexual desire and choice, and unacknowledged exploitation of female labor.

The more sympathetic male historians tended to focus on reascriptions of kinship, property rights, and (de)control of female sexuality, but women reformers were more concerned with forms of physical, personal, and legal autonomy, the power to escape abuse, and rights to shared control of their children. Their accounts of family origins were sketchier, more "pointillist," and more remote from original sources than those of their counterparts in the (essentially all-male) academy, but they brought a fresh breath of living reality to the search for historical "truth" in the ossuaries of past legal systems.

Above all, they offered mordant analyses of the physical and psychological mechanisms through which men enforced women's conformity; relatively blunt accounts of prostitution, sexual violence, and sexually transmitted disease; and much more accurate and differentiated descriptions of the realities of women's "domestic" labor. In their concern with the violent prescriptions and proscriptions of gender roles, in fact, it may have been such Victorian feminists as Caird and Swiney — not Marx or Engels — who provided their century's most "materialist" account of family history.

AFTER THE VICTORIANS

Later feminists have, of course, corrected, extended, and deepened the arguments of Caird, Swiney, and their predecessors. At the end of the Victorian era, for example, the feminist classicist Jane Harrison's *Prolegomena to the Study of Greek Religion* (1903) provided the first full account of female deities in Greek religion, thus confirming and expanding Bachofen's view that the basis of Greek culture had been matrilinear.[18] Twentieth-century works such as Elizabeth Gould Davis's *The First Sex* (1971), Heide Gottner-Abendrott's *Matriarchal Mythology in Former Times and Today* (1987), and Rita Gross's *Feminism and Religion* (1996) have continued to assert the ethical primacy of female-oriented religious traditions.[19] Along a different ideological axis, the work of socialist-feminists such as Michele Barrett or Alison Jaggar remains central to contemporary feminist thought.[20] "Single-shift" explanations of the sort propounded by Bachofen and Engels are no longer in fashion, but contemporary anthropologists have partially confirmed the nineteenth-century reformist view of Caird and Swiney, among others, that women were better situated in many early societies, though they hold militarization of social life rather than the rise of private ownership more responsible for the growth of sexual stratification and oppression.

Cross-cultural comparisons of women's economic situation, similarly, now form the basis of the expanding field of feminist anthropology. Radical assertions of the violence inscribed in seemingly gender-neutral laws have also reappeared in the works of sexuality and reproductive feminists such as Susan Brownmiller and Catharine MacKinnon.[21] MacKinnon, for example, argues in quasi-Swineyan fashion that "the state appears most relentless in imposing the male point of view when it comes closest to achieving its highest formal criterion of distanced aperspectivity. When it is most ruthlessly neutral, it is most male; when it is most sex blind, it is most blind to the sex of the standard being applied. . . . But the legitimacy of existing law is based on force at women's expense" (248, 249).

Assertions of separate traditions of women's spirituality, moreover, have long since become a recognized countercurrent in the work of such contemporary theologians as Mary Daly, Susan Griffin, and Carol Christ.[22] The proto-feminist-pacifist arguments of Swiney, finally, have found refinement and reflection in activist-ecological writers such as Jean Elshtain and Carolyn Merchant.[23]

Caird, Swiney, and other late nineteenth-century women historians of the family, then, focused firmly and clearly on issues of violence, power, and forced labor, and their opposition to standard assumptions of Victorian family history and its preoccupation with legal contracts, ascriptions of paternity, and sexual regulation was clear. However delayed subsequent recognition of their individual contributions has been, no one acquainted with the premises of contemporary gender studies will fail to recognize more recent echoes of these reformers' mordant distaste for idealized representation of the Victorian middle-class family. As a partial result of their efforts, few who read these words would now assert that the legally mandated, biologically bounded nuclear family is the only possible nexus in potential social constructions of sexuality, gender, kinship, and affectional ties.

NOTES

1. Gerda Lerner, *The Creation of Patriarchy* (Oxford and New York: Oxford University Press, 1986), pp. 5–6.

2. Only a few reviews of Caird and Swiney's works, for example, appeared in such socialist and Progressive periodicals as *Commonweal, Justice,* and *To-day.*

3. For a discussion of Victorian views of women, see Robin Sheets, Elizabeth Helsinger, and William Veeder, *The Woman Question: Society and Literature in Britain* (Chicago: University of Chicago Press, 1985).

4. Margaret Shanley, *Feminism, Marriage, and the Law in Victorian England, 1850–1895* (Princeton: Princeton University Press, 1989), p. 159. Other treatments of Victorian marriage and property law may be found in Lee Holcombe, *Wives and Property: Reform of the Married Women's Property Law in Nineteenth-Century England* (Toronto: University of Toronto Press, 1983); Allen Horstman, *Victorian Divorce* (London and Sydney: Croom Helm, 1985); Pat Jalland, *Women, Marriage, and Politics, 1860–1914* (Oxford: Clarendon Press, 1986); Susan Kingsley Kent, *Sex and Suffrage in Britain, 1860–1914* (Princeton: Princeton University Press, 1987); and Joan Perkin, *Women and Marriage in Nineteenth-Century England* (London: Routledge, 1989).

5. Edward Westermarck, *A History of Human Marriage* (London: Macmillan, 1891).

6. J. J. Bachofen, *Myth, Religion, and Mother Right: Selected Writings of J. J. Bachofen,* trans. Ralph Manheim (Princeton: Princeton University Press, 1967), pp. 79, 91.

7. Eleanor Burke Leacock, introduction to *The Origin of the Family, Private Property, and the State,* by Friedrich Engels (New York: International Publishers, 1942). For critiques of Engels from a feminist viewpoint, see Jane Sayers, Mary Evans, and Nanneke Redcliff, eds., *Engels Revisited: New Feminist Essays* (London: Tavistock, 1987); Lise Vogel, *Marxism and the Oppression of Women: Toward a Unitary Theory* (New Brunswick, N.J.: Rutgers University Press, 1983); and Florence and William Boos, "Victorian Socialist-Feminism and William Morris's *News from Nowhere,*" *Nineteenth-Century Contexts* 14, no. 1 (1990): 3–32.

8. (Cambridge: Harvard University Press, 1989).

9. *Woman and Her Master* (Philadelphia: Carey and Hart, 1840), p. 201.

10. Ibid., p. 21; Lydia Child's *Brief History of the Condition of Women in Various*

Ages and Nations (Boston: C. S. Francis, 1854) also provided a pioneering cross-cultural approach to women's history.

11. Eleanor Marx and Edward Aveling, *The Woman Question* (London: Swan Sonnenschein, 1887), reprinted in Joachim Muller and Edith Schotte, eds., *Thoughts on Women and Society* (New York: International Publishers, 1987), pp. 21, 24.

12. Ibid., p. 22.

13. *The Morality of Marriage and Other Essays on the Status and Destiny of Woman* (London: George Redway, 1897), pp. 27–28. Future references to this edition are indicated by page number or numbers within parentheses. See also Lyn Pykett, "The Cause of Women and the Course of Fiction: The Case of Mona Caird," in Christopher Parker, ed., *Gender Roles and Sexuality in Victorian Literature*, pp. 128–42 (Aldershot, Hants: Scolar Press, 1995). Pykett argues that "Caird's novels do not simply transpose into fictional form the polemical rhetoric of her essays; rather they develop what I have described elsewhere as a 'rhetoric of feeling' which similtaneously or by turns represents and explores the complex actualities of women's lives and figures utopian desires" (140).

14. This distinction would have resonated bitterly in the context of current marriage law debates. Fathers retained custody of children, including the right to assign them to guardians other than their mothers, and not until the Matrimonial Causes Act of 1886 could a mother gain custody even upon the father's death. In 1886 also for the first time a woman was permitted custody of children under twelve if the father's violence was sufficiently protracted and extreme as to constitute a threat to their lives. The notion died hard that males, unless proved patently irresponsible and unfit, owned their families.

15. 2d ed. (London: William Reeves, 1903). References to this edition are indicated by page number or numbers within parentheses.

Swiney's other writings included *The Cosmic Procession, or the Feminine Principle in Evolution* (London: Ernest Bell, 1906); *The Bar of Isis; or, the Law of the Mother* (London: Open Road Publishing Company, 1907); *The Mystery of the Circle and the Cross, or, the Interpretation of Sex* (London: Open Road Publishing Company, 1908); *The Esoteric Teaching of the Gnostics* (London: Yellon, Williams, 1909); *Women and Natural Law* (London: C. W. Daniel, 1912); and *Women among the Nations: A Short Treatise* (London, 1913).

16. 152 (July 1899): 69.

17. April 17, 1900, p. 132.

18. (Cambridge: Cambridge University Press, 1903).

19. Elizabeth Gould Davis, *The First Sex* (New York: Putnam, 1971); Heide Gottner-Abendrott, *Matriarchal Mythology in Former Times and Today* (Freedom, Calif.: Crossing Press, 1987); Rita M. Gross, *Feminism and Religion: An Introduction* (Boston: Beacon, 1996). See also Miriam Dexter, *Whence the Goddesses* (New York: Pergamon, 1990); Meredith Powers, *The Heroine in Western Literature* (Jefferson, N.C.: McFarland, 1991); and Anne Jensen, *God's Self-Confident Daughters: Early Christianity and the Liberation of Women*, trans. O. C. Dean, Jr. (Louisville: Westminster John Knox Press, 1996).

20. Michele Barrett, *Women's Oppression Today: The Marxist/Feminist Encounter* (London: Verso, 1980); Alison Jaggar, *Feminist Politics and Human Nature* (Totowa, N.J.: Rowman and Littlefield, 1988).

21. Susan Brownmiller, *Against Our Will: Men, Women, and Rape* (New York: Simon and Schuster, 1975); Catharine MacKinnon, *Toward a Feminist Theory of the State* (Cambridge: Harvard University Press, 1989).

22. Mary Daly, *Beyond God the Father: Toward a Philosophy of Women's Liberation* (Boston: Beacon, 1973); Daly, *Gyn/ecology, the Metaethics of Radical Feminism* (Boston: Beacon, 1978); and Daly, *Pure Lust: Elemental Feminist Philosophy* (Boston: Beacon, 1984); Susan Griffin, *Woman and Nature: The Roaring inside Her* (New York: Harper and Row, 1974); Carol Christ, *Diving Deep and Surfacing: Women Writers on Spiritual Quest* (Boston: Beacon, 1980, 1995); and Christ, *Laughter of Aphrodite: Reflections on a Journey to the Goddess* (San Francisco: Harper and Row, 1987). See also Carol Ochs, *Women and Spirituality* (Totowa, N.J.: Rowman and Allanheld, 1983).

23. Jean Elshtain, *Just War Theory* (New York: New York University Press, 1992); Elshtain, *Public Man, Private Woman: Women in Social and Political Thought* (Princeton: Princeton University Press, 1981); Elshtain, *Women and War* (New York: Basic Books, 1987); and Elshtain, *Women, Militarism, and War: Essays in History, Politics, and Social Theory* (Totowa, N.J.: Rowman and Littlefield, 1990); Carolyn Merchant, *Earthcare: Women and the Environment* (New York: Routledge, 1995). See also Grace Paley, *Long Walks and Intimate Talks* (New York: Feminist Press and the City University of New York, 1991); Birgit Brock-Utne, *Educating for Peace: A Feminist Perspective* (New York: Pergamon Press, 1985); and Cambridge Women's Peace Collective, *My Country Is the Whole World: An Anthology of Women's Work on Peace and War* (London: Pandora, 1984).

Non-European Contexts

DAUD ALI

RECOGNIZING EUROPE IN INDIA:

COLONIAL MASTER NARRATIVES AND THE

WRITING OF INDIAN HISTORY

D espite Frantz Fanon's enigmatic remark that "Europe is literally the creation of the Third World," scholars over the last
ten years have contended that the European colonial project
involved the "invention" of the third world's history and civilization
through a complex manipulation of already existing knowledges and
practices. Edward Said, in his groundbreaking work published in 1978,
has designated the entirety of this process of knowing the Orient as
"Orientalism," which he defined as the complex of knowledges and
institutions "by which European culture was able to manage — and
even produce — the Orient politically, sociologically, militarily, ideolog-
ically, scientifically, and imaginatively during the post-Enlightenment
period."[1] Said analyzed the mass of writings on the Orient as discursive formations instrumental in the maintenance of European imperial
power in the colonized world between the eighteenth and the twentieth
centuries. He also argued that these representations have continued to
play a part in the global hegemony of Western Europe and the United
States in postcolonial times. The great contribution of Said's work has
been the excavation of the concealed political and historical commitments of the academic disciplines that took up the task of "knowing" the
East — disciplines that have consistently represented themselves as disinterested, objective sciences.[2] Said's legacy has been formidable and
complex. It has brought together a long tradition of anticolonial critique with an increasing criticism in the study of English literature of
liberal-humanist approaches to culture, leading to a number of studies
connecting European colonialism to academic disciplines of the human
sciences.[3] In this connection Said's approach has received many criticisms — philosophical, evidentiary, and political (from both the right

and the left) — some of which we shall review in this essay.[4] Perhaps one of the most productive of these criticisms, echoed in a number of works, concerns his tendency to turn East and West into monolithic categories. Many scholars have called for a more complex understanding of what is presumed to be the wholly formed entity of the West, which then acts upon an equally undifferentiated East. Using many of Said's important insights, this essay will work to clarify Fanon's remark that, in fact, the self-image of Europe was in part constituted by the knowledge of its "Other."

What I want to explore here is a contradiction apparent in the rhetorical strategies of the colonialist historiography of India's past and some of its ramifications for later history writing. By the phrase "rhetorical strategy" I do not mean to imply that these authors always consciously deployed particular modes of argument to convince others of their vision of history or that modalities of argumentation were the factors for the particular fates that their historiographies met. Many of the "strategies" are perhaps better understood as "presuppositions" — assumptions that are so taken for granted that their authors never actually call them into question as points of debate. Nevertheless, they do remain, at least on a formal level, rhetorical maps that organize the narratives. We can observe in colonial historiography a constant effort to construct India as Europe's "Other" — a land fundamentally at odds with a number of subject-positions implicitly assumed to represent the "Western Self," on the one hand, but on the other hand a persistent urge to turn India into a version of the West — to contain it within its own historical narratives. This paradox is at the heart of Orientalism.

Relationships of mastery, as Jessica Benjamin has noted in the context of gender, often require the master to reduce the dominated to the inertia of silence but at the same time extract from the dominated the activity and work of recognition, through which the master's own subject position is constituted.[5] Master narratives, then, are incessantly caught up in these maneuvers of othering and incorporating: producing difference in the Other, while at the same time weaving the similitude of the universal. If Europe set itself up as master of the world, then the object of its domination would require careful attention. To reduce India to a totally objectified Other might cause several problems for the colonial historians. The recognition of real difference might challenge the universality of the Western Self and its history. This challenge might take the form of an autonomous Other that would not recognize the Self — a recognition that was crucial not simply for mastery (a point that Said has driven home) but for the very identity of Europe itself. To obtain this recognition it was necessary that the British first acknowledge India as in some sense continuous with Europe, whether through the affinities of race or the universalities of man. Such an appraisal, however, would be not a vision of equality but one that would "discover" in India an imperfect form of Europe. The colonial anxiety over recognition undergirded the unsteady procedures of Orientalist historiography.

Specifically, I take up the discursive "incorporation" of India into the "master narratives" of European history, focusing on how the categories of "social" and "political" have arranged themselves in this relationship. I will pay special attention to the contradictory maneuvers that I have mentioned above and then conclude by briefly outlining what I consider to be the implications of this genealogy of the "social" and "political" for the writing of Indian history since independence. Taking initiatives from some of the recent historiography, we can see how it has moved from debating the place that India has had in the history of Europe to challenging the very autonomy of Europe's master narrative. I hope to point out the incisiveness of Fanon's statement — for the Self's position is established dialectically, only through recognition by its Other.

Orientalism has not been the only way that Europe has known its Others.[6] India, through classical, Christian, and Islamic accounts, for centuries held a distinctive place in the medieval European imagination. India appears in travel accounts, hagiography, geography, and romances as a place of wealth, wisdom, and fabulous life — an oneiric template of medieval Christian society.[7] At the beginning of the nineteenth century Hegel wrote of India that "without being known too well, it has existed for millennia in the imagination of the Europeans as a wonderland. Its fame, which it has always had with regard to its treasures, both its natural ones, and in particular, its wisdom, has lured men there."[8] Hegel, although himself not an Orientalist, was writing at a time when this image of India was being seriously modified and complicated by the scientific apparatus of the expanding European empires. The beginnings of Orientalism as a science of knowing the Orient, concomitant with imperialist European domination over the East, marked a significant break with earlier classical and medieval quests for the "wisdom" of the East. Medieval European thought had constructed India as a land of fabulous wealth, exotic philosophers, and sensual pleasures. These images of India continued into later times, to be sure, but "Orientalism," the science that sought to explain the Orient based on the principles of a rational science, went far beyond the medieval exoticization of the East and was animated by different concerns, the most prominent of which were the attempts to construct a universal human nature dominated by the faculty of reason and to hierarchize the world under its hegemony by using the binaries of a rational, modern West and an irrational, archaic East.[9] This bifurcation, as mentioned above, put Europe in a position of mastery over the East and was intimately tied to the European imperialist projects of the eighteenth to the twentieth centuries.

But Orientalist discourses, despite their concern with the remote and arcane, were integrally tied to the emergence of European modernity. Consequently, they mirrored the shifting struggles that were part of making and remaking European "selves," as well as Oriental "others." Colonialist knowledge of the Orient did not have a single purpose or point of view. Romantics and missionaries differed in their assessments of India precisely because of their divergent visions of what Europe should be. In this sense, we might say that several master narratives have subsumed the colonized.

Most discussions on British interpretations of India include three traditions: Orientalist, Utilitarian, and Evangelical. Here I will treat only the first two because they have had a more formative effect on academic and social scientific thinking about India. The Evangelical, or missionary, perspective on India, while it converged with the Orientalist on the importance of religion as an object of inquiry and with the Utilitarian in its general condemnation of India, was unable to forward its own agendas in the dominant representations of India. Both the Utilitarians and the Orientalists, despite their opposing positions on the value of ancient Indian learning and the role that Sanskrit was to play in the education of Indian civil servants, should be understood as "Orientalist" in the larger, Saidian sense — that is, as embodying modes of knowledge and using schemes and tropes by which the "Oriental is contained and represented by dominating frameworks."[10] In his critique of Indology, Ronald Inden has noted that both of these traditions — the Orientalist, with its romantic and idealist leanings, and the Anglicist, with its utilitarian, empiricist, and positivist inclinations — while seemingly of opposite dispositions toward India (the Romantics taking the position that India had some positive aspects to offer the West and the Anglicists that India was a morass of superstition) — made many of the same assumptions about what constituted the essence of India and thus participated equally in the Orientalist operations that constructed India as the "Other" of Europe.[11]

The first scholarly inquiry into India began in the eighteenth century through the agency of the British East India Company, which required that its officers, in order to administer properly the territories that it had recently acquired, become familiar with the laws, habits, and history of the Indian people. Sir William Jones (1746–94), a judge in the presidency of Bengal who was able to devote time to the study of Sanskrit, perhaps best exemplifies the early tradition of scholarship that was later dubbed "Orientalist." Those in the Orientalist tradition concerned themselves primarily with the study of Sanskrit and Persian languages and literatures, as well as the religions and philosophies of India. Jones was largely responsible for the founding, in 1784, of the Asiatic Society of Bengal for the advancement of research into the culture of ancient India. The study of Sanskrit, called India's "classical" language, was to form the foundation stone of the discipline of Indology. Focus on Sanskrit linked the study of India (which came to be called Indology) with one of the most preeminent sciences of the nineteenth century — comparative philology. Philology, or the science of language, took as its task the classification of world languages into a single taxonomic system. By the middle of the nineteenth century a number of departments for the study of Sanskrit had been founded in various European universities. As a branch of comparative philology, the study of India was integrally involved in the post-Enlightenment establishment of the human sciences.

Philologists accorded India a special status after it was discovered that Sanskrit was related to Greek and other European languages. The ensuing quest for a common Indo-European linguistic and racial heritage was one of the great scholarly fetishes of the nineteenth century, not only calling for a reassessment of India but also altering Greece in Europe's eyes.[12] India came to be seen in this project as a "lost wing" of European culture. The Indo-Aryans, who were said to have migrated south into the Indian subcontinent from Central Asia about the same time as the Doric Greeks moved westward, were thought to have been culturally, linguistically, and racially akin to the earliest European peoples.

Sanskrit, like Greek, was a language of the past. Its texts existed side by side with those of other "living" languages. Philologists and Orientalists thus concluded that Sanskrit was the "classical" language of India that had flourished during the height of India's civilization. Since that moment India had declined. This Orientalist legacy of an Indian classical civilization located in hoary antiquity has been perhaps the most persistent master narrative for Indian history. India, like China and Europe, possessed essential characteristics that were to be found in its ancient past. Scholars believed that once this ancient past had been deciphered, Europe would have the key to understanding all of Indian history. Max Müller (1823–1900), the distinguished Anglo-German scholar and editor of the voluminous *Sacred Books of the East* series, despite never having traveled to India, wrote:

> So great an influence has the Vedic age . . . exercised upon all succeeding periods of Indian history . . . so deeply have the religious and moral ideas of that primitive era taken root in the mind of the Indian nation, so minutely has almost every private and public act of Indian life been regulated by old traditionary precepts that it is impossible to find the right point of view for judging Indian religion, morals and literature without a knowledge of the literary remains of the Vedic age.[13]

Not only did ancient India hold the key to assessing the condition of contemporary India but the Orientalists felt that by studying India's past they could gain a glimpse of Europe's origin, or childhood. But while the Orientalists believed the ancient Aryans might have been a lost wing of European culture, they simultaneously considered their evolution to be different from that of their Doric counterparts. Thus, Indian civilization came to embody characteristics diametrically opposed to those of the Occident. Max Müller argued further that Sanskrit literature embodied a different set of cultural values from those in Greek literature: "not the active, combative, and acquisitive, but the passive, meditative and reflective."[14] Thus, the Orientalists incorporated India into a European master narrative, but at the same time they "othered" it. This incorporation and transformation of India had various uses for the Orientalists; many thought the culture and civilization of ancient India had some instructive aspects for the West. Many Continental Orientalists were Romantics and saw in ancient India a quietistic "idealism," which buttressed their resistance to rationalist thinking at home.

There was, however, another master narrative for India. The scholarly tradition begun by William Jones, which viewed India as a decayed but venerable civilization, was opposed by another group of more empirically inclined Utilitarian scholars. These "Anglicists" dubbed scholars like William Jones and Max Müller "Orientalists." The Anglicist view of India was perhaps best represented in the work of Utilitarian thinker James Mill (1773–1836). Mill, who also had never been to India, published his *History of British India* in 1817. For Mill, the value of a civilization could be measured by the degree to which it exhibited rationalism and individualism. Finding neither of these two values in India, he condemned it severely, arguing that contemporary as well as ancient India, whether in science, religion, government, law, or political economy, was thoroughly unenlightened and barbarous. His text, which was the first comprehensive history of India, became the hegemonic narrative of Indology for nearly eighty years. Reprinted in 1820, 1826, and 1840, it was required reading at Haileybury College, where until 1855 civil servants of the East India Company were trained.[15] The Indian Rebellion of 1857 led to a greater severity in British policy in the colonies and created an environment favorable to the lines of thought on Indian civilization drawn by Mill.[16] Mill's history was instrumental in the dominance that Utilitarian and administratively oriented perspectives came to exert over Indological study in the latter half of the nineteenth century. Along with the work of the Orientalist school, Mill's text would form the other master narrative for Indian history — a narrative in relation to which all subsequent histories would situate themselves.

Mill's *History* eventually became outdated as the British government collected more and more information about India through gazetteers, surveys, and censuses. These investigative modalities, particularly the burgeoning fields of epigraphy and archaeology, prompted a rapid expansion in the discipline of Indology throughout the nineteenth century and did much to "open up" India's past.[17] Several other histories sought to update Mill's narrative. Among the proliferating narratives of Indian history in the late nineteenth century, Vincent Smith's *Early History of India*, published in 1904, was finally able to displace Mill's long outdated account. Culling the fruits of archaeological and textual researches, Smith's work became the dominant history for the next fifty years, after which it was in turn replaced, outside of India, by A. L. Basham's *The Wonder That Was India* (1954).[18] The radical Utilitarian stance of Mill had largely been abandoned by the time Basham was writing. His narrative, produced in the postcolonial era, when nationalist histories arguing explicitly against the positions of Mill and Smith had long held dominance in India, no longer had the inflammatory and condescending tone of the old colonial history. We can see in Basham's text a reawakening of the older Orientalist approach, with its focus on language, literature, and religion. For Basham, however, each civilization had its own unique contribution to make to the great "mosaic of humanity." This liberal humanist approach, enshrined in course syllabi in universities all over the United States, displaced the older colonial attitudes. Mill's critique of India had amounted to a condemnation of the racial characteristics of "Hindoos." Basham often maintained many of the same stances, but his language spoke of "culture" or "civilization" rather than "race," and he deferred his explanations onto other agents, like the environment, rather than onto Indians themselves.[19] So while the invective may have been absent from this new tone, many of Mill's basic assumptions about India remained, though in a euphemized form.

Mill's *History of British India* had as one of its chief projects the refutation of the Orientalist narrative that India had once attained a high level of civilization and that it had since degenerated. Mill maintained that India had always been in the backward and dissolute condition in which the British had found it. But this assertion did not mean that India had no history at all. Mill periodized Indian history into three categories: Hindu, Muslim, and British. Mill's text was the first comprehensive incorporation of India into a European modernist narrative. It explicitly proposed a series of teleologies: progress from barbarism to civilization, religion to science, feminine to masculine, superstition and dependency to reason and individualism. Mill believed that human life in prehistoric times was organized into small bands of disparate families. There then arose monarchial governments, which would eventually be replaced by modern states.[20]

Mill's periodization of Indian history into Hindu, Muslim, and British came to be overlaid, in later Indological studies, with the more familiar epochs of ancient, medieval, and modern.[21] Mill himself would probably not have accepted this translation, since he thought that medieval Europe was still vastly superior to India's level of civilization.[22] Mill's opinion that India was an unchanging land of barbarism, even though his work occupied the preeminent position among histories of India until the turn of the century, was seriously contested by other versions of the Indian past. First, the Orientalist position never completely disappeared. Mountstuart Elphinstone, offended by the "cynical and sarcastic tone" of Mill, attempted to write a more sympathetic "Orientalist" history.[23] His effort failed, however, to challenge Mill's work.

The discourse of the earlier Orientalists and Mill's radical Utilitarianism formed, as it were, the two poles from which subsequent colonial histories of India were written. Indian writers were also beginning to contribute to Indological studies. Although this first generation of Indian historians did not fundamentally question the basic models set by British historians, they were acutely aware of the condemnation that many British historians reserved for Indian history and civilization.[24] The next generation of historians, writing in the 1920s and 1930s, began to offer serious challenge to the narratives of the British, the texts of Mill and Smith in particular. Mill's India was further complicated by the ongoing textual and archaeological studies that formed the "empirical" base of Indological studies. While it is certainly true that the technologies of rulership — the massive archaeological surveys, textual research, and periodic censuses conducted throughout the course of the nineteenth and early twentieth centuries — authorized more completely the imperial voice in India, they at the same time necessitated a more complex negotiation of India's past. Mill's text, written from England at the beginning of the century and claiming that India had never changed, needed to be updated and refashioned to accommodate the "facts" that the very discipline it dominated was "unearthing."

Vincent Smith's text, *The Early History of India*, supplemented Mill's narrative significantly. It accommodated the Orientalist tradition of glorifying India's past while at the same time preserving most of Mill's conclusions. At its outset *The Early History of India* states its task to be the presentation of a "connected relation of national transactions" of pre-Muslim India. Smith presumed, as did Mill and others, the object of his inquiry to be the Indian "nation." His narrative focuses almost entirely on the political transactions of the ancient "states" that composed the natural entity of India. The periodization of Indian history in Smith's work is decidedly more complex than that in Mill's. While his text claims as its concern the "Hindu" period of Indian history (the full title of his work is *The Early History of India from 600 B.C. to the Muhammadan Conquest*), it at the same time folds the European periodization of ancient, medieval, and modern into his narrative. Since the Hindu period forms the chief domain of inquiry, *The Early History of India* ends up telling us the history of the ancient period and *part* of the medieval period, dividing the latter into an "early (or Hindu) medieval" and a "late (or Muslim) medieval." So while presupposing Mill's tripartite Hindu/ Muslim/British scheme, the text also holds to the somewhat different ancient/medieval/modern periodization. From this point forward, the narratives of Indian history, both Orientalist and nationalist, usually adopted some combination of these two periodizations.[25]

The Hindu/Muslim/British and ancient/medieval/modern epochal divisions form two distinct but related discursive incorporations of India within the narrative of European history. The former, originating with Mill, is organized around religion and rationality. India's precolonial history consisted of two religious regimes: Hindu and Muslim. The predominance of religion and the sacerdotal class in a nation's history, according to Mill, was a mark of low civilization.

The priesthood is generally found to usurp the greatest authority in the lowest state of society. Knowledge, and refined conceptions of divine nature, are altogether incompatible with the supposition that the deity makes favorites of a particular class of mankind or is more pleased with those who perform a ceremonial service to himself than with those who discharge with fidelity the various and difficult duties of life. It is only in rude and ignorant times that men are so overwhelmed with the power of superstition as to pay unbounded veneration and obedience to those who artfully clothe themselves in the terrors of religion.[26]

In fashioning this anticlerical invective, Mill seemed to have had in mind not only India but less-remote targets as well.[27] As a Cartesian and a Newtonian secularist, Mill saw organized religion at home as an obsolete holdover from pre-Enlightenment times. As part of his political project, he held up as a bad example the "backward" condition of India, where, he argued, the priestly class (the Brahmins) had gained control of the entire social and governmental system by the fabrication of elaborate and fantastic theologies for consumption by the ignorant masses. "The Brahmens among the Hindus have acquired and maintained an authority, more exalted, more commanding, and extensive, than the priests have been able to engross among any other portion of mankind."[28] But under the tutelage of the British, Mill believed, India might control the excesses that religion had generated in its history. Importantly, Mill bestows upon the final periodization in his history the signification of nationality and not religion (calling it the "British" as opposed to the "Christian" period).[29] Since the Enlightenment, Europe has clothed not only its own past but that of the colonized world in a teleology that moves from religion to science, divine monarchy to the secular state, tradition to modernity. In the postcolonial world this view has enjoyed preeminence in the harder social sciences under the guise of "modernization theory."[30]

The ancient/medieval/modern scheme allowed a more complex narrative for Indian history than Mill's evolution of civilization from religion to rationality. This tripartite periodization, nevertheless, carried a quite similar teleology. A "classical" period, according to nineteenth-century European historiography, was that time in a nation's or civilization's history when it attained its most essential characteristics. Subsequent history would depart from the values and paradigms of this classical epoch. What defines a classical civilization has been a topic of some debate since the nineteenth century — one that is continually raised whenever cultural and historical canons are secured and scrutinized. The most powerful generalizations require some sort of political unity or the emergence of a sovereign state, along with a cultural efflorescence and the birth of a literary and philosophical language. Later political institutions, languages, literatures, and philosophies would derive, but somehow depart, from this classical period.

The "medieval" period, on the other hand, denoted for modern historiography a time when classical values were lost and civilization was cast into an age of darkness — culture declined and polities fragmented. Modernity, the triumph of history, was marked by the reappearance of "classical" values, which in happy marriage with the industrial revolution and the Enlightenment, gave birth to political democracy, capital, and the nation-state.[31] So the story has gone. But in the hands of colonial historians, this narrative attained mastery over India's past as well.

The Orientalist notion of India's ancient glory was to certain extent already indebted to this periodization. The ancient period, as we have seen in Max Müller, was an epoch determinative of India's essence. Philology made its contribution by designating Sanskrit as India's classical language. Colonial historiography constructed India's "ancient period" around two "empires": the Mauryan (320–180 B.C.) and the Gupta (A.D. 350–500). According to historians, it was during this period that India, through the political form of "empire," first attained an approximation of autonomous political unity. Colonial historians such as Smith accorded the later Islamic and British "unifications" of India as perhaps more complete than the Mauryas and the Guptas but disqualified them as "foreign occupations."[32] The *autonomous* unity of India was effected only in the ancient period under the Mauryas and the slightly later

Guptas, the former dynastic era called the Age of Imperial Unity by the foremost nationalist history of India.[33] Colonial and nationalist historians alike have focused on the political accomplishments of such Mauryan kings as Ashoka and Chandragupta and the administrative structures of their empires. But it was also during this time that India attained the essence of its culture, or as one scholar has called it, "the classical pattern."[34] Orientalist, Romantic (and Weberian), and nationalist histories have all constructed this period as a "golden age," based on the model of the "classical" West. The Gupta period, in particular, has enjoyed the position of India's "classical epoch" with regard to culture.[35] Even Vincent Smith, in his *Oxford History of India*, concluded that the "Gupta period is in the annals of classical India almost what the Periclean age is in the history of Greece."[36] During the Gupta period, Indologists tell us, art, science, and literature flourished. Sanskrit attained its "classical" form. The Orientalist obsession with India's glorious past has continued to have force even in post-independence times, in which India's classical period has come to signify the essence of all of its history and peoples. A. L. Basham's text is devoted entirely to the project of elucidating this classical culture, evident from his title — *The Wonder That Was India*. Elsewhere Basham writes of Gupta culture: "The history of civilization is marked by certain periods when in one or other region of the world, human culture reached a peak from which it afterwards in some measure declined."[37] The notion that all great civilizations have a classical age in the ancient past has been one of the founding ideas for "civilization" courses and area studies in postwar academic institutions in the United States.[38] Significantly, it was in the "ancient" period that India made its contribution to world civilization.

If Orientalists believed that ancient India was the high point of Indian history, they saw "medieval" India as the decline of that glory. Following the model of the European Dark Ages, the colonial historiography imagined post-Gupta India as a time when the political unity of the ancient empires fragmented and civilization declined. The two great empires, according to Smith, gave way to the chaos of local dynasties. The death of Harsha, the last great emperor of ancient India, in A.D. 647 heralded an era of political dispersion, in which "a medley of petty states with ever-varying boundaries . . . engaged in unceasing internecine war."[39] The feuding of small dynastic states replaced the glory of despotic empire. This political fracture is ingeniously embedded in all the narratives of Indian history after Smith by the trope of what I would call "regionalization."⁴⁰ The histories of the *medieval* period, beginning with Smith, divide India into three "natural" geographical regions: the north, the south, and the Deccan (central plateau). Whereas for Smith and his successors the field of action in the *ancient* period of Gupta and Mauryan kings was "India" as a whole, the various *medieval* kings were condemned to act within the more fragmented and local political regions of north, south, or central India. The narratives begin by telling us the history of *ancient India*; after the death of King Harsha they relate the separate histories of medieval south India, medieval north India, and the medieval Deccan. Once the authors have named and located these regions, they often backtrack to narrate what was going on there during ancient times. But as discursive entities, the regions enter into the narratives only at the moment of the medieval. Switching the narrative frame from "India" to the three "regions" builds political division and fragmentation into its very structure even before the history itself unfolds.⁴¹

In addition to political decay, the medieval epoch required a degeneration of culture and religion. Accordingly, Indologists have spent great effort in arguing how the religious and cultural innovation of ancient India, namely its philosophical idealism and subtle traditions of Sanskrit literature, took a turn for the worse — becoming stale, turning inward, and most of all, being handed over to the superstitious masses. The trope of the "popular mind" is consistently employed to explain the medieval cultural "decline." The superstitious mental habits of the Indian "masses" had been an axiom of Indology from at least the time of Mill and the Evangelicals. Even the Orientalists, who were more favorably disposed to the "achievements" of Indian civilization, made a sharp distinction between the purveyors of elevated learning, the Brahmins, and the largely ignorant populace. Whatever progress Indian civilization had made during its classical period resulted from controlling those dark forces. But the Indian elite, it turned out, were not up to the task; the popular mind triumphed in the medieval period with the proliferation of mythological theism and "devotional" religion, which displaced the earlier "idealist" philosophical traditions of the ancient period. But these "dark forces" residing in the Indian masses themselves have a genealogy.

The philological assertion that "Indo-European" was the common ancestor of Doric Greek, Old Persian, and Vedic Sanskrit was by no means simply a genealogy of language; it implied a theory of culture and race as well. Martin Bernal has shown the intimate connection of Romanticism and the birth of historical linguistics in the late eighteenth and the nineteenth centuries.[42] Rejecting "reason" as the determinative constituent of human nature, Romantics instead held up feeling and passion, two qualities visceral in nature, located in the collective "blood" of a people. Languages, for the Romantics, were the unique expressions of these particular and incommensurate peoples, or races. As such, they carried the properties of the races by which they were spoken and might be used to tell their histories — that is, their kinship and encounters with other races. The intimacy between language and race can be seen in one of the main metaphors used to articulate the relationship of languages in the nineteenth century — the family. It should not surprise us, then, that the classification of languages in nineteenth-century philology was related to a new systematic racial taxonomy.

Indian history, nearly all the colonial accounts tell us, began with the invasion of the Indo-European Aryans, who had migrated from the steppes of central Asia. Through the "Aryans," racial science gained a foothold in Indian historiography, one that has been difficult indeed to dislodge.[43] According to colonial philologists, historians, and ethnologists, the Aryans did not enter uninhabited territory. They met on the Gangetic plain of North India a race of darker, shorter men with a very different culture, whom they subjugated. Exactly who these people were, however, was at first a matter of some debate. Their identification required a further "advance" in philological scholarship. In 1816 D. Campbell and F. W. Ellis, Orientalists working in the Madras Presidency, published a proof of the existence of a separate language group in south India that was not derived from Indo-Aryan.[44] The discovery of this language group, termed "Dravidian," was greatly popularized by the Reverend Robert Caldwell, who published a grammar of the Dravidian languages in 1856 that, among other things, speculated on the origins of the Dravidian peoples. Caldwell's speculations, although later rejected, prepared the ground for the theory of a pan-Indian civilization that preceded the Aryan incursions.[45] The Sanskritist Gustave Oppert argued in 1893 that these Dravidians were "original inhabitants of Bharatavarsha (India)."[46] By 1901 Herbert Risley (1851–1911), writing a chapter on caste in the *Report on the Census of India for 1901*, simply stated: "The Dravidians were the earliest inhabitants of India."[47] He argued that it was the Dravidians whom the Aryans met as they descended into the Gangetic plain.[48] Soon, the term came to denote "all of the non-Aryan population of India."[49] Even the discovery during the 1920s of archaeological remains in northwestern India that revealed the rise and fall of a complex civilization in the Indus valley before the arrival of the Aryans failed to complicate the racial theories of early Indian history.[50] The Indus valley civilization has most often been understood either explicitly or implicitly as an enclave of Dravidian culture.

Colonial scholars, asserting that the Aryans carried in their veins the same racial stock as the Doric Greeks, bestowed on them the values of classical civilization in the West: rationality and virility. As the Reverend Henry Whitehead, Bishop of Madras, remarked in 1916, "It was not until the Aryan invaders had conquered North India and settled down in the country, that there was in India any growth of philosophic thought about the world as a whole."[51] Dravidians, on the other hand, were the possessors of an animist or totemic religion that was more tied to the earth and village localities and was closer to a feminized nature.[52] Whitehead wrote: "Generally in the Hindu (Aryan) pantheon the male deities are predominant and female deities occupy a subordinate position. This is the characteristic genius of Aryan religion, but in the old Dravidian cults a leading feature was the worship of the female principle in nature. It is possible that this is due to the fact that the Aryan deities were the gods of a race of warriors, whereas the Dravidian deities were the goddesses of an agricultural people."[53]

Indian history increasingly became the ground upon which these two racial essences, Dravidian and Aryan, interacted. After the Aryans had overrun India and the Brahmins had established themselves as a priestly caste, Whitehead wrote, "the old Dravidian cults were influenced by the superior religion of the Aryans, and strongly reacted on them in turn." If the Aryans gained the upper hand socially, religiously the interaction had been at best a "drawn battle."[54] The philosophical and speculative impulses of the Aryans, paralleling the "axial breakthroughs" in Greece, were somehow diluted by the Dravidian religion, the faith of the *masses*, consisting of phallus and goddess worship, fertility cults, and orgiastic dancing.[55] Hinduism as they had encountered it, the British concluded, was a composite religion, consisting of a mixture of lofty Aryan philosophy, on the one hand, "and all sorts of weird notions and customs alien to Brahman tradition," on the other.[56] It was in the medieval period that the Dravidians struck back. The historiography of India almost universally views the medieval period as the time when Brahmanical religion was popularized and mythologized. As Basham writes, the medieval or "final form of Hinduism was largely the result of influence from the Dravidian south." [57]

It was in this stagnant medieval condition that the British discovered India, according to colonial historians. Some extreme Utilitarians and Christians maintained that India had always been stagnant, but the dominant view held that in India's ancient past there had been a moment of light before all was engulfed in darkness. It is here that we may discern that the teleology of Indian history, while mimicking its master, while offering Europe recognition, fails at its final hour. For no sort of modernity could have emerged in India without the aid of the West. According to colonial historians, India would not arrive at modernity on the same terms as Europe had; after all, its modern period was marked not by its own nationality but by Britain's. To achieve this end, the master narrative turned its object into something "other" than itself — a deformation.

If the tripartite teleology of European history was only partially mapped onto India's past, then something had to explain this incompleteness. The constant incorporation and disqualification of India with regard to the European master narrative produced some strange *aporia* in colonialist discourse. The narrative of European history attained its mastery by reproducing not clones of itself but versions, which were slightly different but still recognizable. These versions, however, have had the strange effect of negating one of the main tropes of the master narrative: universality, for the master narrative on the one hand implicitly claims a universal application and on the other tells us how in the case of India it fails.

Mill's text sets up a clear opposition between an enlightened Europe and a barbaric India. India came to signify everything inimical to Mill's secular and utilitarian vision of Europe. Mill's characterization of India, as Javed Majeed has forcefully argued, was undoubtedly intended not only to direct the policies of the trustees of the East India Company but also to attack the "politics of the imagination" (and India's place therein) that underpinned conservative ideology at home.[58] Mill believed religion and the form of government that accompanied it, monarchy — a despotic version of which prevailed in India — to be in direct opposition to the modern state and civil society, which were built on the foundation of rational individualism and representation. Europe's history, to be sure, also included a period of religious dominance (albeit for Mill, one superior to India's), but whereas Europe was emerging from this abysmal state of affairs, India, Mill contended, would never move beyond this condition without the intervention of Great Britain. Mill maintained that India itself had never in fact showed any historical movement: "The Hindus, at the time of Alexander's invasion, were in a state of manners, society, and knowledge, exactly the same with that in which they were discovered by the nations of modern Europe."[59] Even the Muslim period, for Mill, had no real effect on India. Muslim civilization, which he deemed superior to that of the Hindus, was never great enough to change the fundamental effeminacy and superstition of the Hindu people.[60] The root of India's problem, for Mill, was the lack of sound government and law. In India a cruel form of despotism prevailed, buttressed by the scheming of a priestly class: "In short, despotism and priestcraft taken together, the Hindus, in mind and body, were the most enslaved portion of the human race."[61] While assessments were modified, Indology throughout its subsequent history has shared this fundamental suspicion of government and the state, with its "religious" aspect, in Indian history.

Even later colonialist historians who adhered to the ancient/medieval/modern teleology argued that India did not really possess a dynamic history. Vincent Smith and others argued that any political unity or classical values that India had attained were derived from the West to begin with. Early in his narrative Smith "unfolds the wondrous tale" of Alexander's two-year "Indian adventure"[62] (327–25 B.C.), when India was "first disclosed to European observation."[63] What Alexander discovered there, according to Smith, was India's "natural" condition: the aforementioned "medley of petty states engaged in unceasing internecine war."[64] Alexander's conquest, according to Smith, who devotes seventy pages of his four-hundred-page book to his chronicle of the event, introduced the imperial idea to India. Only after Alexander crossed the Indus and planted the imperial seed in India could Indians themselves build an empire. Chandragupta Maurya, who founded the Mauryan polity centered in northeastern India not long after Alexander's campaign, is called by Smith "the first emperor of India, who succeeded to the lordship of Alexander's conquest."[65] Smith tells the colorful story of how at the farthest point of Alexander's advance into India he erected twelve huge altars dedicated to his Greek gods. When Chandragupta Maurya established the first Indian empire five years later, in 320 B.C., he returned "along with his successors for centuries afterwards to venerate the altars, and were in the habit of crossing the river to offer sacrifice to them."[66] The very foundation stone of political unity in India was implanted by Europe. Smith's story, based on a tenuous reading of Plutarch's *Life of Alexander* and not corroborated by any Indian sources, did not survive in subsequent narratives, but the general assertion that the imperial idea was introduced to India by the Alexandrian conquest still has wide currency among many Indologists.[67]

If India's ancient political unity depended on Europe, the high points of its culture were largely derivative. Smith asserts that the literature, coinage, art, and architecture of India's Gupta period, dubbed "the classical age," "were produced in large measure by reason of the contact between the civilization of India and that of the Roman empire."[68] More-mainstream Indologists held that even if India had possessed a high culture, it was only through the British discovery of classical India that they came to realize it. In the mainstream view, when the British arrived, India's classical culture was in abeyance and superstition was widespread. As Lata Mani points out, the colonizing mission sought not only to protect India from its own barbarisms but also to introduce its natives to the truths of their own "little read and less understood" scripture.[69] A. L. Basham begins his work by chronicling the European "discovery" of ancient India. In his conclusion, after mentioning that Islam had no great effect on the regressive medieval mentality, he contends that not until the Europeans arrived on the subcontinent did India "rediscover" the essential elements of its own ancient Hindu civilization: "It was through the influence of Europe that revival came."[70]

Denuded of any agency in its own "glorious" past, India was simply helped along by its various foreign invaders. The only moments of political unity or cultural attainment achieved were through the agency of the invading — and usually Western — powers. India's natural state was one of political chaos and rude superstition. Mill's presence still looms over *The Early History of India*, published nearly one hundred years later. Smith's famous statement on Indian history can now be quoted in full:

Harsha's death loosened the bonds always ready to operate in India, and allowed them to produce their natural result, a medley of petty states, with ever varying boundaries, and engaged in unceasing internecine war. Such was India when first disclosed to European observation in the fourth century B.C., and such it has always been, except during the comparatively brief periods in which a vigorous central government has compelled the mutually repellent molecules of the body politic to check their gyrations and submit to the grasp of a superior controlling force. . . . The three following chapters, which attempt to give an account of the salient features in the bewildering annals of Indian petty states when left to their own devices for several centuries, may perhaps serve to give the reader a notion of what India always has been when released from the control of a supreme authority and what she would be again, if the hand of the benevolent power which now safeguards her boundaries should be withdrawn.[71]

The above preface to India's medieval history argues that political fragmentation was the endemic condition of India. Why would that be so? Before we seek the answer to this question, we must remember that in the nineteenth century history required that the state be its object. If history was the narration of the political transactions of the nation, then Indian history was a tedious ascent up the tower of Babel.[72] Eventually, history itself became a peripheral discipline to Indology. A. L. Basham, Smith's successor, devoted only one of nine chapters to the topic: "History: Ancient and Medieval Empires."[73] Introducing his nine-page treatment of nearly a millennium of "medieval" Indian political history in this five-hundred-page book, Basham tells us, "The history of the succeeding dynasties is a rather drab story of endemic warfare between rival dynasties. It can be followed in some detail, thanks to numerous inscriptions and copper-plate charters, but the detail is monotonous and uninteresting to all but the specialist."[74]

Whereas Smith's narrative busies itself in detailing this tortuous history, reading from it the moral success story of the British empire, Basham dismisses it in one quick stroke. Many British writers in the eighteenth and nineteenth centuries felt compelled to write about Indian history, but by the late nineteenth century Indian history had been effectively eclipsed by another field, which took as its domain not politics but society: anthropology.[75] History for nineteenth-century historians could not be a history of the "social," for its natural object was the state. So while the periodizations of ancient, medieval, and modern were kept, the political history of premodern India was largely jettisoned. To understand how the discipline of political history was peripheralized in Indological studies, it is necessary to look at the way a transhistorical essence that was the "opposite" of Europe was bestowed upon India.

Mill had argued that all mankind, motivated by an acquisitive human nature and the exigencies of survival, progressed through stages. What determined progress on his scale of human cultural evolution was the degree to which any people's law and customs accorded with the principle of utility. According to Mill, mankind, "ignorant and rude," first existed in families and small bands, migrating from Central Asia to Europe and India.[76] When the small numbers of migrants arrived in India they lived on the immense and fertile plains of the subcontinent until "all the most valuable ground was occupied."[77] Slowly it became necessary for families to band together in clans and tribes to protect themselves from the mutually acquisitive natures of their fellow humans. Having reached the status of tribal organization, Indians had entered into a distinct stage in the "evolution of nations." And not long after that, the Hindus made the next natural transition, from the condition of tribal existence to the more regulated and artificial system of a monarchy and laws. But in India something intervened in this "natural" development: "It was probably at not great distance from the time of this important change that those institutions were devised, which have been distinguished by a durability so extraordinary; and which present a spectacle so instructive to those who would understand the human mind, and the laws which, amid all the different forms of civil society, invariably preside over its progress."[78]

Theoretically, the tribal stage of existence was to give way to a higher form of government, monarchy. Slowly tribes were to consolidate into nations, defined not by kinship but by geographical boundaries. In Europe everything moved according to schedule and political consciousness was born. In India, however, there was another story. Caste, the distinctive social system of India, emerged and retarded the further development of Indian society.[79] Caste retained a tribal divisiveness, for its hereditary occupations reinforced tribal and clan kinship or blood relations, which inhibited rather than produced political consciousness. And since the development of the state and its accompanying civil society was predicated upon overcoming tribal organization, India, being unable to do this, never attained to any political consciousness. The caste system was a malignant form of "civil society," post-tribal but prepolitical, which precluded the development of the state. Valentine Chirol (1852–1929), an English journalist who traveled in India between the world wars, put it succinctly: "Hinduism could not build up a nation because the one vital structure that it did build up [caste] was the negation of everything that constitutes a nation."[80]

The caste system and Hinduism were inextricably related, according to Indologists. Hinduism formed the inner mind of India and caste its outer reality. Almost all of Indology agreed that the mind of India, as expressed in Hinduism, was founded on imagination and sensuality.[81] Hegel, who articulated the problem with the Indian mind most succinctly, wrote in his *Philosophy of History* that in India the "unity of subjectivity and [positive] Being — or the idealism of Existence — is established." But he went on to say that the idealism found in India is peculiar, being an "idealism of the imagination, without distinct conceptions."[82] For Hegel, the imagination was not a faculty of the mind commensurate with reason, as it was for the Romantics, but instead a lower form of reason, essentially sensual, which could not distinguish between subject and object, spirit and nature. Human social relations, because of the predominance of the imagination in the Indian mind, were mistaken to be natural and hence divinely or spiritually sanctioned: "The different castes are indeed, fixed; but in view of the religious doctrine that established them, they wear the aspect of natural distinctions."[83] Because of the imagination, argued Hegel, individual subjectivity and freedom, which were associated with reason, were absent in India. There caste precluded the development of that product of proper civil society that was the prerequisite for both political democracy and the modern nation-state: the citizen. Hegel, of course, made much of the fact that in India the "state" was unable to develop as it would in Europe. History and political action were not possibilities in India. For idealists like Hegel, the irrational Hindu mind, dominated by the imagination, stood behind the institution of caste. Empiricists saw the society of caste as the precursor of Hindu religion. Both empiricists and idealists, however, held to the idea that the Indian mind was dominated by the imagination and that it was integral in some way to the predominance of caste and the underdevelopment of the state.

This knowledge was not without its material effects. Through the census, district gazetteers, surveys, and other investigative modalities, Britain was able to transform its vision of India into reality. The "empirical" findings of these modalities were already determined by their presuppositions as to what caste and Hinduism were. Nicholas Dirks has shown how the British, through surveys and censuses, transformed caste, which in precolonial south India was as much a "political" as a "social" institution, into a new phenomenon.[84] The massive amount of data collected from surveys and censuses became the basis for a vast system of rewards, quotas, and discriminations. These colonial restructures became the prison walls of a new caste system — a depoliticized, "social" essence that has been the ongoing patient (and irritant) of the British and postcolonial Indian state.

If caste had precluded the development of political consciousness or a stable system of government in precolonial times, then India could certainly not have attained the political unity necessary to construct a sensible narrative through the ancient, medieval, and modern epochs without, of course, frequent injections from the West. But this conclusion had implications that were potentially troubling for the British. There had to be some entity called India that moved through history. India could not be so dispersed as to escape any attempt to map it out. After all, how were the British to justify rulership over a nation that had never really existed? The answer was provided by locating unity not in the realm of the political but in society and religion.[85] The presence of some sort of societal and cultural unity (based on the caste system and the religion that accompanied it, Hinduism) gave the British some logic of justifying their presence in India — to finish India's historical narrative and provide the "guiding hand" of political order, which India itself had never been able to do.

The terms "social" and "society" obviously have multiple and complex genealogies in European history and social science, and I do not have the space to rehearse them here.[86] In thinking about the category of the social in the historiography of India, I want to outline three dominant senses of the term "social" in the post-Enlightenment human sciences. First is the idea that the social, in its proper functioning as civil society, is distinct or fundamentally separated from the political as represented by the institutions of government and state. In this sense, the social was almost always the passive recipient of the political or, more properly, the state. Here a whole host of related notions of the social might be brought together: the social as an adjunct to the economic; the social as a category, gendered feminine, consisting of customs, manners, civilization, and their reform through education. This sense of the social formed the original domain of inquiry for the nascent disciplines of sociology and anthropology. A second notion of the social in the human sciences has originated from a resistance to the production of the social as a "depoliticized" realm, reading the history of social groups like the working classes, women, or blacks, as in some sense suppressed by the political.

This sort of work has returned politics back to the social and challenged their very separation; to adapt a phrase of the women's liberation movement, "the social is the political." A third notion of the social, or society, has been its association, through the *Annales* school, with "total" history, or a history of society conceived in its broadest sense, including both the state and civil society. Here there has been an attempt to move beyond certain Marxist economisms and bring the recent insights of anthropology in the study of culture to bear on "the history of society."

It should be clear that the notion of the social to which colonial scholars relegated India was the first sense mentioned above, "society with the politics left out." In constituting India as a place determined by a social system (caste) that was prepolitical or antipolitical, Indology was instrumental in the British colonial state's production of a passive, age-old civilization that needed the strong arm of the British state to curb its fissiparous tendencies.[87] Anthropology, until recently, has taken up the constituents of society in India — tribe, village, and caste — with little concern for the political conditions of indigenous peoples, much less for those of anthropology itself. Its erasure of the category of the political and the state from the study of India has been integral to placement of India within the master narrative of European history as a vestigial deformity of Europe's childhood. This "denial of coevalness," as Johannes Fabian calls it, placed the colonized world in a time previous to that of Europe's present.[88] More than that, through the discourses on caste it confined all of India to the space of the social, a space where it became the inert patient of the British colonial state.

It is no wonder that the first major resistance against the colonial state affirmed the very category that India had been denied: the political nation itself. The focus of nationalist history was the reinvestment of ancient and medieval India with the political sovereignty and sound government that European narratives had refused it.[89] If Vincent Smith imagined Alexander's "triumphant progress" in India as demonstrating "the inherent weakness of the greatest Asiatic armies when confronted with European skill and discipline," [90] then nationalists, like Jawaharlal Nehru, contended:

Alexander's invasion of India, in the fourth century B.C. was, from the military point of view, a very minor affair. It was more of a raid across the border, and not a very successful raid for him. He met with such stout resistance from a border chieftain that the contemplated advance into the heart of India had to be reconsidered. If a small ruler on the frontier could fight thus, what of the larger and more powerful kingdoms further south?[91]

Nationalist historiography, as Partha Chatterjee has pointed out, made no substantial changes to the structure of Europe's master narrative but simply contested the claims that India was debased and its sovereignty derivative, reversing its agentive claims.[92] Nationalists claimed that India was a sovereign nation with a both a "history" and a "civil society," just like England, rather than a subject nation incapable of ruling itself. The idea of a stagnant medieval period served nationalist historians well to explain why the British had been able to rule India.

If Europe had sought recognition of the universality of its own modernity and history from the colonies, where it saw a deformed version of itself, the postindependence world of nations seemed to offer that recognition. If there was no longer a single story but a plurality of narratives, it also turned out that all the narratives were basically the same. As Nehru states,

> Every culture and people in the East and West has had an individuality, a message, and has attempted to solve life's problems each in its own way. . . . Ancient India and ancient Greece were different from each other and yet they were akin, just as ancient India and ancient China had kinship in thought, in spite of great differences. They all had the same broad, tolerant pagan outlook, joy in life and in the surprising beauty and infinite variety of nature, love of art, and the wisdom that comes from the accumulated experience of an old race.[93]

This language of liberal humanism, similar to Basham's, has been simultaneously deployed with the "three world" scheme of modernization theory, indicating that the unilinear evolutionary models of the colonial knowledge are by no means a thing of the past. While Britain was no longer the keeper of India's fate, it could still pride itself, as we shall see, on being the benefactor of India.[94] The social in nationalist historiography retained the same relationship to the political as in European historiography. But now it was not the whole of Indian civilization that inhabited the space of the social or spiritual but the same patients of European states — women, peasants, and other subaltern classes — that needed to be educated, regulated, and modernized by its agency.[95]

During and after the nationalist struggle for freedom, the colonialist historiography had to be reworked in light of a newly independent India. History and politics, which had been fading from the picture, disappeared completely from view in Anglo-American studies of ancient and medieval India, while studies of religion, caste, and other elements of "traditional culture" proliferated, often within the emerging paradigm of "development." Regarding modern India and the rise of the Indian nationalist movement, some scholars argued that the nationalists, try as they might, could not invent a "political." They only brought to politics a plethora of caste, religious, community, ethnic — in short, "social" — interests.[96] Anil Seal has written, "As they moved into the secular organisations, they remained riddled with allegiances to caste or community, and what from a distance appear as their political strivings were, on a closer examination, their efforts to conserve or improve the position of their own prescriptive group."[97]

This tradition of historiography, known as the Cambridge School, theorized the nationalist movement as a quest on the part of elite leaders to gain benefits for their particular regional and caste constituencies. This position would have been impossible had not the essence of India already been determined as a congeries of divisive and competing castes or despots, fighting for what little spoils there were in a "Hobbesian war of all against all."[98] This scholarship was the afterglow of an earlier imperialist historical project asserting that there had never been a *political* order in India except for the rule that the British had established. Just as earlier colonial historians had denied political and historical unity to ancient India on account of India's caste system, so too their descendants at Cambridge argued that the nationalist movement had indicated not a political consciousness but only a quest of "social" groups for material advancement clothed in political garb. This explained, they argued, the growing pains of young India.

Marxist historiography offered some alternatives to the earlier nationalist histories.[99] The Marxist view, increasingly focused on modern Indian history after independence, raised crucial questions about the relationship of the nationalist movement to the future patients of the Indian state, the workers and the peasantry. For Marxists, the nationalist bourgeoisie fulfilled a necessary and "progressive" role in catalyzing the formation of state capitalism; it was their unflagging commitment to the national idea and the failure of the left that was responsible for India's unique road to independence.[100] Marxist historians strongly criticized the Cambridge School, who had reduced the antiimperialist struggle to an "interest politics" on behalf of elite or provincial minorities. The Marxist understanding of the capitalist class that led the nationalist movement is expressed by Bipan Chandra:

> Relations between the Indian capitalist class and imperialism evolved during an era of the development of a powerful struggle against imperialism in India. This struggle in its different phases should not be seen in the main as a mere reflection of the contradiction between imperialism and the Indian bourgeoisie. This struggle was basically a reflection of the contradiction between imperialism and all the Indian people, of whom the bourgeoisie constituted merely one important segment. Moreover at no stage from its institution to its later development was the capitalist class the driving element behind this struggle or its militancy.[101]

The antiimperialist movement was the struggle of the Indian people to attain nationhood, and the capitalist class simply formed a single strand of that movement. In the late 1970s, a group of Marxist historians, eventually calling itself the Subaltern Collective, moved away from mainstream historiography and applied new approaches to the question of "history from below." Mainline Marxist historiography in India, according to Subaltern historians, did not theorize strongly enough a conflict of interest between the masses and the leaders in the struggle for independence. In its reaction to the Cambridge School's denigration of antiimperialist struggles, Marxist scholarship had, according to Sumit Sarkar, taken up "a stance rather difficult to distinguish from conventional nationalism."[102] Focusing on the struggle for independence from colonial rule, the Subaltern historians held that nationalists, Cambridge historians, and even some Marxists had all focused on the elites as the makers of history.[103] The Cambridge historians saw the independence struggle as a sort of behaviorist response on the part of the native elite to the institutions, opportunities, and most important, the rewards, established through the agency of the British. The nationalist school, on the other hand, saw the independence movement as a story of the Indian National Congress leading the alternately inert and uncontrollable masses to freedom — what Ranajit Guha, one of the founders of the Subaltern Studies Collective, called the "spiritual biography of the Indian elite."[104] The problem with this elitist historiography, according to Guha, followed "directly from the narrow and partial view of politics to which it is committed by virtue of its class outlook."[105] In other words, elitist historiography failed to recognize politics beyond the institutions of the colonial administration and the political aspirations of the Indian elite they produced. Guha and his companions, coming from the Marxist historiographical tradition, have generally used a concept of the social that would be broadly aligned with the second sense mentioned above. They have attempted to recover the social and "politicize" it by reading agrarian protest, labor unrest, and "religious" millenarianism as forms of political, not prepolitical, action.[106] The social, then, with its colonial genealogy, has continued to haunt the writing of Indian history since independence. But emerging from Subaltern historiography was a confrontation with what Guha calls "the historic failure of the nation to come to its own."[107] In some of the later works of the Subaltern Studies historians and in writing inspired by them, the nation-state, that hallowed beneficiary of the political, has become the object of scrutinizing inquiry.[108]

More recently, Subaltern Studies has increasingly converged with a much wider theoretical stream, current in Western academic circles and composed of scholars of diverse intellectual and political commitments, which brings us in a sense full circle. I have in mind here the poststructuralist critiques of Enlightenment rationality and modernity, and the Saidian literary-critical attacks on Eurocentric racism — what might very loosely be called postcolonial or post-Orientalist criticism.[109] This Saidian and poststructuralist turn, to the extent that it represents a move away from the concerns of historical materialism, has created dissent and conflict within the Subaltern Studies Collective.[110] Critics of the postcolonial developments in Indian history argue that postmodernist and Saidian frameworks tend to reinforce indigenisms that at their best adumbrate nationalist rhetoric and at their worst condone traditionalist and conservative elements in India today.[111] This critique, despite its incisiveness and its compelling call for detailed and theoretically informed Marxist history, has been perhaps too dismissive of a large body of scholarship that arose precisely to solve some of the real problems faced by Marxist historiography in the 1970s.

For our purposes, one of the most productive threads running through this more recent scholarship has been the questioning of the autonomy (and not necessarily the violence) of what I have been calling Europe's master narrative. These scholars have argued that Europe's master narrative was not the possessor of some selfsame identity upon which the colonial world then modeled its own derivative history, but rather that

Europe's historical narrative has been dependent on the deformed versions that it has created for the third world during the colonial era. To use Jessica Benjamin's psychoanalytic language, European history has constantly sought both to distance or "Other" the history of India and at the same time to gain "recognition," or to see itself acknowledged in the history of its Other. It is this quest for recognition, the dependency of Europe's history on its constructions of the third world, that compromises its autonomy. Dipesh Chakrabarty, calling this process the "provincialization of Europe," notes that "Europe's acquisition of the adjective *modern* is a piece of global history of which an integral part is the story of European imperialism." [112] But even the beginnings of Europe's master narrative, the Doric invasions of the Aegean peninsula and the subsequent rise of Periclean Greece, find their origins in a theory of race and language that was dependent on the grammatical structures of Sanskrit! We are beginning to see that the characters in the drama of European history are acting a script that is not entirely of their own making.

NOTES

1. Edward Said, *Orientalism* (New York: Vintage, 1979), p. 3.

2. Said's work was not the first critique of Orientalism but rather the "renewal of a debate" that had its roots in the Arab response to Western scholarship in the nineteenth century. Such a perspective, often from a religious point of view, was later supplemented by the work of anticolonial and socialist critics from the Middle East. For a synthetic review of the pre-Saidian history of the debate on Orientalism, with an analysis of the significance of Said's intervention, see Ulrike Freitag, "The Critique of Orientalism," in Michael Bentley, ed., *Companion to Historiography* (New York: Routledge, 1997), pp. 620–38.

3. The work inspired by Said is far too voluminous to chart here. Several sources of note are Timothy Mitchell, *Colonising Egypt* (Berkeley: University of California Press, 1991); Mary Louise Pratt, *Imperial Eyes: Travel Writing and Transculturation* (New York: Routledge, 1992); J. M. Blaut, *The Colonizer's Model of the World: Geographical Diffusionism and Eurocentric History* (New York: Guilford, 1993); Laura Ann Stoler, *Race and the Education of Desire: Foucault's History of Sexuality and the Colonial Order of Things* (Durham: Duke University Press, 1995); Thomas Richards, *The Imperial Archive: Knowledge and the Fantasy of Empire* (New York: Verso, 1994); and in the Indian context, Ronald Inden, *Imagining India* (Cambridge: Basil Blackwell, 1990); Dilip K. Chakrabarty, *Colonial Indology: Sociopolitics of the Indian Past* (Delhi: Munshiram Manoharlal, 1997); Gauri Visvanathan, *Masks of Conquest: Literary Study and British Rule in India* (New York: Columbia University Press, 1989); various essays in Carol Breckenridge and Peter Van der Veer, eds., *Orientalism and the Postcolonial Predicament* (Philadelphia: University of Pennsylvania Press, 1993);

and Gyan Prakash, "Post-Orientalist Third World Histories," *Comparative Studies in Society and History* 32, no. 2 (April 1990): 383–408.

4. Said's book has drawn sharp criticism from some corners of the Orientalist "establishment." See particularly Bernard Lewis, "The Question of Orientalism," *New York Review of Books*, September 24, 1982, pp. 49–56. For a useful summary and critique of these debates, see Fred Halliday, "Orientalism and Its Critics," *British Journal of Middle Eastern Studies* 20, no. 2 (1993): 145–63; also Freitag, "Critique of Orientalism." For a more general theoretical discussion of Said and Homi Bhabha in the context of structuralist and poststructuralist thought, see Robert Young, "Disorienting Orientalism," in *White Mythologies: Writing History and the West* (New York: Routledge, 1990), pp. 119–40. In the Indian context, with special reference to the work of Ronald Inden, see Aijaz Ahmad, "Between Orientalism and Historicism: Anthropological Knowledge of India," *Studies in History* 7, no. 1 (1991): 135–64; more generally, see Aijaz Ahmad, "Orientalism and After: Ambivalence and Metropolitan Location in the Work of Edward Said," in Ahmad, *In Theory: Classes, Nations, Literatures* (New York: Verso, 1992), pp. 159–220; as well as Sumit Sarkar, "Orientalism Revisited: Saidian Frameworks in the Writing of Modern Indian History," *Oxford Literary Review* 16 (1994): 203–21.

5. Jessica Benjamin, *The Bonds of Love: Psychoanalysis, Feminism, and the Problem of Domination* (New York: Pantheon, 1988), pp. 31–36.

6. For discussions of medieval European views of the Arab world, see Rana Kabbani, *Europe's Myths of Orient: Devise and Rule* (London: Pandora, 1986), ch. 2. For classical and medieval views of Egypt, see Martin Bernal, *Black Athena: The Afroasiatic Roots of Classical Civilization*, vol. 1, *The Fabrication of Ancient Greece, 1785–1985* (New Brunswick, N.J.: Rutgers University Press, 1987), pp. 22–25, chs. 1, 2.

7. For a review of medieval European imagery of the Indian Ocean, see Jacques Le Goff, "The Medieval West and the Indian Ocean: An Oneiric Horizon," in *Time, Work, and Culture in the Middle Ages*, trans. Arthur Goldhammer (Chicago: University of Chicago Press, 1980), pp. 189–200. For two early seventeenth-century missionary representations of India, see Ines G. Zupanov, "Aristocratic Analogies and Demotic Descriptions in the Seventeenth-Century Madurai Mission," *Representations* 41 (Winter 1993): 123–48.

8. From Hegel's *Vorlesungen über die Philosophie der Weltgeschichte II: Die Orientalische Welt*, as quoted in Wilhelm Halbfass, *India and Europe: An Essay in Understanding* (New York: SUNY Press, 1988), p. 2.

9. Unlike the scholar/imperialists of the nineteenth century, "medieval Europeans did not see India as an *inferior* land of the *past*, but as a *superior* land of the *future*, a paradisiac kingdom ruled by a priest-king, Prester John, who might, it was hoped, come to save Christendom"; Inden, *Imagining India*, p. 48.

10. Said, *Orientalism*, p. 40.

11. Ronald Inden, "Orientalist Constructions of India," *Modern Asian Studies* 20, no. 3 (1986): 430.

12. On philology and racism in Europe, see Leon Poliakov, *The Aryan Myth: A History of Racist Ideas in Europe* (London: Sussex University Press, 1974); Maurice

Olender, *The Languages of Paradise: Race, Religion, and Philology in the Nineteenth Century* (Cambridge: Harvard University Press, 1992); and Bernal, *Black Athena*, pp. 29–31, chs. 5–7.

13. F. Max Müller, *The History of Sanskrit Literature*, 1859, cited in Susie Tharu and K. Lalita, eds., *Women Writing in India 600 B.C. to the Present*, vol. 1 (New York: Feminist Press, 1991), p. 42.

14. F. Max Müller, *India, What It Can Teach Us* (London: Longmans, Green, and Co., 1883), p. 101.

15. C. H. Philips, "James Mill, Mountstuart Elphinstone, and the History of India," in C. H. Philips, ed., *Historians of India, Pakistan, and Ceylon* (London: Oxford University Press, 1961), pp. 224–27.

16. Ibid., p. 225.

17. The Archaeological Survey of India was responsible for the collection and translation of thousands of stone and copper-plate inscriptions produced by the imperial polities in the subcontinent from about A.D. 400 to the arrival of the British. These inscriptions contained "dynastic" information, which was used as source material to construct the increasingly complex narrative of pre-British Indian history. For a discussion of the role that archaeology and epigraphy played in Orientalist discourse, see Daud Ali, "Royal Eulogy as World History: Rethinking Copper-Plate Inscriptions in Cola India," in Ronald Inden, ed., *Querying the Medieval: The History of Practice in South Asia* (New York: Oxford University Press, forthcoming), and Tapti Guha-Thakurta, "Monuments and Lost Histories: Archaeology in the Colonial and Nationalist Imagination," in Giles Tillotson, ed., *Towards an Indian Aesthetics* (London: Curzon, 1997), pp. 29–63.

18. The prolific work of nationalist historians became the dominant historical representations in India, while outside India the Indological project had to be reworked in view of nationalist historiography.

19. See especially his remarks on the life negating/life affirming aspects of Indian civilization and their origins in tropical climate, in A. L. Basham, *The Wonder That Was India* (1954; reprint, London: Sidgwick and Jackson, 1985), pp. 3–4.

20. Mill speaks highly of the celebrated political economist Adam Smith and his *Wealth of Nations*.

21. Romila Thapar locates this periodization as the source for the organization of history departments in Indian universities today. See Romila Thapar, "Interpretations of Ancient Indian History," *History and Theory* 7, no. 3 (1968): 5, n. 6.

22. James Mill, *The History of British India (Abridged)* (Chicago: University of Chicago Press, 1975), pp. 63–64, 246.

23. Philips, "Mill and India," pp. 224–25.

24. Chief among these was R. G. Bhandarkar, who wrote the classic *The Early History of the Dekhan* (Bombay, 1894). See Thapar, "Interpretations of Ancient Indian History," p. 11.

25. Perhaps the best example of this is *The Oxford History of India*, which Smith published in 1919, including portions of his own earlier work as well as excerpts from Mill and Elphinstone. This text, meant to be more comprehensive than the *Early History of India*, includes a perfect marriage of the two schemes. The text is di-

vided into (1) "Ancient and Hindu India," (2) "India in the Muslim Period," and (3) "India in the British Period." The narrative gets sticky when in the first section, "Ancient and Hindu India," we come across a subsection titled "The Medieval Hindu Kingdoms." For a discussion of periodization from the nationalist point of view, see U. N. Ghoshal, "Periods of Indian History," in *The Beginnings of Indian Historiography* (Calcutta: R. Ghoshal, 1944), pp. 292–304.

26. Mill, *History of British India*, p. 45.

27. For an analysis of Mill's work as an indirect polemic against the Church of England, see Duncan Forbes, "James Mill and India," *Cambridge Journal* (October 1951), cited in Philips, "Mill and India," p. 219.

28. Mill, *History of British India*, p. 45.

29. Here we can see how the Evangelical and Utilitarian judgments of India differed. While they both would have condemned India's past on the basis of its religion, the Utilitarian narrative ends with the arrival of the British and the eclipse of religion, while the Evangelical conception would have substituted Christian for British.

30. See Carl Pletsch, "The Three Worlds, or the Division of Social Scientific Labor, circa 1950–1975," *Comparative Studies in Society and History* 23, no. 4 (October 1981): 565–90.

31. For a concise presentation and critique of this teleology, see Eric Wolf, *Europe and the People without History* (Berkeley: University of California Press, 1982), pp. 4–7.

32. True political unity, as Vincent Smith emphasized, was not achieved until the British brought the subcontinent under Queen Victoria's crown in 1877. See Vincent A. Smith, *The Early History of India from 600 B.C. to the Muhammadan Conquest including the Invasion of Alexander the Great* (Oxford: Clarendon Press, 1914), p. 5.

33. The great twelve-volume nationalist history of India, *The History and Culture of the Indian People*, devotes two volumes to the ancient period: *The Age of Imperial Unity* (vol. 2) and *The Classical Age* (vol. 3). See R. C. Majumdar, gen. ed., *The History and Culture of the Indian People* (Bombay: Bharatiya Vidya Bhavan, 1951–).

34. Romila Thapar, *A History of India*, vol. 1 (Harmondsworth: Penguin, 1966), pp. 136 ff.

35. For illuminating overviews of Gupta historiography, see David Lorenzen, "Historians and the Gupta Empire," in Chabbra et al., eds., *Reappraising Gupta History: For S. R. Goyal* (Delhi: Aditya Prakashan, 1992), pp. 47–60; and Shankar Goyal, *The Image of Classical India: Its Changing Colours and Contours* (Jodhpur: Kusumanjali, 1997).

36. Vincent Smith, *The Oxford History of India*, ed. Percival Spear, 3d ed. (Delhi: Oxford University Press, 1958), p. 172.

37. A. L. Basham, Introduction, to Bardwell Smith, ed., *Essays in Gupta Culture* (Delhi: Motilal Banarsidass, 1983), p. 1.

38. For an idealist version of this idea based on the theologian Karl Jasper's idea of an "Axial Age," see S. N. Eisenstadt, ed., *The Origins and Diversity of Axial Age Civilizations* (New York: SUNY Press, 1986).

39. Smith (1914), p. 356.

40. For the most recent authoritative histories that chart the rise of regionalism in medieval India, see Thapar, *History of India*, and especially Hermann Kulke and Dietmar Rothermund, *A History of India* (New York: Routledge, 1986).

41. I have elsewhere attempted to destabilize the ancient/medieval political caricatures of Indian history by pointing out that the inscriptions of the "ancient" Mauryan "empire" do not claim hegemony over the "far south" and hence do not take the entire subcontinent as their political domain. And later, inscriptions of "medieval petty kingdoms" like the Rastrakutas, Colas, and Calukyas do make very explicit pan-Indian imperial claims. In short, "regionalism" does not play a role in the formation of historical consciousness in India until the colonial period. But neither were these imperial formations simply prototypes of a modern Indian state, as nationalists might argue.

42. Bernal, *Black Athena*, pp. 224–80.

43. For a useful and comprehensive review of the growth of racial science in colonial historiography and the birth of racial science, see Thomas R. Trautman, *Aryans and British India* (Berkeley: University of California Press, 1997). Also see Chakrabarty, *Colonial Indology*, pp. 54–151. For an account of the more recent political uses of this theory in India, see Romila Thapar, "Some Appropriations of the Theory of Aryan Race and the Beginnings of Indian History," in Daud Ali and Avril Powell, eds., *The Place of the Past: The Uses of History in South Asia* (Delhi: Oxford University Press, forthcoming).

44. On Francis Whyte Ellis's discovery of the Dravidian hypothesis, usually attributed to Robert Caldwell, see Thomas Trautman, "Inventing the History of South India," in Daud Ali and Avril Powell, eds., *The Place of the Past: The Uses of History in South Asia* (Delhi: Oxford University Press, forthcoming).

45. I use the term "prepared" because Caldwell himself believed the Dravidians to be settlers in the subcontinent who were pushed southward by a Scythian invasion long before the Aryans arrived in India. The Scythians, according to Caldwell, were violently subjugated by the Aryans. Although scholars adopted Caldwell's term "Dravidian," they largely ignored his history and dated the Scythian invasions much later. See Rt. Rev. Robert Caldwell, *A Comparative Grammar of the Dravidian or South Indian Family of Languages* (1875; reprint, Madras: University of Madras, 1961), pp. 106–7.

46. Gustave Oppert, *On the Original Inhabitants of Bharatavarsha* (Westminster: A. Constable, 1893).

47. As reprinted in the popular *Imperial Gazeteer of India: The Indian Empire*, new ed., vol. 1, "Descriptive" (Oxford: Clarendon, 1909), p. 299.

48. Ibid., p. 300.

49. Wilbur T. Elmore, *Dravidian Gods in Modern Hinduism* (New York: published by the author, 1915), p. 9.

50. For a critique of the theory of Aryan invasion by an archaeologist, see Chakrabarty, *Colonial Indology*.

51. Rt. Rev. Henry Whitehead, *The Village Gods of South India* (London: Oxford University Press, 1916), p. 12. Following in part the ideas of German Indologist Gustave Oppert, the Reverend Henry Whitehead, bishop of Madras, and Wilbur

Elmore, an American sociologist — writing shortly after the turn of the century — published important studies of "Dravidian" or "Village" Hinduism. Both works sought to unravel the religion of the original inhabitants of India from modern Hinduism of rural India.

52. See Elmore, *Dravidian Gods*, pp. 9–18, and Whitehead, *Village Gods*, pp. 11–20. Both scholars described the religion of the Dravidians as "animist" and "totemic" — designating the most primitive stages that natural religion took on its ascent to monotheism.

53. Whitehead, *Village Gods*, pp. 17–18.

54. Elmore, *Dravidian Gods*, p. 15.

55. Basham, *Wonder That Was India*, pp. 24, 185.

56. Smith, *Early History of India*, p. 8.

57. Basham, *Wonder That Was India*, p. 298.

58. Javed Majeed, *Ungoverned Imaginings: James Mill's* The History of British India *and Orientalism* (Oxford: Clarendon, 1992), pp. 195–96.

59. Mill, *History of British India*, p. 35.

60. Ibid., pp. 233, 241 ff.

61. Ibid., p. 237.

62. Smith (1914), p. 44.

63. Ibid., p. 356.

64. Ibid.

65. Ibid., p. 77.

66. Ibid., my parentheses.

67. As recently as 1986, two German Indologists stated that "the most important indirect consequence of Alexander's campaign was the contribution which it made to the further political development of India" (Kulke and Rothermund, *History of India*, p. 61).

68. Smith (1914), p. 307. The Bactrian Greeks, successors to Alexander's empire, were said to give India art and drama, the Romans, coinage and architecture.

69. As cited in Lata Mani, "Contentious Traditions: The Debate on *Sati* in Colonial India," in Kumkum Sangari and Sudesh Vaid, eds., *Recasting Women: Essays in Indian Colonial History* (New Brunswick, N.J.: Rutgers University Press, 1990), p. 95.

70. Basham, *Wonder That Was India*, p. 481.

71. Smith, *The Early History of India from 600 B.C. to the Muhammadan Conquest including the Invasion of Alexander the Great*, 4th ed. (Oxford: Clarendon Press, 1924), pp. 370, 72.

72. The discursive dismantling of pre-British political practices in South Asia during the colonial period rivals the most thorough postmodern deconstructions.

73. Basham, *Wonder That Was India*, pp. 44–78.

74. Ibid., pp. 69–70. This book deals with the more "interesting topic" of "culture" in ancient and medieval India.

75. Nicholas Dirks, "History as a Sign of the Modern," *Public Culture* 2, no. 2 (Spring 1990): 27.

76. Mill subscribed to the theory, mentioned above, of India's invasion by a race

of fair-skinned peoples, speaking a language related to other languages of the Indo-European family, who migrated from the steplands of central Asia; Mill, *History of British India*, p. 37.

77. Ibid., p. 38.

78. Ibid., p. 39.

79. The literature on caste is voluminous and labyrinthine, without any promise, as Eric Wolf says, of light at the end of the tunnel. For a summary and critique of the different Indological views on caste (racial, occupational, romantic, and positivist), see Inden, *Imagining India*, pp. 49–84.

80. As cited in ibid., p. 65.

81. The Romantics and the Utilitarians, as might be expected, differed in their appraisal of Hinduism. The empiricists (along with the Evangelicals) saw Hinduism as a damnable creed poisoned by the worst superstitions and irrationalities, whereas the Romantics saw it as a misguided but spiritually well-intentioned form of idealism.

82. G. W. F. Hegel, *The Philosophy of History*, trans. J. Sibree (New York: Dover, 1956), p. 139.

83. Ibid., p. 113.

84. Nicholas Dirks, "The Invention of Caste: Civil Society in Colonial India," *Social Analysis*, no. 25 (1989): pp. 42–52.

85. The effect of this relocation of the unity of India has had momentous effects on the academic study of India in the West — as well as on popular notions. The great majority of academicians and Indologists are located in religion and anthropology departments, not in history and political science departments. Most popular images that Americans, for example, associate with India are centered around religion (sacred cows, multiarmed goddesses) and social problems (starving masses, dowry).

86. I have relied primarily on Sumit Sarkar's useful synthetic essay "Social History: Predicaments and Possibilities," *Economic and Political Weekly* 20:25–26 (June 22–29, 1985), pp. 1081–88; also see Wolf, *Europe and the People without History*, pp. 7–23.

87. Space does not permit a treatment of the gendered aspects of this colonial domination and its effects on women's history. See Sangari and Vaid, *Recasting Women*.

88. Johannes Fabian, *Time and the Other: How Anthropology Makes Its Object* (New York: Columbia University Press, 1983), p. 31.

89. See K. P. Jayaswal, *Hindu Polity: A Constitutional History of India in Hindu Times* (reprint, Calcutta: Butterworth, 1924); A. S. Altekar, *State and Government in Ancient India* (1949; reprint, Delhi: Motilal Banarsidass, 1962); R. K. Mookerji, *Local Government in Ancient India* (Oxford: Clarendon Press, 1919).

90. Smith (1914), p. 112.

91. Jawarharlal Nehru, *The Discovery of India* (1946; reprint, Delhi: Oxford University Press, 1985), p. 114.

92. Partha Chatterjee, *Nationalist Thought in the Colonial World: A Derivative Discourse?* (Delhi: Oxford University Press, 1986).

93. Nehru, *Discovery of India*, p. 151.

94. There were, of course, some colonial scholars who felt that the civilizing project in India had largely failed. This admission never included the critique of that project itself. See L. S. S. O'Malley, ed., *Modern India and the West* (London: Oxford University Press, 1941).

95. In his latest work, Partha Chatterjee takes up each of these categories in relation to the Indian nationalist movement. See Partha Chatterjee, *The Nation and Its Fragments: Colonial and Postcolonial Histories* (Princeton: Princeton University Press, 1993).

96. For pre-independence studies, see Verney Lovett, *A History of the Indian Nationalist Movement* (London: J. Murray, 1920); for post-independence historians, see Anil Seal, *The Emergence of Indian Nationalism: Competition and Collaboration in the Later Nineteenth Century* (Cambridge: Cambridge University Press, 1968); John Gallagher, Gordon Johnson, Anil Seal, eds., *Locality, Province, Nation* (Cambridge: Cambridge University Press, 1973). For a critique of this historiography, see Bernard Cohn, "African Models, Indian Histories," in *An Anthropologist among the Historians and Other Essays* (Delhi: Oxford University Press, 1987), pp. 219–22.

97. Seal, *Emergence of Indian Nationalism*, p. 342.

98. Cohn, "African Models, Indian Histories," p. 220.

99. For ancient and medieval India, see D. D. Kosambi, *An Introduction to the Study of Ancient Indian History* (Bombay: Popular Prakashan, 1956); R. S. Sharma, *Indian Feudalism, c. 300–1300* (Calcutta: University of Calcutta, 1965). For the modern period, the classic text remains R. Palme Dutt, *India To-day* (London: Victor Gollancz, 1940); also the works of Bipin Chandra, *The Rise and Growth of Economic Nationalism in India* (Delhi: People's Publishing House, 1966), and *Nationalism and Colonialism in Modern India* (Delhi: Orient Longman, 1979).

100. Bipan Chandra, *Nationalism and Colonialism in Modern India* (Delhi: Orient Longman, 1979), p. 164.

101. "This paper was originally read at the International Seminar on Imperialism, Independence, and Social Transformations in the Contemporary World held in Delhi in March 1972" (ibid., p. 144 n).

102. Sumit Sarkar, *Modern India, 1885–1947* (Delhi: Macmillan, 1983), p. 9.

103. Ranajit Guha et al., eds., *Subaltern Studies*, 9 vols. For a general statement of the goals of Subaltern Studies, see Ranajit Guha, "On Some Aspects of the Historiography of Colonial India," in *Subaltern Studies* (Delhi: Oxford University Press, 1982), 1:1–8; Chatterjee, *Nationalist Thought in the Colonial World*; and Sarkar, *Modern India*.

104. Guha, "On Some Aspects," p. 2.

105. Ibid., p. 3.

106. See Ranajit Guha, *Elementary Aspects of Peasant Insurgency in Colonial India* (Delhi: Oxford University Press, 1983).

107. Guha, "On Some Aspects," p. 7.

108. Partha Chatterjee extended his earlier work on Indian nationalism in his *The Nation and Its Fragments*. See also the analyses of Hindu communalism under

the framework of the "nation" in David Ludden, ed., *Contesting the Nation: Religion, Community, and the Politics of Democracy in India* (Philadelphia: University of Pennsylvania Press, 1996).

109. The literature here is again too vast and the commitment of its authors too diverse to catalog in any comprehensive or systematic manner. Of importance is the work of Gayatri Chakravorty Spivak and Homi Bhabha and the many works they in turn have inspired. Also Breckenridge and Van der Veer, *Orientalism and the Post-Colonial Predicament*. For reviews of these thinkers, see Young, "Disorienting Orientalism." For Subalternist engagement with these trends, see the single essay by Gayatri Chakravorty Spivak in the collection "Subaltern Studies: Deconstructing Historiography," in Guha and Spivak, eds., *Selected Subaltern Studies* (New York: Oxford University Press, 1988), pp. 3–34 (see also Edward Said's preface to the same volume); see also Prakash, "Post-Orientalist Histories"; Gyan Pandey, "In Defense of the Fragment: Writing about Hindu-Muslim Riots in India Today," *Representations*, no. 37 (Winter 1992): 27–55; Dipesh Chakrabarty, "The Death of History: Historical Consciousness and the Culture of Late Capitalism," *Public Culture* 4, no. 2 (Spring 1992): 47–65, and "Of Garbage, Modernity, and the Citizen's Gaze," *Economic and Political Weekly* 27, nos. 10–11 (March 1992): 541–46.

110. For a critique of this trend of Subaltern Studies, see Sarkar, "Orientalism Revisited." For a response, see Dipesh Chakrabarty, "Radical Histories and the Question of Enlightenment Rationalism," *Economic and Political Weekly* 30, no. 14 (1995): 751–59. For a general condemnation of Saidian and poststructuralist frameworks in writing third world history from the vantage point of an apparently orthodox Marxism, see Ahmed, "Orientalism and After"; for an incisive critique of Ahmed's position, see Sudipta Kaviraj's review of Ahmed, "The Politics of Nostalgia," *Economy and Society* 22, no. 4 (November 1993): 525–43.

111. See Sarkar, "Orientalism Revisited"; also Sumit Sarkar, "Indian Nationalism and the Politics of Hindutva," in Ludden, *Contesting the Nation*, pp. 270–94. Hindu nationalists have indeed made use of Saidian critiques of Orientalism to suggest homogenizing and reactionary interpretations of Indian history. Of particular relevance here are the current debates about the historicity and validity of the Aryan invasion. For an example of the Hindu communalist position, which uses the heavy anticolonial rhetoric (without the sophistication) of Poliakov, Said, and Bernal, see Navaratna Rajaram, *Aryan Invasion of India: The Myth and the Truth* (Delhi: Voice of India, 1993).

112. Dipesh Chakrabarty, "Postcoloniality and the Artifice of History: Who Speaks for 'Indian' Pasts?" *Representations*, no. 37 (Winter 1992): 21.

STEPHEN VLASTOS

AGRARIANISM WITHOUT TRADITION:
THE RADICAL CRITIQUE OF PREWAR
JAPANESE MODERNITY

Responding to criticism of Japan's closed agricultural markets, Yamaguchi Iwao, executive director of the Central Union of Agricultural Cooperatives, concluded a ringing defense of the Japanese government's long-standing rice import ban with the following warning: "The principles developed in rice cultivation are the glue of Japanese society. They pervade our social structure, our culture, and our moral code. . . . Without its farms, our society might be fundamentally and irrevocably altered. The pernicious habit of bullying Japanese farmers and ridiculing Japanese agriculture can only lead our nation to ruin."[1]

Threatened by foreign competition, producers the world over are inclined to argue that protection of their industry is in the national interest. What distinguishes the protectionist rhetoric of Japanese farmers is its grandiose assertion of agriculture's historic contribution to Japanese culture. Yamaguchi's defense of the ban on rice imports draws upon a "traditional" trope in the discourse on the social value of Japanese agriculture: the farm village as wellspring of Japan's cultural identity. So commonplace and uncontested is this notion that the lead-in to a recent highbrow journalistic piece on rice imports matter-of-factly reported that mandated reductions of paddy field acreage "deprived farmers of their sense of pride as creators of Japanese culture and history."[2]

This essay critically examines agrarian discourses in modern Japan from the perspective of the invention of tradition. I make three points. First, the idea that Japan's farm villages function as a reservoir of national culture, reproducing the core values and habits that shape Japanese national character, is a relatively recent invention. Although one can find resonance in Tokugawa nativist thought (*kokugaku*), the valorization of the farm village as the heart and soul of Japan belongs to a modern discourse that developed in reaction to social cleavages and national anxieties attendant to industrialization.

The second point concerns the ideological permutations of agrarian thought in the modern period.[3] The dominant agrarian discourse was elitist and conservative, warning that the one-sided development of industry and the neglect of agriculture undermined society's natural bulwark against social revolution. There was also a radical, populist stream of agrarian thought that surfaced around World War I. Largely emerging among angry outsiders, this discourse bitterly criticized the values, culture, and social relations of industrial capitalism. Appalled by the uneven development of the countryside, capitalism's inhumane social relations, and the moral corruption of "great Tokyo," agrarian populists vehemently criticized Japan's trajectory of modern development.

Radical agrarianism, I argue, was a two-voiced position. Running parallel to the furious, apocalyptic polemic against industrial capitalism and urban culture was a utopian discourse on rural harmony and social cohesion. Radical in its critique of capitalism and bourgeois politics, it was not socially revolutionary. Affirming both existing property relations and the sanctity of the farm family, the visionary discourse held conservative values at its core.

The third point is analytic and concerns the rhetorical uses of tradition. In contrast to the dominant-elite discourse on farm and nation, radical agrarianism did not invent a precapitalist golden age of Japanese agriculture. Its lack of nostalgia for the pre-Meiji village, in turn, points to the ideological valence of the trope of invention of tradition. "Tradition" uniquely evokes the authority of "the past"; it can be mobilized by any discourse of reform, or even of revolution, that hinges upon a rhetorical construction of a national past. The rhetoric of utopia, however, posits new social relations in imaginary political space. Tradition, invented or real, has no place.

FROM TOKUGAWA TO MEIJI

Official praise of agriculture in the Tokugawa period (1600–1867), the historical era most closely associated in the popular mind with "traditional" Japan, may suggest that the modern valorization of farming possesses an unbroken lineage. In an often-quoted passage of *Seidan*, Ogyû Sorai (1666–1728), the most influential political theorist of his time, used the Confucian botanical metaphor of root and stem in emphasizing agriculture's importance: "The sages teach us to prize the root and curtail the branches. Agriculture is the root, manufacture and commerce are the branches."[4]

Neo-Confucianism, the official ideology of Tokugawa feudalism, esteemed farming above other mundane occupations because of its social utility and the presumed innocence of profit-seeking. In the Neo-Confucian scheme merchants enriched themselves and impoverished others by their trade, while farmers supported the whole society by producing food and fiber to feed and clothe the entire population. Yet farmers were praised only to the extent that they were law-abiding, diligent in their labor, and dutiful in paying taxes. In the world of Tokugawa feudalism, farming was never more than the mandatory occupation of a politically subordinate and morally inferior social class, and farmers' customs, beliefs, values, and communities were disparaged and viewed with suspicion. It was the warrior class, masters of the literary and martial arts, that embodied virtue.

The Meiji Restoration of 1868, which made economic modernization a top national priority, gave rise to a new discourse on agriculture, shaped by the tenets of economic liberalism. Rejecting the notion that farming possessed special social value, Meiji statesmen promoted rural capitalism. In an often quoted memorial to the emperor dated May 2, 1875, the architect of early Meiji modernization, Ōkubo Toshimishi, argued that enriching and strengthening the nation in the industrial age required "increasing production and building up enterprises" in all sectors, including agriculture.[5] Early Meiji reforms legalized private ownership of land and free movement of labor, imposed a modern land tax based on the market values, and removed all barriers to interregional trade. Some farmers protested, but until the end of the nineteenth century the debate over agricultural policy was largely confined to two issues, technology and taxes.[6]

The first evidence of a counterdiscourse arguing agriculture's unique social value is found in the writings of Shinagawa Yajirô, a conservative member of the Meiji government's inner circle, who warned as early as 1884 against neglecting the countryside. "Agriculture," Shinagawa cautioned, "is the foundation of the family and the foundation of the country."[7] Shinagawa made his remarks in the midst of a massive dispossession of small-farm families in the 1880s, precipitated by the pro-industrial monetary and fiscal policies of Finance Minister Matsukata Masayoshi.[8] In the 1890s, war with China and the continued rise in farm tenancy again focused attention on the perils of uneven development.

With one eye on the manpower demands of modern warfare and the other on the specter of social revolution, bureaucrats in the Ministry of Agriculture and Manufacture developed legislative initiatives — chiefly farm credit institutions and rural industrial cooperatives — designed to stabilize the middle stratum of family farmers.[9]

The most vocal apologist for Japanese farming at the turn of the century was Yokoi Tokiyoshi, a professor of agronomy at Tokyo University's agricultural college. A native of Kyushu who studied at the Kumamoto School of Foreign Studies, Yokoi matriculated at Komaba Agriculture College, where he specialized in soil chemistry. Employed first as a lecturer at the Fukuoka Higher Agriculture School and later as a professor at his alma mater, Yokoi is remembered today as a pioneer of modern Japanese agronomy.[10] In the late 1890s, however, he took on a new role as the vocal critic of rapid industrialization and in 1897 published a short essay titled "Nôhonshugi," which articulated the main themes of the conservative agrarian critique of modern economic development.[11]

Yokoi couched his defense of agriculture in terms of the contribution made by farmimg to the nation-state. One-sided industrial development, he contended, jeopardized the social foundations of the nation. While industry produced greater wealth than agriculture did, he conceded, industrialization frayed the social fabric by making the poor poorer and the rich fabulously rich. "Day by day, month by month," Yokoi warned, "the gulf between poor and rich expands." To his regret, Japan increasingly resembled the "advanced" nations of the West, countries where great disparity of wealth incited revolution.[12] Riches did not guarantee national health and security, he cautioned. On the contrary, "the vitality of a country is fostered by its middle class families; it is particularly well developed among farm families."[13] Farmers, Yokoi contended, were physically and morally best qualified to be soldiers; being closest to the soil, they were naturally the most patriotic. Yet because agriculture could not measure up to industry under conditions of unrestrained competition, inexorably the gap between urban wealth and rural poverty widened. "If this is allowed to go on," he warned, "the pitiful farmers will gradually be oppressed by the urban rich; sacrificed to their interest, they grow weaker and more impoverished year by year." As had already happened in Europe, in Japan the gap between rich and poor was growing. The social cleavage now observed in Japan, he concluded, would soon spawn socialism and violent social upheaval.[14]

Yokoi wrote "Nôhonshugi" in the decade bracketed by the Sino-

Japanese War of 1894–95 and the Russo-Japanese War of 1904–5, a period of rapid urbanization and sustained industrial growth. Yokoi's essay, historian Thomas Havens has written, stands as the inaugural text of modern Japanese agrarianism.[15] But "Nôhonshugi" was not a radical text. Yokoi denounced "industrialism," not capitalism, and looked to the state for the remedy. "It is ultimately the responsibility of the nation state," he advised, "to help the weak and prevent the strong from preying on the weak." If the state fulfilled its social responsibilities, he concluded, "commerce, industry and agriculture can all advance together."[16] This is the rhetoric of a dissenting insider. In 1897, when Yokoi wrote "Nôhonshugi," he spoke from the position of the loyal opposition. At this point he conceived of the problems of the countryside primarily in terms of the excesses of industrialization, and he believed in the efficacy of reform.

THE FIRST RADICAL TURN: YOKOI TOKIYOSHI'S THEORY OF THE JAPANESE "SMALL FARM"

If discourse is as much performance as written word, the November 1914 meeting of the Social Policy Association (Shakai Seisaku Gakkai) enacted the sundering of the Meiji consensus on agriculture's role in national development. Convened at Tokyo Imperial University, the eighth general meeting of the group adopted as its theme "The Problem of Protecting Small Farmers."[17] The first report, delivered by Takaoka Kumao (1871–1961), an eminent agricultural economist and educator, attributed the plight of Japan's small family farmers to their underutilization of household labor. Adopting Wilhelm Roscher's distinction between big and small farming, which hinged on the role of household labor in farm management, Takaoka began by observing that in Japan, 4 to 5 *chô* constituted the upper limit and 1.5 *chô* the lower limit of "small farmer" holdings.[18] The source of the distress of this class, he suggested, was rural overpopulation. Most owner-cultivators simply did not possess enough land to exploit the family's labor power fully, and because little land was left to reclaim, out-migration of farm families appeared to be the only solution. Invoking Gresham's law, the theory that bad money drives out good, he painted a bleak picture: "With advances in education and rising living costs, the most talented and enterprising will leave the countryside for cities, or will move away, so that those who remain in rural areas will be wives and children, the elderly and the very young, and those [adult men] who can't make a go of it."[19] While not a desirable end in itself, Takaoka hastened to assure the audience, out-migration was preferable to the alternative — birth control, which he strongly opposed as injurious to public morals and hygiene.

The second speaker, Soeda Juichi (1864–1929), was nearing the end of a distinguished career in public finance, having served as undersecretary of the Ministry of Finance and president of the Bank of Taiwan and the Industrial Bank of Japan. He began by noting that from the standpoint of production, small-scale farming was not obviously superior to large-scale farming. From the political standpoint, however, small farmers best served the national interest. These farmers, Soeda confidently asserted, were "conservative, filled with loyalty and easily governed. They do not cause problems for political leaders." They were also an important military resource. Unlike the urban masses, farmers were physically fit; and unlike landlords, they did not buy their way out of military service. Sons of small family farmers "exert themselves unstintingly for the sake of their country." A large and economically viable stratum of small farmers, he concluded, provided an important buffer between the upper classes, who by necessity were few in number, and the growing masses of urban poor.[20] Urgent measures, Soeda warned, were needed to shore up the middle farmers, for "if the social disease flares up in Japan a ferocious force will be unleashed."[21]

While Takaoka and Soeda presented utilitarian arguments in the measured tones and reasoned voices of the statesman and the scholar, Yokoi Tokiyoshi seized the occasion to issue a blanket condemnation of Meiji agricultural policy. The Meiji land tax reform of 1873, he declared, was "senseless" and the regulations of the Ministry of Agriculture and Forestry were "arbitrary and meddlesome." Rural credit institutions purportedly established to benefit farmers were in fact "not one whit different" from commercial banks. Subsidy of the sericulture industry only increased farm debt; and in any case, farm by-employment did more harm than good since quick profits promoted sloth and extravagance. The "incomparably stupid" state system of compulsory education only imposed an immense financial burden on farmers. The police "were hopeless," for instead of apprehending "shysters and gangsters" who ensnared village girls, they spent their time interfering with village culture, going so far as to prohibit *obon* dances, plays, and sumo contests. Politicians standing for election in rural districts were "cockroaches" who swarmed out at election time to buy themselves a seat in the Diet.[22] Every government official and agency with the exception of the emperor, it would appear, had a hand in creating the "present situation where farmers had no choice but to leave in droves."[23]

How did the distinguished gentlemen of the Social Policy Association respond to Yokoi's tirade? The absence of the notation "applause followed" in the published proceedings provides a clue. At least one member, Dr. Fukuda Tokuzô, professor of economics at Tokyo Higher College of Business and Industry, was deeply offended. In his address the following day, Fukuda appended to his prepared remarks a blistering rejoinder. Dr. Yokoi's lecture, Fukuda asserted, violated all norms of "impartial scholarly inquiry" by interjecting such vulgar epithets as "gangster" and "cockroach" into the serious discussions of a "purely scholarly body like the Social Policy Association." Hadn't Yokoi, Fukuda asked sarcastically, "taken upon himself the role of physician administrating emergency care"?[24]

The bitterness, pessimism, and alienation that leap out from Yokoi's text expose the limits of the generalization that a consensus on national priorities prevailed during Japan's modernization. Even within the elite membership of the Social Policy Association, deep divisions of opinion existed on the agricultural question — and this was in 1914, a decade before the onset of the interwar agriculture depression.

The vehemence of Yokoi's complaint and Fukuda's rejoinder strongly suggests that values rather than policy were being contested. Dripping with sarcasm, Fukuda's put-down of Yokoi employed exactly the right metaphor: emergency-ward physician. Fukuda analyzed the problem of Japanese small-scale farming from the standpoint of market capitalism and questioned whether measures to shore up small-scale farming indeed addressed the urgent national task of "advancing" agricultural production. Yokoi viewed farming as a living organism struggling to survive in a hostile environment. In his last published work, *Shônô ni kansuru kenkyû* (Studies concerning small farming), a book that Yokoi proudly claimed to be the fruition of "research started fifty-two years ago," he plainly stated his conviction that agriculture held out the possibility of preserving a segment of Japanese society from the dehumanizing forces of capitalism. "Japan is a country of small farmers," he wrote in the introduction, and "small-scale farming is not based on capitalism's profit motive; in fact, its essence is anti-capitalist." In every other sector, "the profit motive prevails" and "one class exercises absolute control over other classes." Under capitalism, there are only two classes: the laborers, who "produce food and clothing," and the capitalists, who "make others work to produce life's essentials." The capitalist entrepreneur, whether industrialist or landlord, is motivated exclusively by the profit motive. He treats "labor, property and credit as factors of production, bending every effort to reduce costs and maximize profit."[25]

Shônô ni kansuru kenkyû forcefully argued that Japan's small family farms resisted the dictates of capitalism. Coining the term "labor-power management" (*rôsaku keiei*), Yokoi categorically asserted that small-scale farming was governed by a fundamentally different logic: the maximum utilization of household labor. Only in the case of "big farming" did the principle of profit maximization prevail. In Yokoi's formulation the size of holdings did not dictate the character of social relations in farming. The distinction between "big" and "small" farming was qualitative, reflecting the following criteria: Is a price attached to individual labor? Are farm products treated as marketable commodities? Do farmers depend on capital for the factors of production? In Yokoi's imaginary world of Japanese "small farming," utilization of farm labor was a moral imperative, not a strategy of profit maximizing. His approach freed farming from compulsion, strife, and alienation. Everyone "willingly puts out the maximum labor, takes pleasure in work, is in sympathy with the environment, and finds happiness in nurturing the growth of plants and animals."[26] Japan's small family farms, in other words, were conceived as a social space immune to what Marx identified as the most dehumanizing effects of social relations under capitalism: exploitation and alienation.

Acknowledging that the husband exercised authority over his wife, Yokoi nevertheless asserted that in small-farm households, in actual practice "there are no bosses or underlings; just plain workers who, without regard to status, will do what needs to be done." Because value is calculated in terms of household production "reflecting the contributions of men and women, the weak and strong," farm villages do not show "the great gap between rich and poor evident in cities." Adding the qualification that too much equality can be socially debilitating, "only in the countryside," Yokoi said, "can one find people of more or less equal economic circumstances." Where everyone, whether landlord or tenant farmer, is motivated by the single desire to utilize family labor fully, "a kind of spirit and a way of thinking" arise that bind villagers together in cooperation and harmony. This "spiritual element," the enabling condition of harmony and cohesion, frees farming from the social conflicts of capitalism "even within a developing capitalist economy." When the spiritual element is lost, however, "the cohesiveness of the farm community slackens, agriculture itself collapses, and non-capitalist farming is necessarily transformed into capitalist management."[27]

Yokoi developed his theory that "small farming" escaped the laws of capitalism at a time of sharply escalating conflict between tenant farmers and landlords over rents. In the five years preceding the publication of *Shônô ni kansuru kenkyû*, more than ten thousand disputes between landlords and tenants were recorded; in 85 percent of the disputes tenants demanded either permanent or temporary reduction in rents. Obviously, the issue of distributing farm profits was very much on people's minds. Village youth, moreover, appeared to be leaving the countryside in record numbers to take factory and service-sector jobs in cities. In some cases youths were forced out by their family's poverty or when the family's holdings were so small that their labor was largely redundant. But rural young people, especially women, increasingly left voluntarily in search of an easier, more pleasurable, and freer life than was possible within the patriarchal farm family. Yokoi's theory of "labor-power management" and his insistence that this principle generally prevailed required a massive denial of the actual social divisions in Japanese agriculture.

Yokoi Tokiyoshi died in November 1927, five months after the first printing of *Shônô ni kansuru kenkyû*. The year 1927 also marked the onset of the second agricultural recession of the decade. Farm commodity prices, which had just begun to recover from their post–World War I collapse, began a downward slide in 1926 that turned into free fall after 1929. One can only speculate how Yokoi's thinking might have developed in the crisis years of early Shôwa. As it was, Yokoi bequeathed a potent legacy in developing a utopian theory of agricultural economy grounded in a moral critique of capitalism. Yokoi's later writings display the distinctive double voice that would characterize depression-era agrarian populism. One voice, angry and alienated, warned in apocalyptic tones of the imminent destruction of Japanese farming, and hence of Japan itself. The other voice, urgent and exhortative, promised agricultural renewal, rural harmony, and national salvation.

THE SECOND RADICAL TURN: TACHIBANA KÔZABURÔ AND AGRARIAN POPULISM

In the context of the deepening agricultural crisis, agrarianism took a second turn around 1930. Agrarianism, as we have seen, surfaced in Japan at the end of the nineteenth century as a minority critique of one-sided industrial development from within the Meiji establishment. The first turn in agrarian thought, which occurred in the Taishô period (1912–26), is illustrated by Yokoi Tokiyoshi's utopian conception of Japanese farming and his moral critique of capitalist social relations. At the end of the 1920s, however, embattled farmers and rustic intellectuals transformed agrarianism into a movement of economic renewal and political activism. Farmers desperately searching for practical solutions to the very real problem of economic survival and rural polemicists certain that capitalism and city culture were the root causes of the crisis developed their own brand of agrarianism.

Tachibana Kôzaburô (1893–1974) and the farm cooperative movement that he founded exemplify the radical turn of agrarianism in the early Shôwa period. The son of a wealthy dye merchant in Mito City, the capital of rural Ibaraki prefecture, Tachibana took up farming to find spiritual salvation. In February 1915, just before graduating from Tokyo First Higher School, the premier college preparatory institution in Japan, Tachibana dropped out. Forgoing matriculation that spring at Tokyo Imperial University, he returned home and began farming a seven-acre tract of fallow land in nearby Tokiwa village that belonged to the family. Tachibana married in 1916, and the next year his boyhood friend Hayashi Shôzô, who had just graduated from Tokyo Arts University, joined him at the farm. Over the next five years their brothers and sisters followed, creating a thriving farm commune known locally as Kyôdaimura.[28]

Looking back on his new life of relentless farm labor, Tachibana spoke in terms of religious conversion: "I saw God, and guided by the spirit of the divine was received in the warm embrace of the great natural universe. My heart and whole being were filled with brotherly love for my neighbors and dear friends. In a word, human being that I am, I had at last found my spiritual home."[29] In the late 1920s, as the agricultural recession deepened, however, Tachibana was drawn into a life of political activism. Convinced that agricultural production cooperatives organized and run by farmers held the key to revitalizing small-scale farming, and informed by his voluminous reading of world history and political economy, Tachibana began to publicize his ideas on the causes and cures of the farm crisis.

Believing that "only farmers can save themselves," Tachibana founded the Aikyôkai farm cooperative movement in 1929. The Aikyôkai quickly became the focal point of agrarian activism in northern Ibaraki. At its peak in 1932 it had twenty-five village chapters and four hundred to five hundred dues-paying members, and it published a thick monthly journal, *Nôson kenkyû*. Both a newsletter with technical advice on new farming methods and a platform for political and cultural commentary by the membership, *Nôson kenkyû* offered an intimate view of the thinking of Shôwa-era agrarianism at the grass roots.

The tone of Tachibana's writings and of many of the essays in *Nôson kenkyû* penned by village-level leaders is apocalyptic. Japan's farm villages confronted "imminent and total collapse," Tachibana warned in the lead essay of the first issue, and because "Japan and [its] farm villages [were] like fish and water," the nation itself was in peril.[30] Writing late in 1930, Tachibana attributed the "sick condition" of Japanese society to capitalism, arguing that capitalism historically caused "the destruction of villages and the decline of agriculture. While [capitalism] brings prosperity to industry and cities, it has precisely the opposite effect on farm villages."[31]

Passages like this one demonstrate the polemical conflation by depression-era populists of capitalism, industrialization, and the modern city. Under capitalism, Tachibana insisted, the relationship of city to village could be only parasitic and destructive. Modern cities, "the very crystallization of capitalism's materialistic civilization," Tachibana declared, "demand the sacrifice of villages; there is absolutely no mutually beneficial developmental relationship."[32] This was a favorite theme. In an essay titled "The Age of Urban Tyranny," Yamakawa Tokio, a frequent contributor to *Nôson kenkyû*, identified the nineteenth century as the beginning of "the era of the capitalist state." How did farm villages fare under this regime? "Bourgeois scholars of agricultural science," Yamakawa warned, claimed that the relationship between city and village was symbiotic. Although "a comforting theory," it is all a lie. In the age of the capitalist state, all economic transactions by farmers, whether trade, taxes, insurance, or even savings deposits, were means by which the city exploited the countryside. Cities, Yamakawa concluded, had become "the ruling class, the superstructure."[33]

The climactic metaphor of "The Age of Urban Tyranny" is a city likened to a "monstrous three-legged idol stained crimson with the blood of farmers." Not only the agent of rural economic exploitation and political domination, the city was also the producer of a mass culture of hedonism that attacked the village from within by colonizing farmers' minds. When Yamakawa sarcastically queried, "Is there anything more to cities than prostitutes, cafes, geisha houses, dance halls, cinemas, theaters and department stores?" he gave voice to a deep and pervasive fear of Japanese farmers: the out-migration of village youths. The prosperity and luxury of cities represented more than wealth gained by an economic exploitation of the countryside. Cities stole away village youths by offering a more exciting and easier way of life. An anonymous poem, "Guarding the Village," in the inaugural issue of *Nôson kenkyû*, for example, expressed the profound feeling of loss experienced by a family whose only son had fled the ancestral home for "the bright lights of the city."[34] Daughters, too, were being enticed away. "What is the world coming to," Tachibana Kôzaburô cried out in frustration, "when village maidens who are our pride and joy" desire only to become "servants in Tokyo, or, even worse, cafe waitresses?"[35]

In 1931, when *Nôson kenkyû* began publication, the crisis of Japanese farmers was real as well as imagined. Farm income declined steeply as prices of rice and raw silk, the largest cash crops, plummeted. The wholesale price of rice, which stood at 35 yen per *koku* in 1927 and 29 yen in 1929, fell to 18 yen in 1930. The decline of raw silk prices, which depended largely on exports to the United States, was even steeper. At the same time, taxes, interest payments, and fertilizers, farmers' principal costs, held steady or declined moderately.[36] Although not as deep or as long-lasting as the agricultural depression, the industrial recession dealt an additional blow to poor farm families, especially tenant farmers who depended on their sons' and daughters' factory wages. Escalating conflict between landlords and tenants added to the crisis atmosphere. Landlord-tenant disputes, which had declined somewhat in the latter half of the 1920s, exploded, more than doubling in number between 1928 and 1933.[37]

The crisis of the world capitalist system created in the minds of many Aikyôkai members the possibility of a new social order. Writing in January 1931, Yamakawa Tokio reassured readers that "the collapse of capitalism and also of the urban culture is not the same as the end of all civilization." In fact, the present crisis harbingered epochal change. "Necessarily, the road will open to a new age of local self-government and economic self-sufficiency. The nineteenth century was the era of the city, centralized polity and large industry. But the twentieth century will be the age of agriculture, the farm village and the devolution of political authority to localities."[38] In a postscript to the February 1931 issue of *Nôson kenkyû*, the editor, Sugiura Takashi, sounded the same theme.

Capitalism had reached a historic impasse, and its self-destruction, rooted in internal contradictions, had already begun. "But rising from the ruins of capitalism, is the banner of the agricultural cooperative movement held high by the new-awakened farming masses [who will] build a society with agriculture as the essence."[39] At the vanguard of the historic movement of Japan's farmers, Sugiura boasted, was "our Aikyôkai," which had blazed the trail of farm village regeneration one year earlier by establishing the first true production cooperative, the Aikyôkai livestock cooperative.[40]

Agriculture production cooperatives organized locally and managed entirely by farmers formed the core of the Aikyôkai program of farm village renewal. Production cooperatives offered farmers more than the economic advantages of market leverage and economies of scale. By bringing people together in collective labor, they made it possible to transcend the destructive ethos of acquisitive individualism. "When performed with a pure heart, diligent farm labor," Tachibana proclaimed, "spiritually and materially harmonizes the interests of self and other" and thereby "bestows the riches of true brotherhood." Unlike socialist alternatives to capitalist organization, production cooperatives arose "directly from human nature." A life of working and living together such as Tachibana experienced at Kyôdaimura enabled people to grasp "the true meaning of human existence and its attendant joys. It fills people with virtue and secures their livelihood."[41]

Production cooperatives offered Aikyôkai members practical advantages, but the compelling attraction was their promise of spiritual fulfillment and new beginnings. It was a vision, moreover, that did not look to the past for legitimation or guidance. There was no talk of restoring a lost golden age. On the contrary, the figure of the traditional Japanese village in Aikyôkai discourse was uniformly negative. For example, an article in the March 1931 issue of *Nôson kenkyû* welcomed the "collapse of the old feudal village" and approvingly noted the "uninterrupted efforts of our Aikyôkai to build new farm villages." References to tradition (*dentô*) are negative. In recounting the history of the Aikyôkai chapter in Yanagikawa village, the writer explained that as long as farmers "failed to free themselves from the shackles of tradition," no progress was possible.[42] In the November issue, Shôji Hajime, a leader in Kuji district, where the movement was particularly strong, praised Tachibana for showing the way to a bright future by "shucking off the old skin of traditional customs and habits and articulating a vision of rural renewal."[43]

When the Aikyôkai evoked an image of the past to explain the present, it was not a lost golden age but rather "hundreds of years of exploitation of the feudal peasant." [44] Nor in the view of Kawamata Seitarô, director of the Aikyôkai production cooperative, did the Meiji Restoration bring much improvement. "The Meiji Restoration was a movement from the top down, carried out by a minority at the center." The Aikyôkai movement, he insisted, was the exact opposite: "a movement of farmers from the bottom up and from the provinces to the capital." While the goals of Meiji statesmen were military strength and industrial development, the Aikyôkai's mission was "to build a truly free, unified and equal Japan." [45] Until recently, another writer insisted, farmers lived lives of "blind obedience, not believing in themselves or taking the initiative." Now that farmers had become consciousness of their historical condition, he continued, "[the] time when farmers can be hoodwinked by such pure cant as 'Farmers are the Treasure of the Nation' is long gone." [46]

Aikyôkai members imagined their movement as "the bright light of dawn breaking over the sleeping villages." [47] At times Tachibana spoke as if the new agrarian order spelled the end to capitalism, even predicting that "an international movement of farmers will sweep the world clean of capitalism." A few pages later, however, he defined his mission in terms of "the fundamental rectification of capitalism," implying that reform was possible.[48] Moreover, Tachibana and other writers explicitly rejected materialist solutions to the economic crisis and affirmed conservative gender relations. Private property and the patriarchal farm family still constituted the social foundations of the farm village.

Made up largely of owner-cultivators, the Aikyôkai insisted that the rural renewal did not require land redistribution. The Marxist analysis of the rural crisis, Tachibana protested, was all wrong, since "tenants do not sell their labor and large landowners do not purchase labor power." Denying that capital produced social divisions in farming, Tachibana insisted, "We farmers are simply farmers, neither capitalists nor the proletariat." Because the tenant used the same technology as his landlord, Tachibana argued, "tenants do not need to look upon landlords as the enemy." [49]

The conception of the family, too, was ultimately conservative. "History," Tachibana wrote, "tells us that all culture is preserved within the family and all culture will dissipate when the family dissolves." [50] Tachibana's idea of the family was not the authoritarian ie sei based on lineage that Meiji conservatives advocated. Rather, he imagined the ideal farm family in terms of the late Meiji-invented tradition of "home" (*katei*): domesticity as opposed to lineage and cohesion arising from love rather than the legal authority of the male household head.[51] Nevertheless, in Tachibana's ideal farm family, order and harmony were achieved through a distinctly Confucian conception of a natural moral hierarchy, not through relations of equality. The family and farming were inseparable in this conception. "In the last analysis what most distinguishes farming [from industry] is the essential family element of small [farm] management. It is a fundamental principle that farm management cannot be separated from family life."[52]

The social construction of agriculture as an enterprise that uniquely fused family solidarity and economic production conveyed a strong message. Japanese agriculture anchored the entire society by reproducing both harmonious relations and gender hierarchy. "Japan," Tachibana warned, "must return to the sacred family system that nurtures the very life of the Japanese nation. This, I must insist, is the starting point for a fundamental reform of economic relations and [social] organization."[53]

This was a message that broad segments of Japanese opinion in the 1930s welcomed as an antidote to capitalism's erosion of the relations of social authority. The enshrinement of agriculture and village as the wellspring of authentic Japanese culture occurred in the context of military aggression in northeast Asia, international censure, and intensified ideological mobilization for war with American and England. But the 1930s were also a time of social and cultural turmoil: disputes between landlords and tenants reached unprecedented heights; rural youths poured into cities, attracted by service-sector employment; and in cities men and women experimented with new gender roles.[54] Under these conditions, the reassuring image of harmonious and productive farm families served the ideological needs of many sectors of Japanese society.

The underlying social conservatism of agrarian populism helps to explain its right-wing trajectory. Morally offended by capitalism's values, antagonistic to central authority, cool toward the military, and suspicious of overseas expansion, the Aikyôkai despised representative government, loathed Marxism, and feared social revolution. As long as the Aikyôkai stayed local, eschewing a broader politics, the movement managed to contain these contradictory ideological vectors. When Tachibana lurched into national politics, however, he pulled the movement hard to the right. In 1932, nineteen Aikyôkai members secretly enlisted by Tachibana joined army and navy officers in the "May 15 Incident"— attacks against government officials and installations in Tokyo intended to ignite a general insurrection. The army and navy officers assassinated Seiyûkai prime minister Inukai Tsuyoshi, whose murder brought down the last party cabinet of the prewar period.

The operational assignment of the Aikyôkai conspirators — to bomb power transmitters — was consistent with Tachibana's subsequent explanation of why he allied with the militarists. He desired, he later confessed, to awaken the metropolis to the desperate plight of villages by "plunging great Tokyo into darkness." Although the Aikyôkai saboteurs failed to dim even one offensive neon sign with their primitive explosives, if Tachibana's goal indeed was to move the farm crisis to the center stage of national politics, the gambit succeeded. The mass media played an important role, sympathetically reporting the trial of the young army and navy assassins who claimed to have acted to save "village Japan." Political parties and the bureaucracy, which had given farmers short shrift before the spring of 1932, sprang into action. Appropriations for rural relief provided some material benefit — 420 million yen between 1932 and 1934. Equally important, village representatives and government bureaucrats found common ground in a rhetoric of self-reliance and self-help on the one hand and cooperation and collective effort on the other.[55] The public relations offensive that accompanied the campaign reinforced the identification of Japan's farm villages with core conservative values, and the anticapitalist message was diluted. Soon afterward, the bureaucracy launched a new campaign to recruit up to a million poor farmers to the imperial cause of colonizing Japan's new puppet state of Manchuria.[56] By the time of the Pacific War the propaganda machine could persuasively identify Japan's villages as "spiritually and demographically the incubator of national strength."[57]

NOTES

This essay was first published in Stephen Vlastos, ed., *Mirror of Modernity: Invented Traditions of Modern Japan* (Berkeley: University of California Press, 1998). Reprinted with minor revisions by permission of the University of California Press. I wish to thank Deirdre McCloskey, David Arkush, Shelton Stromquist, and Betsy Scheiner for comments and criticisms.

1. Quoted from Yamaguchi Iwao, "Don't Push Our Farmers Too Far," *Japan Echo* 14, no. 1 (1987): 26. Originally published in *Bungei Shunju* (January 1987): 188–201.

2. Ni'ide Makoto, "Rice Imports and Implications," *Japan Quarterly* 41, no. 1 (1993): 19.

3. Thomas R. H. Havens, *Farm and Nation in Modern Japan* (Princeton: Princeton University Press, 1974), p. 7. Readers are referred to Havens's comprehensive study of Japanese prewar agrarian thought and the lucid discussion of bureaucratic agrarianism and state policy.

4. Cited in Tsunasawa Mitsuaki, *Nihon no nôhonshugi* (Tokyo: Kinokuniya Shinsho, 1971), p. 17; See also Havens, *Farm and Nation*, pp. 18–21.

5. Quoted in Denda Isao, *Kindai Nihon nôsei shisô no kenkyû* (Tokyo: Miraisha, 1969), p. 59.

6. In the 1870s the Meiji government promoted the English American model of large-scale, capital-intensive farming and encouraged the importation of Western farm machinery, but these efforts met with little success. By the mid-1880s advocates of small-scale farming prevailed and the policy shifted to developing technologies suited to small-scale, labor-intensive farming and promoting their diffusion. See Havens, *Farm and Nation*, pp. 36–41. The Meiji land tax was initially set at 3 percent of land value and was reduced to 2.5 percent in 1877 to appease restive farmers at the time of the Satsuma Rebellion. See Stephen Vlastos, "Opposition Movements in Early Meiji," in Marius B. Jansen, ed., *The Cambridge History of Japan*, vol. 5, *The Nineteenth Century* (Cambridge: Cambridge University Press, 1989), pp. 372–82.

7. Quoted in Havens, *Farm and Nation*, p. 65.

8. According to data compiled by Paul Mayet, a German agricultural expert employed by the Japanese government, during the period from 1883 to 1890 some 367,744 farmers were forced into arrears in their payment of the land tax, resulting in foreclosure on more than 115,800 acres of farmland. Cited in E. H. Norman, *Japan's Emergence as a Modern State*; reprinted in John W. Dower, ed., *Origins of the Modern Japanese State* (New York: Pantheon, 1975), p. 251.

9. See Havens, *Farm and Nation*, pp. 66–83.

10. Yokoi Tokiyoshi is primarily remembered today for developing techniques of brine seed assortment, fertilizer application, and tillage. The entry for Yokoi Tokiyoshi in *Nihon kingendai shi jiten* (Tokyo: Tôyô Keizai Shimpôsha, 1978), for example, lists only his scientific achievements, not his writings on political economy. Yokoi's collected writings are published in *Yokoi Hakushi zenshû*, 10 vols. (Tokyo: Yokoi Zenshû Kankôkai, 1925), hereafter, *Yokoi zenshû*.

11. Yokoi, "Nôhonshugi," in *Yokoi zenshû*, 8:225–35.

12. Ibid., pp. 227–28.

13. Ibid., p. 229. Quoted in Havens, *Farm and Nation*, p. 101.

14. Yokoi, "Nôhonshugi," p. 228.

15. Havens, *Farm and Nation*, p. 101.

16. Yokoi, "Nôhonshugi," p. 232.

17. Reprinted in Ôuchi Tsutom, ed., *Shônô hogo no mondai* (Tokyo: Nôsangyoson Seisaku Gakkai, 1976). Hereafter, *Shônô hogo*.

18. 1 *chô* = 2.45 acres.

19. Takaoka Kumao, "Hôkoku dai'ichi seki," in *Shônô hogo*, p. 75.

20. Soeda Juichi, "Hôkoku daini seki," in *Shônô hogo*, pp. 80–81.

21. Ibid, p. 97.

22. Yokoi Tokiyoshi, "Hôkoku daisan seki," in *Shônô hogo*, pp. 103–6.

23. Ibid., p. 111.

24. Ibid., pp. 205, 208.

25. Yokoi Tokiyoshi, *Shônô ni kansuru kenkyû* (Tokyo: Maruzen, 1927), pp. 1, 5–6.

26. Ibid., pp. 3–4, 10–11, 34–35, 47.

27. Ibid., pp. 48–49, 52, 252, 235.

28. Havens, *Farm and Nation*, pp. 234–37. The most detailed and insightful study of Tachibana Kôzaburô's life and thought is Matsuzawa Tetsunari, *Tachibana Kôzaburô: Nihon fuashizumu genshi kaiki ron ha* (Tokyo: San'ichi Shobô, 1973).

29. Tachibana Kôzaburô, *Nôsongaku* (Tokyo: Kensetsusha, 1932), preface, p. 4.

30. Ibid., p. 10.

31. Ibid., pp. 142, 87.

32. Tachibana Kôzaburô, *Kôdô kokka nôhon kenkoku ron* (Tokyo: Kensetsusha, 1932), p. 9.

33. *Nôson kenkyû* (January 1931): 12–13.

34. Ibid., p. 30.

35. Tachibana, *Kôdô kokka*, p. 17.

36. Itô Masanao, Ökado Masakatsu, and Suzuki Masayuki, *Senkanki no Nihon nôson* (Tokyo: Sekai Shisôsha, 1988), pp. 151–54.

37. Ann Waswo, *Japanese Landlords: Decline of a Rural Elite* (Berkeley: University of California Press, 1977), p. 100.

38. *Nôson kenkyû* (January 1931): 15.

39. Ibid. (February 1931): 52.

40. Aikyôkai members dismissed the state-sponsored agricultural producers associations as "not real cooperatives but another form of capitalism." See essay by Kawamata Sietarô in the inaugural issue of *Nôson kenkyû* (January 1931): 55–56.

41. Tachibana, *Nôsongaku*, p. 20.

42. *Nôson kenkyû* (March 1931): 20.

43. Ibid. (September 1931): 11.

44. Ibid. (February 1931): 55.

45. Ibid. (September 1931): 23.

46. Ibid. (April 1931): 25–26.

47. Ibid. (February 1931): 62.

48. Tachibana, *Nôsongaku*, pp. 11, 45.

49. *Nôson kenkyû* (August 1931): 6–7.

50. Tachibana, *Nôsongaku*, p. 243.

51. For a discussion of *ie sei* and *katei* and the invented tradition of "home," see Jordan Sand, "At Home in the Meiji Period: Inventing Japanese Domesticity," in Stephen Vlastos, ed., *Mirror of Modernity* (Berkeley: University of California Press, 1998), pp. 191–207.

52. Tachibana, *Nôsongaku*, p. 25.

53. Tachibana, *Kôdô kokka*, pp. 244–45.

54. See Miriam Silverberg, "The Cafe Waitress Serving Modern Japan," in *Mirror of Modernity*, 208–25.

55. For an important revisionist interpretation of the farm village rehabilitation movement, see Kerry Douglas Smith, "A Time of Crisis: Japan, the Great Depression, and Relief Policy" (Ph.D. diss., Harvard University, 1994).

56. See Louise Young, "Colonizing Manchuria: The Making of an Imperial Myth," in *Mirror of Modernity*, pp. 95–109.

57. Furukubo Sakura, "Senzen, nôson ni okeru 'bosei' o meguru 'shisô,'" in Miyoshi Masayoshi, ed., *Shônô no shiteki bunseki* (Tokyo: Fumin Kyôkai, 1990), p. 226.

CHARLES W. HAYFORD

THE STORM OVER THE PEASANT: ORIENTALISM AND RHETORIC IN CONSTRUING CHINA

After Mao Zedong died in 1976, his body was put on display in one of those see-through coffins that Lenin made popular. Shortly after, on the NBC evening news, David Brinkley termed this "peasant under glass"—a racist flippancy that would not have been accepted (or probably even thought of) for the dead leader of a Western state. Moreover, Mao was by no means a peasant. He never made his living with a hoe (if anything he was a landlord); he earned the highest educational degree available in his home province at the time; he was successively a librarian, a teacher, and a school principal; and for most of his career he was a professional politician and paid government official. Mao was no more a peasant than was Gandhi, though they both created and deployed rural symbols. Mao saw himself in the tradition of rulers and state builders like Qin Shi Huangdi and George Washington. Mao is a peasant only if *all* Chinese people are peasants in essence, simply by virtue of being Chinese. (Curiously, for some of the same Orientalist reasons, Mao and his successor, Deng Xiaoping, were also held to be "emperors." That is, *all* rulers in Beijing were emperors by virtue of being Chinese.)

China was so strongly perceived as being a country of "peasants," held by a peasant revolution, that it came as a surprise to find that the use of the word "peasant" (rather than "farmer" or an Anglicized Chinese word) is relatively new; I found virtually no English-language application of the word "peasant" to China before the 1920s, even though the word was commonly used in Europe, Russia, and even the Mediterranean world. The word and the concepts behind it were brought to China during the 1920s; the usage spread in ways we will examine briefly here, and by the 1940s it had become habitual. Although never limited to Marxists, the "peasant" construction of the countryside built cultural and ideological legitimacy for Mao Zedong's political and organizational revolution.[1]

In the West, a dismissal of Mao's 1949 revolution as peasant and therefore backward was shared by European and Soviet Marxists as well as liberal modernizers; that attitude was challenged in the 1960s during American involvement in Vietnam, by reversing the valence on the word "peasant" but not discarding it. Antiwar activists often saw the peasant as an ecologically sound antidote to bourgeois imperialism; more serious theorists built on the rediscovered analysis of the peasant household economy started by liberal Soviet economist Alexander Chayanov in the 1920s.[2] Post-Mao critiques, some written by recovering Maoists possibly as part of a twelve-step program, charged the China field with naïveté and revolution pandering; some saw a dominant "revolution paradigm"; one charged that the "paramount myth" of the Chinese revolution was the "promise of peasant salvation." John K. Fairbank, seen as a scholarly bellwether, is taken to task for remarking that "valued in the Chinese peasant's terms, the revolution has been a magnificent achievement, a victory not only for Mao Zedong, but for several hundreds of millions of the Chinese people."[3]

Yet the use of the term "peasant" is now under fire. Supporters of Deng Xiaoping's reforms claim that the peasant stage has been left behind; a writer in *China Daily* wrote in 1985 that "from now on, the word peasant no longer suits China's rural population." For different reasons, an American historian recently called "peasant" a "quaint taxonomic term that Americans usually used and that served to keep the Chinese apart — and ranked vaguely below — the 'farmers' at home."[4] Still others challenge its applicability anywhere. The prominent anthropologist Polly Hill, whose fieldwork deals with Africa, attacks the term "peasant" as overly broad in two ways: first, it mixes together all residents of the village, regardless of whether they farm, peddle, weave, cook, or lend money (or do each in succession), and second, it puts into one category villagers in Africa, Latin America, and Asia who are actually in wildly different situations.[5] Moreover, we cannot justify "peasant" as the translation for the Chinese term *nongmin* (which was introduced from Japan in the early twentieth century) on the grounds that it is the official translation; this would be to simply accept the Chinese Marxist parti pris.

Must we therefore forswear "peasant"? Stop our subscriptions to *Peasant Studies*? Burn Eric Wolf's *Peasant Wars of the Twentieth Century*?

Heavens, no. But I will argue that too often we mistake "peasant" for a primary category of nature rather than a contingent intellectual tool; the term is what Raymond Williams calls a "keyword,"[6] one that encapsulates and collapses history and argument and must be used as a choice only by those aware of its trade-offs and limitations. I have already begun a study of "Chinese pastoral"— the "ambivalent and sometimes tortured attempts of educated Chinese to understand and uplift their country cousins"— in which I discuss Chinese language materials.[7] In this essay I will examine the rhetorical and political background of the term "peasant" in English-language, primarily American, usage during the period leading up to the establishment of the People's Republic in 1949.

First, an observation: Tracing the recent history of the keyword "peasant," not simply what it *means* but what it *does*, runs us into a general dilemma of cultural relativism: we may make things appear exotic or uniquely Chinese, when those things are actually merely local or particular — Chinese apples taste different but fall from trees at the same rate as Wisconsin or Nigerian apples. On the other hand, we may force round Chinese phenomena into square Western concepts that we mistake as universal — understanding Chinese religion, to take but one example, can proceed only when we abandon definitions and assumptions drawn from Europe. Given that no two places in the world are entirely alike, what is the nature of the "China difference"?[8] When does a concept falsely "-ize" China — exoticize, essentialize, Orientalize — and when does one particularly describe it?

PAST AND PEASANT

The choice of "peasant" is not from lack of alternative English words. Any number have been used to designate cultivators of one sort or another — one study found 1,515 of them![9] Many fighting words and terms of abuse started as meaning rural inhabitant or cultivator —"villain," "clown," "clod," "hodgepodge"— though it's not clear that Hamlet means anything rural (or Slavic) when he calls himself a "rogue and peasant slave."

The word is generally given as deriving from the Latin *paganus*, the Roman imperial term meaning outlying administrative district. When the cities of the empire became Christian by decree, the term "pagan" came to mean non-Christian, and eventually any rural dweller, thus mapping class and morality onto geography. Incidentally, the word "farmer" did not originally designate an agricultural worker, but one who bought the right to carry out some economic activity — a meaning that survives in "tax farmer" or to "farm out." The word "country" is said to derive from *contra* (against, opposite).[10]

Thus a particular use of "peasant" may or may not be rhetorically significant. William Cobbett, the early nineteenth-century reformist and rural radical, objected to the use of what he called the "French" word "peasantry." Originally, he wrote, it had simply meant "country folk," but had come to mean a *"distinct and degraded class of persons,* who having no pretension whatsoever to look upon themselves, in any sense, as belonging to the same *society* or *community*, as the *Gentry*, but who ought always to be 'kept in their proper place.'" Further, Cobbett told his readers, "the insolent wretches call you the *peasantry*, or the *population*; they never call you the *people*."[11]

This still leaves our basic question: why and how did the word "peasant" come to replace the word "farmer" in English-language usage for China?

First let us essay an easier question: why did Americans mostly see themselves as farmers but Europeans as peasants? This was more than a verbal quibble; the distinction between "farmer" and "peasant" was central to Jeffersonian democracy. Jefferson's own distrust of city and industry — "the mobs of great cities add just so much to the support of pure government as sores do to the strength of the human body" — and faith in the husbandman — "cultivators of the earth are the most valuable citizens" — was transmuted in the course of the nineteenth century into a vague but politically powerful myth of the "virgin land" as the economic basis of republican government.[12] Old World despotism was based on the landless peasant who could not stand up to the dukes, lords, barons, and kings. A "peasant" worked under European ("medieval" or "feudal") conditions, a "farmer" under free or democratic rule.

When Americans looked across the Pacific with Jeffersonian eyes, construing the Chinese village was a problem. China was neither the New World nor the Old, but sui generis. The set of assumptions that generated American China discourse until the 1920s grows out of this view that China was unique; it is hard to choose any one word to characterize them, but these assumptions can be put under the heading "Orientalist." Edward Said has recently popularized the word "Orientalism" in the powerful sense of Western scholarship used to construct an Oriental "Other," treating it as an exotic, unchanging essence in order to encompass and subdue it. This is an indispensable insight.[13] But

"Orientalist" also had an earlier, eighteenth-century sense. Some in the British East India Company chose that term to describe themselves; they argued that Oriental cultures were of great (though not equal) value but of a different nature from European cultures. The argued logic of the earlier Orientalist position was that Asian countries need not and should not simply import British ways but had to parallel the European Renaissance by reviving their own ancient cultures — the first Sanskrit dictionary was compiled by a Baptist missionary, and the British East India Company sponsored the first college of Sanskrit studies.

This respect for Oriental culture, qualified and limited though it was, earned these Orientalists the ridicule of Thomas Babington Macaulay and Karl Marx, who flew the newly unfurled banner of Progress. Macaulay claimed to be "ready to take the Oriental learning at the valuation of the Orientalists themselves" but "never found one among them who could deny that a single shelf of a good European library was worth the whole native literature of India and Arabia." The solution? The British must form a "class who may be interpreters . . . a class of persons, Indian in blood, and color, but English in taste, in opinions, in morals, and in intellect." These "interpreters" would present their native masses with science in terms "borrowed from the Western nomenclature." Marx took the Progressive argument a step further. He argued that England "has to fulfil a double mission: . . . one destructive, one regenerating — the annihilation of old Asiatic society and the laying of the material foundations of Western society in Asia."[14]

The key difference between Orientalist and Progressive concepts was not in their respect for the Other; either of these clusters can show respect or contempt, often side by side, sometimes indistinguishable. Each side could be, and was, used to develop colonial hegemony. The point here is the Orientalist insistence that Asia was sui generis, of a different nature from Europe, and the Progressive reply that all history was governed by the same universal (read European) laws. Over the course of the nineteenth century, before, as Michael Adas puts it so well, machines became the "measure of man,"[15] Orientalism in a broad sense flourished. It is a pity that Edward Said's strong definition, because of its basic soundness, has come to dominate, for the authentic cross-cultural dilemma is obscured. Whether respectful, or exploitative and racist ("East is East . . ."), or chinoiserie romantic, Orientalists agreed that China was a different *type* of place from the West in race and history.

Recognizing this Orientalism allows us to reconceive our problem of why there were farmers in China but peasants elsewhere: China was not Europe, the unconscious logic seemed to argue, and it operated outside history; the peasant was a feudal European phenomenon; China was not feudal or European; ergo, China had farmers, not peasants.

But this still does not answer the further question of *timing*: Why did nineteenth-century Orientalists and Progressives both see "farmers," but after the 1920s virtually everyone saw "peasants"? Let us take some examples to see the role played by the village in different Orientalist China stories.

PIDGIN ORIENTALISM AS A PEKING CANARD

Each type of Orientalism spun a variation on the China story in a characteristic, though overlapping, vocabulary; keyword and metaphor expressed and shaped history and moral judgment. The historian Jacques M. Downs, for example, argues that early nineteenth-century American Canton traders — ex-slavers, narcotics merchants, and pirates — developed a myth of their own seafaring history and of the Chinese as heathen, alien, powerful, rich (or, alternately but to the same end, powerless and poor), cruel, and depraved. This myth made the Chinese into "fair game," to whom one could sell opium with no guilt.[16]

These China coast traders did their business on the seacoast; Canton and Shanghai had more in common with Boston, Calcutta, and London than with inland China. Traders literally constructed their own physical treaty port "China" and literarily construed a story "China" for the home audience. During the boom for California, the Pacific, and China in the 1840s, the American demand for exotica was insatiable; over the following century survivors of even brief China stays turned their glimpses into books, public attention, and cash. The Chinese farmer played at most an offstage role; blue-and-white willowware, mass-produced by Chinese craftsmen to the specifications of American markets, showed only trees, bridges, birds, and lovers, not sweating rice farmers. This was a story of lovely, exotic, eternal China — almost not a story at all, for little happened in it.

"Pidgin" — business — English was the lingua franca, a necessity, given the many languages and dialects of the long-established trading world. One of the last of the China hands was Carl Crow, best known for his best-seller, *400 Million Customers*. In his *Foreign Devils in the Flowery Kingdom*, he describes Treaty Port China.[17] To our point here, Crow prefaces the book with a glossary, called "The China Coast Vocabulary," which conveniently lists the "strange and curious" language of the China coast, "unavoidable" because "there are no other words which mean exactly the same thing"— the China difference. In his *China Handbook*,[18] Crow explains that pidgin is the "attempt" (he repeats the word) of Chinese people to pronounce English words, an attempt in which they naturally and comically fail. The China story here is burlesque. The countryside again does not appear. As one recent historian put it, "Crow's China had no misery, wretchedness, poverty or . . . revolution. He looked for 'Four Hundred Million Customers,' but perhaps found 'Four Hundred Million Number One Boys.'"[19]

"The China Coast Vocabulary" reinforced a pidgin Orientalist idea that China was a different *type* of place from Europe, an upside-down kingdom where dessert came first and soup last, people ate dogs and wrote backward, white was for mourning, and normal history did not apply.

EVANGELICAL ORIENTALISM
AND THE VILLAGE MISSION

Missionary and merchant operated in different Chinas and wanted different things from them; they used different words (even different sets of words) to tell different China stories, assume different histories, and construe different Chinas. One example will have to do.

Arthur H. Smith, D.D., was sent by the American Board of Commissioners for Foreign Missions to China in 1872, equipped with a Protestant trinity of evangelism, populism, and Orientalism. His populism led him to ignore the imperial lords and Confucian scholars in order to set the Gospel before the powerless — later the entry point for Mao Zedong's revolution. He preached on any street corner to "farmers, hawkers, coolies, barbers, yamen runners, and loafers." When these proved slow to convert, a mission colleague suggested that "Asiatics" might have a racial inability to understand the Gospel. Smith demurred, "Christ was an Asiatic."[20]

Nor did Smith believe in the redemptive value of Western technology or progress. The first generation of American missionaries, in the 1840s, had come to a China in which technology was not much different from that of the farms they had grown up on, although China's cities were bigger and more cosmopolitan. Even after the American Civil War, when American technological pride came to have more substance, it was still hard to find apt metaphors and comparisons with which to conceptualize the China difference. Many wrote home in terms drawn from the Bible, describing the scenes as familiar from the Old Testament. But Smith, writing at the time when machines became the measure, did not equate the importation of Western technology with progress for China: "Commerce, diplomacy, extension of political relations, and the growing contacts with Occidental civilization have, all combined, proved totally inadequate to accomplish any such reformation as China needs."[21]

Smith's position was Evangelical Orientalism: China needed technological change but not Western culture; China could go through "reformation" on its own terms, if only — looking back, we can see that this is a big "if" — Christianity gave a New Life to the people. This variety of Orientalism ignored what we now have discovered or invented as an anthropological reality that "culture" (whatever that is) is an integral whole, and no strand of its web can be changed without affecting all of it. On the other hand, we must give Smith credit for seeing, at least on the intellectual level, that Asian change must proceed from Asian values; in an age when traders and diplomats seriously suggested that China import knives and forks, pianos, or the American Constitution, Evangelical Orientalists must be accorded some respect.[22]

Liberal missionaries would soon focus on cities and the middle class as the foundation for a strong new nation; influenced by the Social Gospel and American technology, they held that in order for China to absorb modern technology, Western values first had to be installed in middle-class students, much like Macaulay's "interpreters." But Smith settled in a village. Since he felt Christianity had worked its way up from the bottom in the West, the village was the building block — "The Chinese village is the empire in small." A Chinese Christianity could be cultivated only slowly, by creating Christian homes, by educating Christian leaders to lead, not leave, the village, and by building Christian village communities.[23] The Social Gospel of the Progressive era would later equate America, modernity, and the future of bourgeois China, just as Marx and Macaulay had seen Britain as India's future; Smith maintained a China difference. In his 1894 *Village Life in China* he wrote:

> Our ancestors may have perhaps have been peasants [This is the only use of the word "peasant" that I see in the book; it does not refer to the Chinese, who are "villagers," "rustic country people," or simply

"Chinese"], but they were an integral part of the land in which they dwelt. . . . A Chinese village is physically and intellectually a fixture. Could one gaze backward through a vista of five hundred years . . . , he would probably see little more and little less than he sees today. The buildings standing are not indeed five hundred years old, but they are just such houses as half a millennium ago occupied the same sites. . . . Those who now subsist in this collection of earth-built abodes are the lineal descendants of those who lived there when Columbus discovered America . . . , doing what their ancestors did, no more, no less, no other.[24]

Smith remained poised between, on the one hand, a vision of an eternal (in the face of his own contradictory evidence), Orientalist China, one that Christianity could transform without changing, and, on the other hand, the emerging, resisted suspicion that the reason China's villages were so slow to accept the Gospel was that only comprehensive "progress" could make any difference.

ANTIIMPERIALIST ORIENTALISM

For still another story built on Orientalism, let us look at a domestic figure from an unfamiliar vantage point: Mark Twain, whose writings struggle between an American faith that equated progress with technology and a cultivated skepticism of civilization as, in Huck Finn's words, "dismal regular and decent" (chapter 1). In A Connecticut Yankee at King Arthur's Court (1889), Twain transports his machine-making hero back to Arthur's medieval kingdom to be appalled by feudal filth, ignorance, backwardness, and oppression — reminiscent of Americans going to China, though (and this is just the point) none of his readers would have made that connection.

Twain has his Yankee exclaim: "Why it was like reading about France and the French, before the ever-memorable and blessed Revolution, which swept a thousand years of such villainy away in one swift tidal-wave of blood" (chapter 13). This argues that material progress created morality; the passage goes on to justify the blood of the French Revolution as a small price for the liberation of society from injustice. At the end of the book, the barons, knights, and their lackeys rise up to resist Yankee progress. Twain's hero deals with this by inventing dynamite: "We will kill them all" (chapter 43).

Yet Twain's reaction to the events of 1900 in China showed quite a different principle — we might call it "antiimperialist Orientalism." Japanese, German, Russian, British, and American troops invaded China to lift the Boxer siege of the Peking Legations. Missionaries of the American Board — Arthur Smith's colleagues — then convinced their Marines (fresh from crushing nationalist "rebels" in the Philippines) to tour villages where Christian Chinese had been massacred. The Marines confiscated village property and distributed this "loot"[25] to the survivors. Twain was exasperated beyond humor by these "reverend bandits" and wrote "To a Stranger Sitting in Darkness," whose concern went beyond respect for China's political independence. Twain did not concede that the Chinese needed change at all: "Leave them alone, they are plenty good enough just as they are; and besides, almost every convert runs a risk of catching our civilization."[26] King Arthur's Europe was to be destroyed in order to reform it, but China was "plenty good" as it was. It is hard to accuse Twain of racism in making this distinction, yet clearly he treated China and Europe as being separate and essentially different — Orientalism in action.

CHINA RECONSTRUED — FROM ORIENTALISM TO PROGRESSIVISM

Progressive Americans of the early twentieth century dreamed of a new and special relationship with China. Whereas Orientalism asserted that China did not need Western civilization, Progressive America evolved what the historian Michael Hunt analyzes as a paternalistic vision of reforming and defending China; only a China transformed along American middle-class lines could defend itself against imperialist Europe, Japan, and Russia.[27] The cultural logic of the Open Door seemed clear: uplift, technology, prosperity, and Christianity, like all good things, went together, forming a system that was variously called Civilization, the American Way of Life, or, later, Modernity. A political and economic Open Door would free Westernized Chinese, like Macaulay's "interpreters," to lead their backward nation along the yellow brick road to modern civilization.

This shift from Orientalist to Progressive discourse involved reworking the China difference. In 1911, Professor E. A. Ross, president of the American Sociological Society, toured China. The introduction to his resulting China book pooh-poohed the argument that China was unique and criticized the "old China hand" for saying that the West could never understand the Chinese. China could be construed in social science terms:

> The fact is, to the traveller who appreciates how different is the mental horizon that goes with *another stage of culture or another type of social organization* [emphasis supplied] than his own, the Chinese do not seem very puzzling. . . . The theory, dear to literary interpreters of the Orient, that owing to diversity in mental constitution the yellow man and the white man can never comprehend or sympathize with one another, will appeal little to those who from their comparative study of society have gleaned some notion of what naturally follows from isolation, the acute struggle for existence, ancestor worship, patriarchal authority, the subjection of women, the decline of militancy, and the ascendancy of scholars.

The first sentence of the first chapter of Ross's book is "China is the European Middle Ages made visible."[28]

In the ten to twenty years after 1911, with hardly anyone noticing it as such, the universe of keywords, stories, and metaphors used by Americans to construe China shifted, and not merely because of the introduction of Marxist vocabulary in the 1920s. Orientalists of various stripes had defined China as exotic and autonomous, capable of generating its own future but perhaps unwilling to do so — proud but pickled. A new Progressive discourse emerged, with a new China difference: China was behind, on a lower step of the historical ladder, poverty-stricken, and culturally vapid — *medieval*. The difference was no longer mapped only onto geography — the "Far" East — but onto historic time as well; China was now what the West had been, China's future was the modern West.

The process of conceptual change was ragged and never complete or consistent. Exotic, unchanging China was still usable, but more often as a source for ancestral wisdom critical of bourgeois vanity. An example: The most persuasively favorable view of Chinese farming came from F. H. King, a University of Wisconsin professor of agriculture — the redoubtable, still saleable *Farmers of Forty Centuries: or, Permanent Agriculture in China, Korea, and Japan*. King preached the Progressive gospel of efficiency, repeated the century-old observation that Oriental agriculture more resembled gardening than farming, and was enchanted with the wise frugality with which the Japanese and the Chinese recycled every possible nutrient — can the American fixation on "night soil," a virtual cloacal obsession, be explained only in Freudian terms?[29] China was the Shangri-la of organic farming.

But with an increasing tendency to define agriculture in terms of industrial fertilizers, chemical pesticides, and machines, and with a now settled tendency to unwittingly agree with Karl Marx that the advanced countries represented the future of mankind, Progressive Americans began to construe a little-changed, literal, visible China in different terms. Liberty Hyde Bailey, the Cornell agronomist, at the request of King's widow, had written a preface for King's book. He visited China in 1917 and reported that he "went to China filled with expectations of its wonderful centuries." But where King saw frugality, Bailey found a "wasteland": "One is constantly impressed everywhere by the merciless skinning of the land to get every last fragment of fiber and root for fuel. He has never seen such sacrilege of the earth." Typical of titles in the following years is Walter Mallory's *China: Land of Famine*.[30]

THE CHINESE PEASANT: INVENTED OR DISCOVERED?
The Chinese people of the New Culture Movement (1916–23) came to see the Chinese village not as the basis of glorious tradition but as dark, backward, and shameful. They searched for a new political force powerful enough to destroy traditional culture and to repel imperialism. This destruction and regeneration, much like the "double mission" that Marx had called for, was what many of them meant by "revolution." The social construction of *feudal* China, populated by *peasants*, was under way.[31]

You may feel impatient at this point: Isn't the difference between "farmer" and "peasant" a mere quibble? The importance is that from at least the sixteenth century the Chinese rural economy had been basically commercialized, with free markets in land and labor, a civilian-controlled bureaucratic government, with politics centralized and national — anything but feudal. True, by the mid-1920s, the Chinese village and rural economy had been shaken by political disarray, deflation, inflation, drought, flood, famine, warlords, taxes, pestilence, opium, and sociologists. But the solution proposed to these terrible realities depended on the terms in which they were construed as *problems*.[32] To put it baldly, reconstruing China as "feudal" made "feudalism" a curable structural malady, made the revolutionary destruction of the landlord class the solution, and made the man with the hoe into a "peasant."

Historians resist the claim that China was feudal. "Feudal" applied to

China was, as John K. Fairbank put it, merely a "useful swear word," and Paul Cohen sees the argument over feudalism as evidence of "the residual grip of the nineteenth century." [33] True, but not the point. "Feudalism," in this Progressive argument, was not a technical description but a metaphor, and a devastatingly effective one at that. For the American followers of Jefferson and Mark Twain, just as for an apostle of Stalin's revised standard Marxism, to say that China was "feudal" was to reject Orientalism and to assert that it consigned China to a dungeon of exotic stagnation, that China, far from being unique, shared universal history, that the Chinese people had to be liberated from feudalism through revolution, that revolution was possible, that the formation of a nation was liberating, and that a vanguard should lead it. Stalinists and American Progressives simply disagreed about method (principally, the role of violence) and about whether the leaders should be a vanguard middle class or a vanguard proletariat.

Mao Zedong presented the aroused countryside as a source of national power. As part of his Autumn Harvest Uprisings in 1927 he predicted in his "Report on an Investigation of the Peasant Movement in the Hunan Countryside":

> In a very short time, in China's central, southern and northern provinces, several hundred million peasants will rise like a mighty storm, like a hurricane, a force so violent that no power, however great, will be able to hold it back. They will smash all the trammels that bind them and rush forward along the road to liberation. They will sweep all the imperialists, warlords, corrupt officials, local bullies and evil gentry into their graves.

The "peasant-feudal" view of China did not convince all young Chinese. James Yen, though in the same generation as Mao and equally committed to making a powerful Chinese nation, turned to America as an inspiration from which to select and adapt. To make "new citizens," Yen went to the countryside at almost the same time as Mao, but he did not see "peasants": "Unlike the serf-peasant of Imperial Russia or the depressed classes of India, the Chinese farmer is a free being. . . . Though poor, he is thrifty and industrious. Though unlettered, he is intelligent and an expert in intensive farming." [34]

From 1926 until the Japanese invasion of 1937, Yen and his Rural Reconstruction Movement lived in villages of Ting Hsien, a North China county, to crossbreed tradition with "modern" knowledge. They set out to develop Chinese forms of modern organization for education, health, government, and economics. Over the course of nearly a decade, they effectively transformed these North China villages without destroying (or even assuming the existence of) a feudal landlord class. Yet Mao's revolution came to power in 1949 using a vision of feudal peasantry that justified revolution but eventually, in the Great Leap Forward of the mid-1950s, led to disaster.

The late 1920s saw the nominal unification of China under Chiang Kai-shek's Nationalist Party, which agreed with the decimated Communist Party that imperialism and feudalism could be defeated only by a nation-state, one that followed Japan, Prussia, and Russia in organizing and controlling village cohorts of militarized (though sometimes folk-dancing), sanitized peasants purged of rebelliousness, superstition, and backwardness.[35] The China story was the pageant of the Chinese nation; the peasant danced center stage but did not write the script.

Chinese discourse on history, nation, and the peasant is beyond the scope of this essay, but foreign works provide a useful reflection of its development and the problems that foreign friends had in seeing it. R. H. Tawney, a British non-Marxist socialist, visited China in 1930–31, sponsored by the new Institute of Pacific Relations. He appears in our largely American discussion because his *Land and Labor in China*, first prepared as a research memorandum for the institute's 1931 Shanghai conference, indicates a tipping point in the change from "farmer" to "peasant." After spending time in the library of China's leading American-inspired economic research institute in Tientsin, Tawney spent several days in James Yen's Ting Hsien and visited John Loessing Buck and Pearl Buck in their home at Nanking University, and thanked both for their "counsel and inspiration."[36]

Land and Labor uses both terms — "farmer" and "peasant." Tawney admired both Yen's rural reconstruction experiments and Buck's extensive surveys of the Chinese farm economy; he acknowledged their suggestion that technological change, not revolution, was the answer for the village crisis. Still, Tawney only sidles up to the issue of the China difference. He concedes that the "hackneyed reference to the Middle Ages is sadly overworked," since it "implies a comparison of stages of development, as though the Chinese version of civilization, instead of differing in kind from the European, were merely less mature," and proceeds to spell out significant contrasts between Europe and China. On the other hand, he can't resist leaving the way open for seeing the "peasant" as characteristic of an immobile, feudal China, which only revolution could liberate.[37]

Whatever the case, after the early 1930s, references in English to Chinese "farmers" are few. We will now weigh the last major example.

WHAT'S SO BAD ABOUT *THE GOOD EARTH*?

Pearl Sydenstricker Buck wrote *The Good Earth*, published in 1931, a few hundred miles from Mao's 1927 Autumn Harvest Uprisings, in the house where her husband was compiling his rural survey and where she welcomed and informed R. H. Tawney. The daughter of missionaries, raised in China, she challenged the Progressive American Open Door vision of a passive China awaiting uplift; she loudly and skeptically asked, "Is there a case for missions?" and answered, "No." Nor did she reject this American uplift in favor of its equally progressive revolutionary antagonist; she must be counted one of the last of the Orientalists.[38]

Pearl Buck wrote that she lived in "several worlds."[39] That statement should put us on the lookout. What she wrote in the attic of her faculty cottage on the Nanking University campus is not what the American public read. The American audience of *The Good Earth* reads a story about "peasants," a word that does not appear in the book. "I am Wang Lung, the farmer," says our hero; when city people or servants of the rich revile him, they call him a garlic eater or pigtailed lout, never a "peasant."[40]

The Good Earth implicitly argues an Orientalist view of the farmer as the heart of eternal China. In *The Exile* (1936), a moving, aggrieved biography of her mother, Pearl Buck puts an almost perfect Orientalist creed in her mother's mouth. As she views the countryside, she cries out, "As Christ cried, 'O Jerusalem, Jerusalem!'":

> It doesn't need to be so very different from this. . . . So little needs really to be changed in these villages — the houses, the streets, the fields, they are all good enough in themselves. I want them kept as they are. But, oh, if the people would not kill their girl babies and keep their women ignorant and bound of foot and if they would not worship blindly through fear only — if only the filth could be cleared from the streets and the half-dead dogs killed, even — it's a beautiful country if only they use what they have! [102]

Buck must be respected here for resisting the racism of reducing China to "feudal culture" to be transformed by kindly American uplift.

Perhaps she had seen too many pious missionaries raise money with Sunday night slides of Chinese bound feet, orphans, and judicial torture.

But Orientalism also contains an opposite danger — that of not allowing China the capacity to change and ridiculing or belittling nationalism and revolution. In 1924 Buck wrote: "Bolshevism? No, I think not. The young Chinese rants a little and philosophizes a great deal, but he has an inner foundation of unemotional, hard commonsense, a practical gift from his ancestors, which will make him stop and see what Bolshevism has done thus far, and finding it barren of fruit, he will cling to a saner, slower order of progress."[41]

The Good Earth presents a phlegmatic Chinese farmer with no interest in politics. Several passages resonate with Arthur Smith's *Village China*, in their Orientalist respect for eternal China. Wang Lung and his wife, O-lan, are in the fields: "He had no articulate thought of anything; there was only this perfect sympathy of movement, of turning this earth of theirs over and over to the sun, this earth which formed their home and fed their bodies and made their gods." The field contains bits of wood, brick: "It was nothing. Some time, in some age, bodies of men and women had been buried there, houses had stood there, had fallen, and gone back into the earth. So would also their house, some time, return into the earth, their bodies also. Each had his turn at this earth" (33–34).

Because he is so (almost literally) grounded, Wang Lung evenhandedly rejects change in the form of either radical agitation or Christianity. When Wang takes his wife, sons, and retarded daughter to "the great city" as refuge from drought and famine, Buck shows us his reaction to a missionary tract and a revolutionary pamphlet: he gives each to his wife as paper to patch shoes. Wang Lung resists the agitator's attempt to define him as a peasant whose "poverty" is caused by a landlord. His lack of money, reasons Wang, is caused by drought. Was it the landlord who kept the rain from falling?

Unlike Dickens, her literary hero, Miss Buck offers us the tale of only one city and no revolution. "When the rich are too rich there are ways, and when the poor are too poor there are ways" (123). Pushed too far by war, conscription, and starvation, the poor become a mob. "Common people" howling a "deep, tigerish howl" woke Wang Lung one night, swept him along (like Mao's "hurricane"?), into a house of the rich. As Wang Lung wanders dazed through courtyard after courtyard, he comes across "a great fat fellow, neither old nor young, and he had been lying naked in his bed, doubtless with a pretty woman, for his naked body gaped through a purple satin robe." He "fell upon his knees and knocked his head on the tiles of the floor" and pled with Wang Lung to take not his life but his money: "Money . . . *the land!*" (142–43).

This is one of the most revealing scenes in an American China book. Written only a few years after Mao's "Report on an Investigation of the Peasant Movement in the Hunan Countryside," the incident is a failure of nerve, observation, and imagination. It does not confront the issues that surrounded Buck when she was writing the book. Wang Lung achieves the fruits of revolution — "the land" — with no taint of class war or even collective action. As one of my students once put it, "Mao Zedong's revolution could never have taken place in Pearl Buck's China." (Perhaps Mao's revolution couldn't take place in his China either, but that is a matter for another day.)[42]

Pearl Buck's works written in China — especially the twin biographies of her parents — show her as far more complex than the common impression of the grandmotherly, sugary hack (which she may later have become). Her China writings explore American foreign relations and cultural issues using a vision of Chinese "farmers" (not "peasants") as existing for themselves, not for a liberal nation-state or for foreign ideas or for progress. Her style and Orientalism, however, opened her to scorn from the wartime generation of popular China-ologists and to being ignored by the following generation of China professionals.[43]

REVOLUTIONARY CHINA — THE PEASANT A KEY

Still another China story appears in the classics of American Progressive wartime reporting, which rejected Orientalism: Edgar Snow's *Red Star over China* (1937); the reportage of Anna Louise Strong and Agnes Smedley; Theodore White and Annalee Jacoby's *Thunder out of China* (1946); William Hinton's *Fanshen*, conceived in the 1940s but published in 1966; and Jack Belden's *China Shakes the World* (1949), which presents the most complex view of revolution in any of these sources. These writings represent the abandonment of half-conscious Orientalism in favor of a Progressive definition: China is feudal, the peasant its essence, and peasant revolution its destiny.

Edgar Snow's *Red Star over China* is almost too well known: familiarity keeps us from seeing it. Even so, it seems clear that the book was more than the "Message from Mao" that it has been recently called.[44] Compared with the books emerging from China after Mao's death in

1976, *Red Star* indeed seems naive and blinkered, but compared with earlier Orientalist work, it represents a step forward by recognizing revolutionary nationalism and portraying the grimy politics of nation-building to an American public that had previously seen a willowware exoticism.

Snow landed in Shanghai on an around-the-world tour in 1929 and stayed on to report the revolution. In 1933 he visited James Yen's village work in Ting Hsien and proclaimed that "rural China is being remade." He did not see feudalism as an obstacle; he did not use the word "peasant."[45] By the time of *Red Star*, written in 1936–37, when China and Snow were looking for strong leaders against the Japanese, the story had changed: social revolution will come because the "basic conditions which have given it birth carry within themselves the dynamic necessity for its triumph." Snow concluded that "what this 'communism' amounted to in a way was that, for the first time in history, thousands of educated youths . . . 'returned to the people,' went to the deep soil base of their country, to 'reveal' some of their new-won learning to the intellectually sterile countryside, the dark-living peasantry, and sought to enlist its alliance in building a 'more abundant life.'" Revolution was the uplift of the "dark-living peasantry" by the educated vanguard.[46]

Theodore White went from Harvard to China in 1939, shortly after the Japanese had driven the Nationalist government upriver to Chung-king. He saw wartime terror and collapse, then returned with Annalee Jacoby to the United States after the war to write *Thunder out of China*, free of Chiang Kai-shek's censors and *Time* magazine's editors. Chapter 1 of their best-seller was titled "The Peasant." It begins: "The Chinese who fought this war were peasants born in the Middle Ages to die in the Twentieth century." White and Jacoby complained, echoing E. A. Ross, that many Western and Chinese students have looked at China through the eyes of Buck's classics, and have "regarded China as 'quaint' and found a timeless patina of age hanging over the villages and people." They condemned this picture as "both false and vicious" (32). Then, echoing the Mark Twain who put the social morality of the French Revolution into American technological terms, they argued: "Less than a thousand years ago Europe lived this way; then Europe revolted" (xix). The Chinese government was controlled by "feudal minded men" who ran it in the interests of "feudal landlords" (310–13). Failing the development of a middle class, the only other organized group was the Communists, who represented a new French Revolution: "We revere the memory of that Revolution, but we regard such uprisings in our own time with horror and loathing" (20).

By 1950, American nonrecognition was cultural fact as well as diplomatic policy. Americans did lose a China, after all — the China construed in their heads. None of the American writers, whether Orientalist or Progressive, construed a China that conveyed the dilemma of culture and nation-building. American and Chinese liberal progressives, who accept revolution, modernity, and the nation-state as clearly natural and maybe good, have shared a vision of the peasant that makes it difficult to see the village and to deal with the human problems of the country and the countryside. Still, the earlier Orientalists, from Arthur Smith to Pearl Buck, for all their shortcomings, may yet have some value. By showing that the construction of the peasant in a feudal China was neither simple nor inevitable, the Orientalists examined issues that open questions that have not been seen to exist.

NOTES

This essay, prepared for the Workshop on the Rhetoric of Social History at the University of Iowa, June 1992, draws on an evolving manuscript, "America's Chinas: Construing China from the Opium Wars to Tiananmen." I have published parts of this project as "Chinese and American Characteristics: Arthur H. Smith and His China Book," in Suzanne Wilson Barnett and John King Fairbanks, eds., *Christianity in China: Early Protestant Missionary Writings* (Cambridge: Harvard University Press, 1984), pp. 153–67, and as "'The Good Earth,' Revolution, and the American Raj in China," in Elizabeth J. Lipscomb, Frances E. Webb, and Peter Conn, eds., *The Several Worlds of Pearl S. Buck* (Westport, Conn.: Greenwood Press, 1994), pp. 19–27.

1. This is a general theme in my book *To the People: James Yen and Village China* (New York: Columbia University Press, 1990) and is taken up by Myron Cohen, "Cultural and Political Inventions in Modern China: The Case of the Chinese Peasant," *Daedalus* 122, no. 2 (Spring 1993): 151–70.

2. Chayanov's influence is represented in Teodor Shanin, ed., *Peasants and Peasant Societies: Selected Readings*, 2d ed. (Oxford: Basil Blackwell, 1987). Daniel Little, *Understanding Peasant China: Case Studies in the Philosophy of Social Science* (New Haven: Yale University Press, 1989), accepts as given that China is a "peasant" society. Kathleen Hartford and Steven M. Goldstein, (introduction to *Single Sparks: China's Rural Revolutions* [Armonk, N.Y.: M. E. Sharpe, 1989]) helpfully examine work on the village revolutions leading up to 1949 without a generic "peasant" analysis.

3. Ramon H. Myers and Thomas A. Metzger, "Sinological Shadows: The State of Modern Chinese Studies in the United States," *Washington Quarterly* (Spring 1980):

88; Steven Mosher, *Broken Earth* (New York: Free Press, 1983), pp. 299–300, excerpting (without ellipses) from John K. Fairbank, *China Perceived* (New York: Random House, 1974), p. xvii. I regret not having space here to discuss the evolution of Fairbank's complex views.

4. Randall Stross, *Stubborn Earth: American Agriculturalists on Chinese Soil, 1898–1937* (Berkeley: University of California Press, 1986), p. xi.

5. Guo Liyu, "Farmers Reap Rewards of Reform," *China Daily*, May 1, 1986, p. 4; Polly Hill, *Development Economics on Trial: The Anthropological Case for a Prosecution* (London: Cambridge University Press, 1986).

6. For an early and general suggestion on how to apply Williams's concept, see Charles W. Hayford, "Outward and Visible Signs: Provocations to Social and Cultural History of Republican China," *Chinese Republican Studies* 1, no. 3 (June 1976): 35–46.

7. Hayford, *To the People*, p. ix. See also Helen Siu, comp. and ed., *Furrows: Peasants, Intellectuals, and the State — Stories and Histories from Modern China* (Stanford: Stanford University Press, 1990).

8. I take this phrase from Ross Terrill, ed., *The China Difference* (New York: Harper and Row, 1979).

9. John T. Schlebecker, "The Many Names of Farmers," *Agricultural History* 55, no. 2 (April 1981): 147–55.

10. For the derivation of "country," see Raymond Williams, *The Country and the City* (New York: Oxford University Press, 1973), p. 307. I owe much to the spirit of Williams's book.

11. Quoted from the *Register*, April 7 and 14, 1821, in Gertrude Himmelfarb, *The Idea of Poverty* (New York: Knopf, 1983), p. 220. For Cobbett, see Raymond Williams, *Cobbett* (Oxford: Oxford University Press, 1983).

12. Jefferson, quoted in A. Whitney Griswold, *Farming and Democracy* (New York: Harcourt, Brace 1948), pp. 30–31. For the agrarian myth, see Henry Nash Smith, *The Virgin Land: The American West as Symbol and Myth* (1950; reprint, Cambridge: Harvard University Press, 1970).

13. I have discussed some of the implications of the term "Orientalism" in "The Open Door Raj and Post-Semi-Colonial Historiography: Chinese-American Cultural Relations, 1900–1945," in Warren Cohen, ed., *Pacific Passage: The Study of American–East Asian Relations on the Eve of the Twenty-first Century* (New York: Columbia University Press, 1996).

14. Karl Marx, "The Consequences of British Rule in India," reprinted from the *New York Daily Tribune*, June 10 and July 22, 1853, in d'Encausse and Schram, eds., *Marxism and Asia* (London: Allen Lane, 1969), p. 117. Macaulay, "Minute on Education (1835)," reprinted in Stephen N. Hay, ed., *Sources of Indian Tradition*, vol. 2 (New York: Columbia University Press, 1958), pp. 45, 49. For the Orientalists, see David Kopf, *British Orientalism and the Bengal Renaissance: The Dynamics of Indian Modernization, 1773–1835* (Berkeley: University of California Press, 1969), and Garland Cannon, *The Life and Mind of Oriental Jones* (London: Cambridge University Press, 1990). Gauri Viswanathan, *Masks of Conquest: Literary Study and British Rule*

in India (New York: Columbia University Press, 1989), is among those who demonstrate that Orientalist and Progressive concepts differed but were both used in British imperialist rule.

15. Michael Adas, *Machines as the Measure of Men: Science, Technology, and Ideologies of Western Dominance* (Ithaca: Cornell University Press, 1989), describes largely European thought; for Americans, the timing appears to be different.

16. "Fair Game: Exploitative Role-Myths and the American Opium Trade," *Pacific Historical Review* 41, no. 2 (May 1972): 133–49.

17. Carl Crow, *Four Hundred Million Customers: The Experiences — Some Happy, Some Sad — of an American in China, and What They Taught Him* (New York: Harper and Brothers, 1937) and also *Foreign Devils in the Flowery Kingdom* (New York: Harper and Brothers, 1940).

18. Carl Crow, "Shanghai," in Kelly and Walsh, *Handbook for China*, 5th ed. (1933; reprint, with an introduction by H. J. Lethbridge, Oxford: Oxford University Press, 1984).

19. Jerry Israel, "Carl Crow, Edgar Snow, and Shifting American Journalistic Perceptions of China," in Jonathan Goldstein, Jerry Israel, and Hilary Conroy, eds., *America Views China: American Images of China Then and Now* (Bethlehem, Pa.: Lehigh University Press, 1990), pp. 148–68.

20. Smith, "The Best Method of Presenting the Gospel to the Chinese," *Chinese Recorder* 14, no. 6 (November–December 1883): 431. For Smith's career, see Hayford, "Chinese and American Characteristics" and Theodore D. Pappas, "Arthur Henderson Smith and the American Mission in China," *Wisconsin Magazine of History* 70, no. 3 (Spring 1987): 163–86.

21. Arthur H. Smith, D.D., *Village Life in China: A Study in Sociology* (New York: Fleming H. Revell, 1899), p. 5.

22. In fact, the Chinese New Culture leader Lu Xun, Mao Zedong's favorite author, recommended in 1926 that his students read Smith's *Chinese Characteristics* (New York: Fleming Revell, 1894), which had been quickly translated into Chinese. For a fascinating discussion of this process of linguistic and social translation, see Lydia Liu, *Translingual Practice: Literature, National Culture, and Translated Modernity: China, 1900–1937* (Stanford: Stanford University Press, 1995).

23. Smith, *Village Life*, p. 5.

24. "The Monotony and Vacuity of Village Life," p. 316.

25. The word "loot" seems itself a piece of Orientalist vocabulary, taken from Hindi, implying that to rape and plunder was simply to follow local custom.

26. "To a Stranger Sitting in Darkness," *North American Review* 172 (1901): 161–76, quoted in Arthur Schlesinger, Jr., "The Missionary Enterprise and Theories of Imperialism," in John K. Fairbank, ed., *The Missionary Enterprise in China and America* (Cambridge: Harvard University Press, 1974), p. 358.

27. Michael Hunt, *The Making of a Special Relationship: The United States and China to 1914* (New York: Columbia University Press, 1983), p. xi.

28. Edward Alworth Ross, *The Changing Chinese: The Conflict of Oriental and Western Cultures in China* (New York: Century, 1911), pp. xvi, 3. The book does not use the word "peasant."

29. F. H. King, *Farmers of Forty Centuries: Or, Permanent Agriculture in China, Korea, and Japan* (reprint, Emmaus, Pa.: Rodale Press; Madison: University of Wisconsin Press, 1911). Daniel Harrison Kulp II, *Country Life in South China: The Sociology of Familism* (New York: Columbia University Teachers College, 1925), is dedicated "To the Farmers of Forty Centuries."

30. Bailey's article carried the good Jeffersonian title "Permanent Agriculture and Democracy" and concluded that "no man should be sentenced to one sixth of an acre of land," for "on the basis of five cents a day and food, there can be no satisfactory agriculture." L. H. Bailey, "Permanent Agriculture and Democracy," *American Museum Journal* 17, no. 8 (December 1917), reprinted in C. F. Remer, ed., *Readings in Economics for China* (Shanghai: Commercial Press, 1922), pp. 541–51. See also Mallory, *China: Land of Famine* (New York: National Geographic Society, 1929).

31. Hayford, *To the People*, especially pp. 60–65; Cohen, "Cultural and Political Inventions in Modern China"; Arif Dirlik, "The Universalization of a Concept: From 'Feudalism' to Feudalism in Chinese Marxist Historiography," *Journal of Peasant Studies* 12, nos. 2–3 (1985): 197–227.

32. Philip C. C. Huang, *The Peasant Economy and Social Change in North China* (Stanford: Stanford University Press, 1985), esp. pp. 3–32, summarizes the issues; for another view, see Ramon Myers, "The Agrarian System," in *Cambridge History of China* (Cambridge: Cambridge University Press, 1986), *Republican China 1912–1949*, 13:230–69.

33. *United States and China*, 4th ed. (Cambridge: Harvard University Press, 1976), p. 25; *Discovering History in China: American Historical Writing on the Recent Chinese Past* (New York: Columbia University Press, 1984), pp. 91 ff.

34. James Yen, *Ting Hsien Experiment, 1934* (Peiping, 1934), quoted in Hayford, *To the People*, p. 141.

35. See Prasenjit Duara, *Culture, Power, and the State: Rural North China, 1900–1942* (Stanford: Stanford University Press, 1988), for the nationalization of the masses in the countryside.

36. Randall E. Stross, *The Stubborn Earth*, has an illuminating chapter on J. L. Buck.

37. R. H. Tawney, *Land and Labor in China* (London: Allen and Unwin, 1932; reprint, with an introduction by Barrington Moore, Jr., Boston: Beacon Press, 1966), pp. 8, 91. In 1938, Tawney wrote the introduction to *Agrarian China: Selected Source Materials from Chinese Authors*, compiled and translated by the research staff of the Secretariat, Institute on Pacific Relations (Chicago: University of Chicago Press for the Institute on Pacific Relations), which translated essays arguing feudal-peasant China.

38. Buck, "Is There a Case for Foreign Mission?" *Harpers*, January 1933; William R. Hutchison, *Errand to the World: American Protestant Thought and Foreign Missions* (Chicago: University of Chicago Press, 1987), pp. 166–69; Charles W. Hayford, "'The Good Earth,' Revolution, and the American Raj in China," in Elizabeth J. Lipscomb, Frances E. Webb, and Peter Conn, eds., *The Several Worlds of Pearl S. Buck* (Westport, Conn.: Greenwood Press, 1994), pp. 19–27.

39. *My Several Worlds: A Personal Record* (New York: John Day, 1951).

40. Buck recalled that the words "coolie" and "amah" were not allowed to be used in her home when she was growing up (not to mention "Chinaman") (introduction to the Modern Library edition, originally *New York Times Book Review*, January 15, 1933. All quotes are from this edition).

41. Pearl Buck, "China the Eternal," *International Review of Missions* (October 1924). In *The Young Revolutionist* (New York: Friendship Press, 1932), commissioned and published by the YMCA, Buck explicitly and crudely attacks revolution as destructive anarchy. See also Alfred Dixon Heininger, *Youth and Revolution in China: A Course for Leaders of Intermediate Groups based on 'The Young Revolutionist' by Pearl S. Buck* (New York: Missionary Education Movement, 1932). By the 1940s Buck's attitude had become more complex, and she repudiated *The Young Revolutionist*.

42. Buck endorsed the views of James Yen in *Tell the People: Talks with James Yen about the Mass Education Movement* (New York: John Day, 1945); Yen's resemblance appears in her novel *Kinfolks* (New York: John Day, 1948).

43. Upon her return to the States, she fought for the rights of women and minorities and (with Eleanor Roosevelt) against anti-Japanese racism. John Dower, *War without Mercy: Race and Power in the Pacific War* (New York: Pantheon, 1986), p. 7.

44. Jonathan Mirsky, "Message from Mao," *New York Review*, February 16, 1989, pp. 15–17, reviews of *Edgar Snow: A Biography*, by John Maxwell Hamilton (Bloomington: Indiana University Press, 1988).

45. Snow, "How Rural China Is Being Remade," *China Weekly Review*, December 13 and 30, 1933; quoted in Hayford, *To the People*, pp. x, 141.

46. Ch. 5, "Red Theater."

The Uses of Synthesis

RUTH CROCKER

UNSETTLING PERSPECTIVES:
THE SETTLEMENT MOVEMENT,
THE RHETORIC OF SOCIAL HISTORY,
AND THE SEARCH FOR SYNTHESIS

To many historians, the outpouring of scholarly work in social history since the 1960s testifies to the vitality of the field, but to others it has signaled the fragmentation of historical writing and the loss of a wider vision. In a provocative 1986 essay, historian Thomas Bender deplored the "proliferation of intensely parochial, nearly hermetic discourses around a series of social units far smaller than either societies or nations." How were these studies related to each other and to the master narrative of "American history," he asked? [1]

Peter Novick, surveying the history of the profession in *That Noble Dream* (1988), also deplored fragmentation and the loss of a "center." Novick wondered whether history any longer constituted a coherent discipline. "[It was] not just that the whole was less than the sum of its parts," he wrote, "but that there was no whole — only parts." [2]

Defenders of traditionalism joined the conversation; they were quick to detect a challenge to the national purpose in the explosion of "parochial" and "narrow" social history studies. What use was a social history that could not "even" explain such major events as the founding of the American Republic, Gertrude Himmelfarb asked? And William Bennett called on intellectuals to "reclaim a legacy." But many demurred at the implication that American history lay there waiting to be reclaimed, a seamless narrative whose meaning was transparent and uncontested. [3]

Since Bender's essay appeared, controversy over whose history should be written, taught, and celebrated has become increasingly acrimonious — witness the disputes over such national remembrances as the Smithsonian Institution's commemoration of the dropping of the atomic bomb on Japan in August 1945, or the controversies over the proposed national History Standards. [4] In view of this new public scrutiny of history, as well as of the debates within the historical profession over how much historians should concede to the destabilizing vision of postmodernism, which views experience as constituted through language, so that all stories are equally worth telling, it may be useful to revisit the question of synthesis and fragmentation in history writing a decade after Bender's essay appeared.

There are two obvious explanations for the explosion of social history narratives since the 1950s. First, social historians asked new questions about new groups, using new "sources," that is, previously unused bodies of evidence. And they wrote about what Peter Stearns has called "modes of existence," creating subfields that reproduced the range of topics developed in sociology: work and leisure, family, ethnicity, education and voluntarism, delinquency and crime.[5] Second, social history often signaled the arrival of new practitioners of history. Peter Novick's *That Noble Dream* raised the issue of diversity among historical practitioners by acknowledging the relationship between who has practiced history and what was taught as history.[6] Former outsiders to academia often (though not always) created new narratives in place of familiar ones, so that what to some looked like "fragmentation" in fact resulted from the democratization of the profession. Bender's proposal that groups other than the dominant elite (white males) could become part of the historical narrative (part of "History") at the point where their histories entered the public realm did not mollify his critics. As Nell Painter and others pointed out, only the earlier exclusion of others' stories from "History" had made synthesis seem natural and unproblematic.[7]

The critics of fragmentation assumed that wholes were preferable to parts, a single narrative to many "parochial" narratives. And indeed, for those who looked to history for an account of how political institutions evolved by means of a "rational, deliberate attempt to organize public life so as to promote the public good," history simply became far too messy once other groups claimed agency as historical actors.[8]

But rhetoric also helps to construct these alternative narratives, for it functions epistemically, bringing some issues forward and eclipsing others. By "rhetoric" I do not mean a lapse into shoddy tactics or partisanship — "mere rhetoric" — for if political engagements prefigure the historian's engagement with texts, rhetorical ones also help to structure historical inquiry.[9] Social history narratives multiply because different subfields of social history help constitute distinct audiences of readers.

"Fragmentation" thus results from both new practitioners and new readerships, and calls for synthesis overlook the constructedness of these new social history subfields. Black history, women's history, and ethnic history all have their own political and rhetorical commitments as well as their ruling paradigms, their authorities, and their germinal texts.[10]

If we recast the question of fragmentation into an inquiry about what historian Jeff Cox has called "comparative and competitive storytelling," then the problem becomes a matter of understanding how successive communities of interpretation produce new knowledge about the past. An optimistic view of historical knowledge as incremental holds that each generation of scholars sees further by standing on the shoulders of its predecessors. A more gloomy assessment is that even standing on the shoulders of their predecessors they may still be looking in the other direction. Are communities of historians engaged in a "conversation" or a shouting match? Do they stand on each other's shoulders — or (as D. N. McCloskey has quipped) on each other's faces?[11]

The Progressive Era settlement movement offers some advantages for examining the production of social history narratives. This discrete episode in American reform has been the beneficiary (or the victim — it is the purpose of this essay to explore which) of multiple social history narratives. I discuss how the narratives of the first settlement workers became hegemonic so that scholarly as well as lay enthusiasm continued to be centered on Hull-House and its residents. This Chicago settlement came to represent Progressive reform at its most articulate and disinterested. But competing narratives about the settlements also emerged, characterized by different rhetorics and appealing to different readerships; often we can identify them with specific subfields of social history. This essay analyzes the persistence of the Hull-House story amid competitive storytelling and asks whether we might usefully recast the question of synthesis-fragmentation as one of competing rhetorics. Such an approach can both help explain alternative narratives and stem the anxious quest for synthesis or metanarrative.

"THE SETTLEMENT IMPULSE": PARTICIPANT-OBSERVERS GO TO THE SLUMS AND FIND THEMSELVES

The earliest narratives of the settlement movement were written by the participants themselves. Jane Addams, Alice Hamilton, Graham Taylor,

Vida Scudder, Mary Simkhovitch, and Lillian Wald were among a dozen or more settlement workers who wrote their autobiographies.[12] While a few of these workers (Robert Woods, for example) represented the group as heirs to the English intellectual reform tradition of Carlyle, Ruskin, and Morris, of Christian Socialism and the revolt against industrialism, others represented themselves as missionaries on an urban frontier between the civilized and the savage. At the heart of their account was the "settlement impulse," the splendid, romantic gesture of college-educated men and women serving the poor by going to live among them.[13]

Vida Scudder, founder of Boston's Denison House, described the settlement impulse in terms of a secular conversion experience. Her account warrants quoting at length because it shows how the settlement workers' journey "to the depths" involved the search of these intellectuals for their own psychological integration. She wrote:

> Ever since my Oxford days, I had been beating my wings against the bars, the customs, the assumptions, of my own class. . . . I wanted to escape, where winds buffeted, blowing free. The spirit of adventure drives some men to explore the Gobi desert, or to seek the Pole; others to research in the buried past, or to travel among alien races. Me, it filled with a biting curiosity about the way the Other Half lived, and a strange hunger for fellowship with them. Were not the workers, the poor, nearer perhaps than we to the reality I was always seeking?[14]

Others who went to the settlements employed a rhetoric of passivity, of a great cause seeking out its instrument. Lillian Wald claimed that when she began settlement work she had "little more than an inspiration to be of use in some way or other." Wald ascribed her entry into settlement work to altruism and naturalized it as an instinctive response to a suffering fellow-human: "A sick woman in a squalid tenement . . . determined me to live on the East Side."[15] And Jane Addams also used the passive voice in the preface to *Twenty Years at Hull-House* (1910): "This volume endeavors to trace the experiences through which various conclusions were forced upon me."[16] Florence Kelley, on the other hand, entered Hull-House because it enabled her to continue work she already had in hand (labor legislation) and because it met her need to live apart from her abusive husband. For Kelley, residing at Hull-House between 1891 and 1898 and then at Henry Street until 1926 made possible a remarkable political career.[17]

THE HISTORIANS AND HULL-HOUSE

When historians accepted Jane Addams's view of the settlements, they were not only accepting the most self-consciously intellectual and democratic view, but they were also letting these early narratives set the terms of their own inquiries into the settlement movement.[18]

Twenty Years at Hull-House, which offered Addams's version of the "settlement impulse," positioned Hull-House as the archetype of the settlement house and identified her completely with it.[19] Addams's portrait of Hull-House, nuanced and brilliant, established the settlement rhetorically both as a way of knowing and as an agent of change. Her account moves from description to prescription and from a rhetoric of uncertainty to one of reform. By segmenting the city into discrete areas of life and different groups ("Immigrants and Their Children," "Public Activities and Investigations," and so on), the narrative cast the settlement and its middle-class residents as an agency of intervention and amelioration.

Telling the story from the point of view of settlement residents, these participant-observer narratives depict working-class life elliptically so that the poor have what Alan Mayne calls a "glimpsed-at" quality.[20] While they surveyed and quantified poverty, *Twenty Years* and other founding narratives of the movement effected a distancing from the poor. They both aestheticized the poor and represented settlement clients episodically, sketching a few individuals or relating curious or unique incidents (the "devil baby" of *Twenty Years*, for example).[21] The settlement's working-class neighbors enter the narrative only long enough to teach the residents different lessons about life.[22] Letters home to a middle-class readership, the vignettes depict the city as a disorderly place where fallen women brush against the respectable, innocent children play in the dangerous streets, strangers (lodgers) invade the privacy of immigrant families, men "lounge" in saloons instead of coming home, and contagion bred in one filthy slum court spreads to respectable poor families living nearby. And as middle-class reformers entered the slums, they constructed new typologies of city folk — "the neglected child," "the shiftless husband," "the overworked mother," the "dull-witted Slav"— out of a combination of pity, outrage, and intellectual curiosity and with what one historian has called "that objectifying elite gaze" of the social investigator.[23]

These firsthand settlement narratives reflected the enthusiasms of an evangelical and imperialistic age. Many settlement workers had planned missionary careers, only to go instead into "home missionary work," and their accounts bear titles that suggest the danger of their enterprise — *On Journey, Exploring the Dangerous Trades, Pioneering on Social Frontiers.* Self-conscious "pioneers on the urban frontier," settlement workers wrote for an audience of readers who believed themselves distant morally as well as geographically from the objects of these narratives. A visitor to Graham Taylor's University of Chicago settlement in the 1890s observed, "Missionaries in the heart of Africa would hardly present a greater contrast with their surroundings than did these cultured and refined people in such a neighborhood."[24]

Settlement histories emplotted as progressive narratives began by problematizing the city as a slum, a place of frightening disorder and crime, only to recast it rhetorically as a "neighborhood," a small world where social order has been restored.[25] Others, like Lillian Wald's *The House on Henry Street* (1915) and Jane Addams's *Twenty Years*, are stories about wise and sympathetic women making their homes among the poor.[26] Narratives like these, which identify settlements with women and home — which stress the settlement *house* rather than the *movement* — effect a strategic rhetorical transposition from metaphors of danger and journey to those of home and neighborhood. They make the story of reform safe for incorporation in the celebratory narratives of public history. Progressive Era female settlement workers were on the defensive, after all: most were women living "alone" (that is, without men), in parts of the city where respectable women did not go. A story about unmarried female economists, policy experts, and physicians living and working collectively in little urban policy institutes — this was a story that could not be told, especially after 1919, with the disappearance of a coherent women's movement and the rise of antistatism and anti-feminism.[27] It was only by tolerating, and even encouraging, such confusing images of herself as "Mother to the Poor" and "the Protestant Nun," that Jane Addams, a never-married woman, an intellectual, administrator, and lobbyist, legitimated her public career.[28]

As for Florence Kelley, a Ph.D. who had translated a seminal socialist text, then divorced her husband and left her children in order to pursue the work of reform — how could her story be told at all during a conservative age? How could Kelley be an "American heroine" like Jane Addams? A moving force in dozens of Progressive reform initiatives, Kelley was nevertheless notably absent from the public-history narratives of the settlements until a revived feminism created a readership for narratives of women reformers. The recent biography by Kathryn Kish Sklar finally recounts Kelley's long and important reform career, making it emblematic of a progressivism defined by women's political culture.[29]

LATTER-DAY PROGRESSIVES
DISCOVER THE SETTLEMENTS

Interest in the Progressive Era settlements had first revived in the 1950s, when meliorist liberals in search of an American reform tradition rediscovered the movement. In 1956, Robert H. Bremner staged the settlements as part of a late-nineteenth-century "discovery of poverty" that could inspire and validate one in his own time. *From the Depths: The Discovery of Poverty in the United States* established the rhetorical engagement for the histories that followed. Bremner addressed three communities of readers: the "do-gooders — the responsible Americans in every generation who have heard and heeded the cry from the depths," the poor, and "the rest of us." By "the rest of us," Bremner rhetorically designated a readership of liberal intellectuals who would find in the settlement workers' engagement with the poor seventy years earlier a working-out of their own "subjective necessities."[30] At the same time, he called attention to the poverty (though not the racism) of his own time, praising the Progressive Era "generation of factfinders" for their work of social investigation and legislative enactment.[31]

Allen F. Davis's *Spearheads for Reform* (originally a 1959 University of Wisconsin dissertation) shared Bremner's commitment to reform. Exhaustively researched and persuasively argued, *Spearheads* documented the contribution that settlement workers had made to numerous Progressive reform causes and focused on those cities "where the movement was strongest and most concerned with reform."[32] This was accomplished rhetorically through a mode of presentation that surveyed the activities of the settlements topically (immigrants, labor, children, and so on) and positioned the settlements as a source of solutions — an approach that replicated that of *Twenty Years at Hull-House*. Davis's settlement workers continued to engage in reform activities during the conservative 1920s (as Clarke Chambers and others have shown) and played important roles in the New Deal.[33] The foreword by Richard Wade called readers' attention to the parallels between the Progressive Era settlements and the Peace Corps and VISTA, later examples of secular mission. The existential gesture of these intellectuals' going "to the people" resembled contemporary antipoverty initiatives, including community organizing in the War on Poverty. "Few historical studies . . . have such clear and present relevance to our own time," Wade wrote. Their history demonstrated that American capitalism might still be reformed and saved.[34]

A different kind of engagement with the settlements led Christopher Lasch to make Jane Addams a central figure in his reinterpretation of the history of American intellectuals, *The New Radicalism in America*.[35] For Lasch, Addams was emblematic of the rise of a new "social type," whose journey "to the depths" accomplished her own psychological integration. Lasch was the first to take seriously Addams's description of how founding Hull-House after eight years of aimless travel and "nervous" illness solved her problems of life, work, and love. He portrayed the settlement impulse as an episode in the history of American intellectuals, for whom "the discovery of the poor was bound up with the discovery of the self."[36] Settlement workers rebelled against "living at second hand," and in contemplating the Other, they achieved their own salvation.

But the laudatory progressive accounts of the settlements as community-based reform movements that could revive a participatory democracy proved more enduring than the more problematic narratives that saw the settlements as part of the psychological quest of intellectuals. These depictions privileged the settlements that had an impact on national reform politics and overlooked the numerous settlements engaged in such essentially conservative work as Americanization, proselytizing, and moral reform.[37] Jane Addams's story of Hull-House, shorn of its psychological dimensions, became a story that eclipsed the variety and range of settlements in other cities. It imposed order on a congeries of individual organizations. Even labeling them a "movement," though links between agencies were weak and funding was local, rhetorically begged the question of whether activist settlements were representative or exceptional. Moreover, a commitment to the settlements as instruments of reform caused religiously affiliated settlements to be marginalized or excluded from these accounts.[38] Historians overcame the problem of typicality by simply omitting hundreds of institutions that called themselves settlement houses, especially black settlements, missionary settlements, and those in the South. Instead, they mapped the history of the settlements onto the historiography of Progressivism by representing the settlement workers as the leading wedge of the movement's "social-justice wing."[39]

SOCIAL-WORK HISTORY AND THE DISCOURSE OF PROFESSIONALISM

A different set of narratives about the settlements arose within social-work history, a subfield whose practitioners were affiliated with professional social work.[40] Ontologically biased toward the triumph of professionalism and of casework over group work, social-work historians staged the settlements as part of the prehistory of their profession and the settlement workers as admirable, if somewhat eccentric, forerunners of modern social workers.[41]

Readership shaped the new histories of the settlement movement as it had the old ones. Judith Trolander's *Professionalism and Social Change: From the Settlement House Movement to Neighborhood Centers* (1987) addressed two audiences, social workers and social historians. Positioning herself as an heir to the movement as well as its historian, Trolander, who had lived in a settlement house for a time, argued that American cities needed and continue to need the kind of cross-class alliances that, in her view, the settlement promoted. Progressive citizenship could serve as an alternative to Marxist class consciousness.

Professionalism and Social Change marked a departure from earlier narratives because it analyzed institutional and structural factors, such as funding and federation, rather than the extraordinary leaders who had dominated earlier accounts.[42] Rhetorically, it broke away from the older narratives by staging the settlements as a century-long "movement," not a brief outburst of reform enthusiasm coterminous with the Progressive Era. Trolander was also the first to address the exclusion of blacks from the Progressive Era white settlements, the post–World War II transition of city neighborhoods, which forced settlements to serve black clients, and the eventual transition to black leadership in the movement.[43]

Like the Progressive Era narratives and their liberal, reformist descendants, narratives of social-work history and of social policy shared a "top-down" perpective that paid little attention to questions about the impact of settlement programs on the people receiving the service.[44] These somewhat linear modes of presentation portrayed the settlements as important as much for what they anticipated as for what they achieved; they framed the settlements as harbingers of the welfare state, nurseries for the social-policy experts of the New Deal and beyond. Social-work historians who identified with the role of professionals in naming and solving urban ills tended to read the amateurish and feminized settlements out of the history of the profession. In Roy Lubove's *Professional Altruist* (1965), in which professionalism was defined as the rejection of reform enthusiasm and of female styles of reform and female leadership, the settlements were a diversion from the road to professionalism. Jane Addams and her colleagues were altruists, but not "professional altruists."[45] Stanley Wenocur and Michael Reisch signaled their own professionalism by using the bloodless language of market theory to trace the professionalization of social work, or how professionals gained power through "monopolistic control over a specialized competency." They attributed the later decline of the settlements and the rise of casework to the settlements' lack of a clear "service commodity."[46] But for Progressive social-work advocates Harry Specht and Mark Courtney, the history of the social-work profession is one of declension, and the Progressive Era settlements symbolize the profession's lost opportunity to reshape democracy.[47]

MULTIPLE REGRESSIVE? SOCIAL SCIENCE HISTORY

Two conflicting developments shaped narratives about the settlements in the 1970s and 1980s. The first, social science history, emphasized empirical measurement and hypothesis testing and dealt with aggregates rather than the exceptional. Adopting a rhetoric of inclusion, quantitative history promised to "fill in the gaps" and provide a corrective to top-down histories of social-work institutions.[48] The settlements seemed suitable for the application of the methods of quantitative social science history: membership, budgets, attendance, personnel — all could be described statistically.

Some historians produced "case studies" of individual settlement houses. Sharing the rhetoric of generalizability, small-scale, local studies suggested that an authoritative and complete history of the settlements could be constructed from the building blocks of empirically based histories of individual institutions. But these had little cumulative impact on the dominant Hull-House paradigm for a readership that, by the 1980s, was primarily interested in the settlements as women's history and the history of reform movements.[49] Thus, although Allen Davis had gathered statistics about 724 settlement workers for his 1959 study, his efforts found few imitators — perhaps because a statistical portrait of the settlements would have diminished the significance of the exceptional settlements like Hull-House. And an interest in the settlement movement as a "reform crusade" was what drew scholars and readers to the subject in the first place. The result was that the Hull-House paradigm persisted amid new and competing narratives.[50]

THE NEW SOCIAL HISTORY AND
THE HISTORY OF INSTITUTIONS

A second development of the 1970s and 1980s, the new social history, rhetorically evoked history as the "lived experience" of "ordinary people" in the past. More romantic than Marxist, new social history offered a bottom-up perpective that viewed institutions with distrust and portrayed social work as an intrusion into functioning, culturally autonomous ethnic and working-class communities. New social history often relied on the notion of agency to explain how powerless people could nevertheless have some control over their lives and proclaimed the self-sufficiency of the immigrants, blacks, and workers who were its subjects.[51]

From Stephan Thernstrom's recovery of the experience of "the common man" to James Borchert's careful reconstruction of the cultural anthropology of the Washington slum, these new social histories insisted on lower-class groups as actors, not merely as acted upon.[52] Unlike the Progressive master narratives and their modern descendants, which told the story of the settlements from the point of view of the settlement workers, these descriptions told it from the perspective of the clients, previously little heard from in social-work history. They deployed a rhetoric of exposure or (sometimes) of giving voice to the previously silenced; they promised readers a glimpse of a hitherto obscured reality, a journey "below the surface of things" that recalled the appeal of the turn-of-the-century muckraking journalist. The psychological worlds of settlement workers, vividly portrayed by Christopher Lasch and Natalie Davis, were forgotten in narratives about the lives of slum dwellers, the settlements' target population.[53]

This turning away from heroic narratives of the settlements was further accentuated in left-Progressive social histories of the 1980s, which, while sympathetic to settlement workers' reforming intentions, pointed out that as advocates of poor people, the settlements were constrained by their financial dependence on business and other conservative elites.

They also showed how settlements got swept up in early-twentieth-century Americanization campaigns as allies of business and the public schools in the suppression of ethnic differences and how settlements also contributed to the conservative refashioning of family and community, the contours of which became clear in the 1920s.[54]

Emerging social-work institutions, including the settlements (but also the social survey and casework), signaled the rise of new technologies of order rather than a blossoming of upper-class benevolence or middle-class radicalism, according to this view. After all, the settlement impulse was from the first a drive to investigate as well as to serve the poor, and settlement workers' writings created new knowledge about the poor, which became available to policymakers and social experts of all kinds. Robert Woods, in a classic statement of the settlement house's work of investigation that described it as "a shaft sunk through the deepest part of society to examine its lowest strata," summoned up an almost Foucauldian vision of surveillance of the poor by social experts based in settlement houses.[55] These narratives situated the settlements in a metanarrative about the rise of a new, corporatist social order. John McClymer, for example, called settlement workers "the first generation of social engineers," and others showed how goals of efficiency, meliorist welfare capitalism, and 100 percent Americanism obtained the support of social workers, government, and business alike.[56]

SETTLEMENTS IN WOMEN'S HISTORY: SPACE, POWER, COMMUNITY

Women's history, emerging as a field in the 1960s, dramatically transformed the way historians wrote about the settlements. Women had been overlooked as long as histories of Progressivism had focused on formal politics; with broader definitions of the political, women suddenly appeared in large numbers as reformers and professionals.

Feminist scholarship on the settlements at first took the form of biographies that limned the personal and political lives of female settlement residents. Biographies probed their psyches, traced their networks, and recorded their friendships. The emphasis on biography and on the settlements in the years before 1914 was still evident in Mina Carson's sensitive 1990 reprise of the movement.[57]

This focus on the settlement workers rather than on the settlements' work had been prefigured in a widely reprinted essay by Jane Addams that later became a chapter of *Twenty Years*, in which Addams revealingly explained how settlement houses served the needs of their residents. She called the settlements an institutional solution to the "subjective necessity" of college women, doomed by convention "to live out but half the humanity to which we have been born heir and to use but half our faculties."[58] She also portrayed the settlements as a sign of women's evolutionary emergence into a public realm that needed their gender-linked moral vision to cleanse and save it.[59]

Addams's essay had compelling interpretive power to historians who were beginning to trace a women's presuffrage politics from the nineteenth into the twentieth century. In this Progressive narrative, rhetorically represented as an emergence from a private (or domestic) to a public "sphere," the settlements functioned as a halfway house — what Estelle Freedman in her famous essay "Separatism as Strategy" (1979) called a "female public sphere."[60] Taking a different perspective, Martha Vicinus emplotted the settlement houses as a narrative about women's communities organized for useful work — and work, for 1970s feminists as for their Victorian sisters, was "the means out of the garden, out of idleness, out of ignorance, and into wisdom, service, and adventure."[61]

Interest in Hull-House was heightened by new scholarship on lesbian identities and histories, notably essays by Carroll Smith-Rosenberg (1975) and Blanche Cook (1977).[62] Earlier accounts of Jane Addams and her circle had been either dismissive or uncomprehending. For example, Ray Ginger's *Altgeld's America* (1957) had pilloried the women of Hull-House as "virginal" or, worse, "sexually unemployed." Even Allen F. Davis, writing in 1973, had remarked that Jane Addams sacrificed passion to her life's work — without noticing that her long-term relationships with Ellen Starr and later with Mary Rozet Smith grounded her life and work for forty years.[63] Narratives of the emerging subfield of gay and lesbian history took Hull-House as typical of other settlements, which were assumed all to be institutions of woman-identified women, evidence that a women's culture had flourished in the years before the dark night of the twenties with its propaganda of companionate marriage and its compulsory heterosexuality.[64] For example, in their history of sexuality in America, John D'Emilio and Estelle Freedman wrote of the settlements: "Here was a female world of love and passion, different from the same-sex ties of the mid nineteenth century in that its participants were freed from the bonds of matrimony, able to live and work independently of men."[65]

When historians wrote about nineteenth-century women they employed a rhetoric of access — to public space and to power — that produced narratives of emergence. The trope of "separate spheres" was useful in identifying areas of women's autonomy and in arguing for the existence of women's political power before the vote.[66] The "fit" between this rhetoric of access and the Progressive Era settlements allowed women's historians to view Hull-House (and, by extension, other settlements) as a women's space, a center of women's reform networks, a means of access to the public sphere, and an institution that enabled professional women to combine work and family — all vitally important to the rhetoric of women's history and to its modern practitioners. By the 1980s, most feminist scholars rendered the Progressive Era settlements "communities of women reformers," the material expression of sisterhood, its institutional setting, and its facilitator. The settlements fostered a remarkable "women's political culture," which simulaneously advanced reform causes and provided satisfying careers for women reformers.[67]

Women's history created other kinds of narratives about the settlements. Several influential accounts emplotted Hull-House, Henry Street, and other activist settlements as the culmination of women's presuffrage power in a narrative about the gendered origins of the state and state policies.[68] To historians bent on "putting the state back in" to social history, the settlements provided the crucial link between nineteenth-century women's voluntarism and twentieth-century political participation. Often it seemed that Hull-House *was* the settlement movement and all settlements were "like Hull-House."[69] In a history of the settlements that echoed the Bremner-Davis "spearheads for reform" account, with women reformers cast as the main protagonists, Robyn Muncy persuasively sketched what she called a "female dominion in American reform," an institutional nexus extending from Hull-House and Nurses' Settlement to the new schools of social work and into the Children's Bureau in the U.S. Department of Labor. She argued that the settlements enabled Addams, Kelley, Lathrop, the Abbotts, and Wald to become players in state and national reform politics.[70]

PUTTING "RACE" BACK IN

The "Progressive" ("mainstream") settlement histories had paid little attention to African Americans except to note the presence of a handful of black settlement houses. But in 1991, historian of religion Ralph Luker presented a dissenting history of the settlements that traced them to an indigenous source: the missions for freedpeople established in the South after the Civil War. Luker was unable, however, to dislodge the meta-narrative of the settlements focused on the Northeast and Midwest or to disrupt what Jacquelyn Dowd Hall has called "the entrenched habit of making the South a proxy for race, and reducing racism to a regional issue."[71] When black settlements were written about, it was under the rubric "Southern history," "social gospel," or "self-help," and the racial politics of the Northern, "mainstream" settlement movement went unexamined, even though Hall's fine discussion of Methodist churchwomen's settlements in the South in *Revolt against Chivalry* (1978) should have destabilized the racialized construction of settlement history. Instead, new subfields created "comparative and competitive storytelling" rather than new syntheses. For example, when the subfield of black urban history developed, it did so, to begin with, separately from social-work history or women's history, for it generally ignored the role of women.[72] It is hard to escape the conclusion that the terms on which blacks had been included in the unitary narratives of the "mainstream" settlement movement and the ways in which, conversely, settlements figured in histories that identified themselves as African American revealed the profound divisions created by rhetoric and the ideological commitments it prefigures.[73]

Celebrating "agency," narratives of black history reinterpreted the previously unexamined and ambiguous transactions between white social/settlement workers and black clients. Were white settlements helping blacks or oppressing them? If the white settlement leaders of the Progressive Era were racial liberals, why did blacks appear only episodically in their narratives of the movement?[74] And why did black settlements appear only on the periphery of the major modern narratives of the movement from Bremner (1956) and Davis (1967) to Carson (1990)? Before 1980, only Trolander discussed how white-dominated settlements first accommodated to racial segregation, then, after World War II, served black neighorhoods and hired black social workers and administrators.[75]

Why did settlement history resist the incorporation of blacks for so long? Because it reflected the whites-only definition of Progressivism of which it was part. Settlement history was for-whites-only, not because the black settlements were few ("statistically insignificant")— if that were so, then Hull-House, too, would be displaced from the center of the settlement narrative. But the emplotment of the settlement movement as a Progressive Era white-led liberal reform crusade was incompatible with the emplotment of the major narratives of black history, in which the same era had traditionally been inscribed "the nadir."[76] My own work on the racial dynamics of early twentieth-century social work points to the need for historians to distinguish between black settlements that were self-help organizations of blacks and those created as segregated, black-only institutions by whites. Such white-controlled settlements could not easily be included in the metanarrative of African American history, that of racial progress. Instead, they provide evidence for the construction of a quite different story, one about how social-work agencies have functioned as part of the apparatus of white social control of blacks and poor people of all ethnic groups.[77]

"Gendering" black history produces yet other social history narratives. Historians of black women celebrated black-run settlements as the creation of female community builders and service providers.[78] The rhetorical engagement of Elisabeth Lasch-Quinn's *Black Neighbors* (1993) with "interracial work," that is, with the reform work of black and white women, stages the settlements as arenas of racial cooperation in a history of the settlements that includes the South.[79] At the same time, this perspective continues the traditional preoccupation with the impact of the settlements on the consciousness of the service providers rather than on clients and eclipses ways in which agencies may have helped to reproduce structures of racial and economic inequality. Emphasizing race and gender, it loses sight of class and social-policy concerns. Historians' disagreements over the significance of the black settlements depend on the metanarrative that each is telling.

Clearly, including the black settlements in "mainstream" settlement history destabilizes the narrative of a secular, white-led, Progressive reform "crusade." It shifts attention from the nondenominational movement to the religious missionary settlements and from New York, Chicago, Boston, and Philadelphia to the South.

Audience was also important in the construction of these narratives: feminist historians found validation in reading of an earlier group of educated women who both controlled their own space and made it a base from which to fashion a critique of industrial society. But in histories of working-class and poor women, where class and race were axes of oppression as salient as the axis of gender, the settlement houses seemed to demonstrate that elite women's newfound power as professionals and experts could be deployed at the expense of poor women and women of color. Eileen Boris and others exposed the racialized construction of Progressive Era feminism, and Linda Gordon's history of welfare policies demonstrated that "women's power does not always promote all women."[80] For example, the heroic work of the settlements in tackling the problem of unemployment among blacks becomes complex and multivalent once we take into account that their "solutions" included founding agencies to train black women as domestic workers.[81]

Similarly, historians of immigration were disinclined to privilege the narratives of middle-class, native-born, white women (the settlement residents) whose avowed purpose was Americanization. Because the rhetorical engagement of these histories was with ethnic survival, they excluded as irrelevant the good intentions of Anglo female settlement workers, and neither were they concerned to detail how settlements helped the settlement residents' own identity crises. Rivka Lissak's demythologizing study of Hull-House, *Pluralism and Progressives* (1989) is a narrative about ethnic identity and survival that ignores the conventional staging of Hull-House as a "woman's space," instead emplotting the settlement in a narrative about Americanization and ethnicity.[82]

As competing narratives about the settlements multiplied, the rhetorical commitments that shaped these narratives hampered conversation between subfields. For example, "community" in feminist history referred to the collectivist institutions of female settlement residents. The term was crucial to an argument that evoked the friendships of women, empowered by the shared disabilities of sex.[83] But other social historians also continued to use "community" to mean a neighborhood or a self-conscious group, and historians of working-class leisure and culture were beginning to view settlement houses as alien institutions that disrupted working-class communities even while making them objects of study.[84] And so with the word "family." Social historians who had portrayed the family as the (romanticized) functioning institution that enabled immigrants and blacks to create vital communities in the industrializing city were bound to conclude that settlement workers and social investigators of these working-class families were either menacing or ineffective.[85]

CONCLUSION: WHO'S AFRAID OF FRAGMENTATION?
The proliferating subfields of social history have yielded a rich but fragmented history of the settlements. A recent study, Lissak's *Pluralism and Progressives* (1989), illustrates the pitfalls and the benefits of the new pluralist perspectives. Using the omniscient voice of social-scientific history, Lissak sets out to demythologize Hull-House, the paradigmatic

settlement and the source of the most powerful myth about the settle-ment movement. Her rhetoric, one of unmasking, replicates the Pro-gressives' own search for reality. Lissak examined the theories of Ameri-canization held by the Hull-House circle and the settlement's practice of Americanization in order to critique the pretensions of Hull-House lib-eral progressivism to be the cultural pluralism of its day (or ours).[86]

But *Pluralism and Progressives* also shows how increasing special-ization takes us ever further from synthesis. Written by a scholar who identifies with ethnic aspirations, the study challenges the central place of Jane Addams and Hull-House in the movement, but it does so from a perspective different from that of recent work in women's history and for a different purpose. It is an example of scholars working not in con-versation but in parallel yet different rhetorical and ideological tradi-tions. Paradoxically, *Pluralism and Progressives* reinforces rather than challenges *Twenty Years* as the canonical text of the movement, for in trying to debunk Addams's account, Lissak again falls captive to her categories, putting the Chicago story and Addams herself at the center of settlement historiography and determining that settlements that did not resemble Hull-House were not settlements at all. Similarly, Mina Carson's *Settlement Folk* (1990) presents a compelling intellectual por-trait of the movement but retains the focus on Hull-House.[87]

Indeed, perhaps it is the persistence of the Hull-House story, not its fragmentation, that needs explanation. Comforting, comfortable stories such as that of Jane Addams and Hull-House survive alongside the mul-tiple narratives of social history and amid the onslaughts of revisionists, partly because public-history narratives about the settlements were a self-conscious attempt to keep the memory of Hull-House alive. A Hull-House centennial volume, *One Hundred Years at Hull-House* (1990), was designed to appeal to a broader public, a readership that reveres Jane Addams as a famous American "social worker," pacifist, and Nobel Prize winner.[88] Consisting of firsthand accounts of the settlement by ob-servers as various as Beatrice Webb, Edmund Wilson, and Studs Terkel, the volume would surely have met with Jane Addams's approval — her own account, *Twenty Years*, consisted of loosely strung anecdotes of life. In choosing to tell about Hull-House in a series of fragments, the editors replicated Addams's classic account of her encounter with the reality of Chicago's poor.[89]

But they also brought us even further from synthesis. The critics of social history called for narratives that would link local events to national developments and "large processes."[90] But as I have suggested here, the fragmentation of history is more than a matter of historians' not thinking of large processes, nor can it be cured by exhorting them to do so. It is not so much that historians of the same phenomenon come up with different answers as that they begin with different questions. The search for one, synthetic story, a metanarrative, thus appears futile, since alternative narratives may use the same "data" but emplot it in different stories.

Several scholars have been critical of synthetic narratives altogether as somehow undermining the goals of a multicultural America, "an America of endless multiplicity."[91] Others have suggested that in this postmodern era all legitimation becomes "plural, local, and imminent."[92] This is not a position that I hold. A historian aware of the constructedness of alternative narratives can still "listen in" across the boundaries dividing subfields enough to propose a working interpretation, free from the anxious search for synthesis.

A new multivocal narrative of the settlements — a settlement house history for the 1990s — could incorporate insights from many social histories of the last decades. It should take seriously the "subjective necessity" of settlement workers, pay attention to the impact of the settlements on working-class communities, listen to the clients' point of view, and also give weight to the contribution of the settlements to the emerging American welfare state and to twentieth-century corporate capitalism.

In the new settlement histories, the term "settlement" might include many different kinds of cross-class interventions in which turn-of-the-century reformers traversed the city or the land and moved geographically to be among an alien population, many of whom were undergoing their own migrations. These incursions, whether directed to Italian immigrants in Boston, Jewish immigrants in Chicago, Appalachian migrants in Indianapolis, blacks in Alabama, or by field matrons to Native Americans on Indian reservations, resulted in small colonies of self-conscious reformers, or "settlements."[93] Not confining the term "settlement" to member agencies of the National Federation of Settlements (as did most earlier accounts) opens the inquiry to hundreds of Catholic and Protestant missions that were excluded from earlier histories because they combined social work with religious work. And because such missions were more numerous in the South and the Southwest, a broader understanding of the term also breaks the regional barrier that has confined "the settlement movement" for the most part to the urban Midwest and Northeast.

But a new narrative of the settlements also examines other kinds of "crossings." Contemporary observers, some of them hostile, unwittingly gave us clues about how the settlements were sites for a reexamination of gender. One described the settlements as places for "young ladies with weak eyes and young gentlemen with weak chins flittering confused among heterogeneous foreigners."[94] Feminist scholars depicted the settlements as surrogate families for their residents and experiments in cooperative living that were a "creative solution" to the dilemmas of work and living for single professional women.[95] The settlement, from this perspective, was a site for the turn-of-the-century search for new working definitions of womanhood and manhood beyond the Victorian. For women, this meant combining work and love in new ways; for men, it was a search for new definitions of manhood beyond money-making and competition, "where the male prerogative of economic self-assertion did not exhaust the meanings of self-hood."[96] As such, we glimpse the settlements not only as generators of reform but also as sites for the fashioning of modern selves. The settlement house and its history thus return to the role of "public place" in Bender's meaning: a site where meanings are contested and where public culture is remade.[97]

NOTES

I was an NEH fellow at the Workshop on the Rhetoric of Social History, held at the University of Iowa in June 1992. This essay is a revised version of the paper presented there. I acknowledge with sincere thanks the hard work of workshop organizers Jeffrey Cox, Shelton Stromquist, and Linda Kerber, and fellow workshop participants Daud Ali, Florence Boos, Charles Hayford, Barbara Laslett, D. N. Mc-Closkey, Allan Megill, Adriana Méndez, Judy Polumbaum, Randolph Roth, and Stephen Vlastos. Michael Grossberg and anonymous readers for the *American Historical Review* made this essay stronger than it would have been. I would especially like to thank Jackson Lears, Larry Gerber, and Susan Reverby for their thoughtful comments and suggestions, and Guy Beckwith for keeping the conversation going.

1. Thomas A. Bender, "Wholes and Parts: The Need for Synthesis in American History," *Journal of American History* 73, no. 1 (June 1986): 126–27, 129.

This essay does not attempt to explore definitions of the social. For two analyses of the terms "social" and "political," see Nancy Fraser, *Unruly Practices: Power, Discourse, and Gender in Contemporary Social Theory* (Minneapolis: University of Minnesota Press, 1989), p. 160, n. 32 and passim; and Denise Riley, '*Am I That Name?*': *Feminism and the Category of Women in History* (Minneapolis: University of Minnesota Press, 1988).

2. Peter Novick, *That Noble Dream: The "Objectivity Question" and the American Historical Profession* (New York: Cambridge University Press, 1988), pp. 440–45, 584. The final chapter, on the profession since the 1960s, is revealingly titled "There Was No King in Israel"; Linda Gordon, AHR Forum: Comments on *That Noble Dream, American Historical Review* 96, no. 3 (June 1991).

3. Gertrude Himmelfarb, "History of the American Revolution," AHR Forum: Some Reflections on the New History, *American Historical Review* 94, no. 3 (June 1989): 662–63; William Bennett, "To Reclaim a Legacy," *Chronicle of Higher Education* 29, no. 14 (November 28, 1984): 16–21.

4. The most recent of several excellent works on history and memory is Genevieve Fabre and Robert O'Meally, eds., *History and Memory in African-American Culture* (New York: Oxford University Press, 1994). See also Michael Kammen, *Mystic Chords of Memory: The Transformation of Tradition in American Culture* (New York: Knopf, 1991); John Bodnar, *Remaking America: Public Memory, Commemoration, and Patriotism in the Twentieth Century* (Princeton: Princeton University Press, 1992); S. P. Benson, Stephen Brier, and Richard Rosenzweig, eds., *Presenting the Past: Essays on History and the Public* (Philadelphia: Temple University Press, 1986); and the special issue, David Thelen, ed., "Memory and American History," *Journal of American History* 75 (March 1989): 1117–1201.

5. Peter N. Stearns, "Toward a Wider Vision: Trends in Social History," in Michael Kammen, ed., *The Past before Us: Contemporary Historical Writing in the United States* (Ithaca: Cornell University Press, 1980), pp. 221–22; Olivier Zunz, introduction to *Reliving the Past: The Worlds of Social History*, ed. Olivier Zunz (Chapel Hill: University of North Carolina Press, 1985), p. 8. Social history was long preoccupied with questions about mobility. See Stephan Thernstrom, "Notes on the Historical Study of Social Mobility," *Comparative Studies in History and Theory* 10 (January 1968): 162–72. Others analyzed class formation; see Michael B. Katz, *The Social Organization of Early Industrial Capitalism* (Cambridge: Harvard University Press, 1982), and Mary P. Ryan, *Cradle of the Middle Class: The Family in Oneida County, New York, 1790–1865* (New York: Cambridge University Press, 1981). Some community studies paid attention to changing modes of work and meanings of community; see Daniel Walkowitz, *Worker City, Company Town: Iron and Cotton-Worker Protest in Troy and Cohoes, New York, 1855–84* (Urbana: University of Illinois Press, 1978). A useful summary is Kathleen Neils Conzen, "Community Studies, Urban History, and American Local History," in Kammen, *The Past before Us*, pp. 270–91. Alice Kessler-Harris summarizes and synthesizes recent social history writing in Eric Foner, ed., *The New American History* (American Historical Association; Philadelphia: Temple University Press, 1990), pp. 163–84.

6. Novick, *That Noble Dream*, pp. 440–45; "The Objectivity Question and the Future of the Historical Profession," AHR Forum: Peter Novick's *That Noble Dream, American Historical Review* 96, no. 3 (June 1991): 675–708. And more recently, Bonnie G. Smith, "Gender and the Practices of Scientific History: The Seminar and Archival Research in the Nineteenth Century," *American Historical Review* 100 (October 1995): 1150–76.

7. Bender, "Wholes and Parts," p. 129. For reactions to Bender's essay, see David

Thelen, Nell Irvin Painter, Richard Wightman Fox, Roy Rosenzweig, and Thomas Bender, "A Round Table: Synthesis in American History," *Journal of American History* 74, no. 1 (June 1987): 107–30; Eric H. Monkkonen, "The Dangers of Synthesis," *American Historical Review* 91 (December 1986): 1146–57. See also Thomas Bender, "'Venturesome and Cautious': American History in the 1990s," *Journal of American History* 81, no. 3 (December 1994): 992–1003.

8. One scholar confessed to "a feeling of intense despondency" at what he called "overproduction" by historians; Frank R. Ankersmit, "Historiography and Postmodernism," *History and Theory* 28 (1989): 139–40. For similar complaints, see Gertrude Himmelfarb, "Denigrating the Rule of Reason: The New History Goes 'Bottom-Up,'" *Harper's*, April 1987, pp. 84–90. A more balanced view is Linda Kerber, "Diversity and the Transformation of American Studies," *American Quarterly* 41, no. 3 (September 1989): 415–31. See also Elizabeth Fox-Genovese, "The Great Tradition and Its Orphans," in Taylor Littleton, ed., *Rights of Memory* (University: University of Alabama Press, 1986), pp. 185–213, and "Between Individualism and Fragmentation: American Culture and the New Literary Studies of Race and Gender," *American Quarterly* 42, no. 1 (March 1990): 7–34.

9. Allan Megill and D. N. McCloskey, "The Rhetoric of History," in John S. Nelson, Allan Megill, and D. N. McCloskey, eds., *The Rhetoric of the Human Sciences* (Madison: University of Wisconsin Press, 1987), p. 223. Megill wittily uses the term "immaculate perception" to refer to the assumption that doing research is epistemologically unproblematic; Allan Megill, "Recounting the Past: 'Description,' Explanation, and Narrative in Historiography," *American Historical Review* 94, no. 3 (June 1989): 627–53.

10. Clarence E. Walker, *Deromanticizing Black History: Critical Essays and Reappraisals* (Knoxville: University of Tennessee Press, 1991); Darlene Clark Hine, ed., *The State of Afro-American History, Past, Present, and Future* (Baton Rouge: Louisiana State University Press, 1986); August Meier and Elliott Rudwick, *Black History and the Historical Profession, 1915–1980* (Urbana: University of Illinois Press, 1986); Thomas C. Holt, "African-American History," in Foner, *New American History*, pp. 211–32. On immigrant and ethnic history, see Ewa Morawska, "The Sociology and Historiography of Immigration," in Virginia Yans McLaughlin, ed., *Immigration Reconsidered: History, Sociology, Politics* (New York: Oxford University Press, 1990), pp. 187–240; and Donna Gabaccia, "American Immigrant Women: A Review Essay," *Journal of American Ethnic History* 8 (Spring 1989): 127–33.

Scholars are exploring the question of how female historians have constructed the historical subject and themselves in relation to it. See Joan Scott, "American Women Historians, 1884–1984," in *Gender and the Politics of History* (New York: Columbia University Press, 1988), pp. 178–98; Nina Baym, *American Women Writers and the Work of History, 1790–1860* (New Brunswick, N.J.: Rutgers University Press, 1995).

11. For "comparative and competitive storytelling," see Jeffrey Cox and Shelton Stromquist, introduction" to this volume. For "communities of interpretation," see Thomas L. Haskell, *The Authority of Experts: Studies in History and Theory* (Bloomington: Indiana University Press, 1984).

12. The most famous are Jane Addams, *Twenty Years at Hull-House* (New York: Macmillan, 1910) and *Second Twenty Years at Hull-House* (New York: Macmillan, 1930), Graham Taylor, *Pioneering on Social Frontiers* (Chicago: University of Chicago Press, 1930) and *Chicago Commons through Forty Years* (Chicago: Chicago Commons Association, 1936); Lillian Wald, *The House on Henry Street* (New York: Henry Holt, 1915) and *Windows on Henry Street* (Boston: Little, Brown, 1934); Mary K. Simkhovitch, *Neighborhood: My Story of Greenwich House* (New York: W. W. Norton, 1938); Alice Hamilton, *Exploring the Dangerous Trades* (Boston: Little, Brown, 1943). Biographies and autobiographies written by American settlement workers are usefully listed in Allen F. Davis, *Spearheads for Reform: The Social Settlements, and the Progressive Movement, 1890–1914* (New York: Oxford University Press, 1967), pp. 213–14. For the Christian Socialist roots of the English settlements, see Robert Woods, *English Social Movements* (New York: Scribner's, 1897), and Mina Carson, *Settlement Folk: Social Thought and the American Settlement Movement, 1885–1930* (Chicago: University of Chicago Press, 1990).

13. Clarke A. Chambers called this the settlement workers' "existential gesture" (keynote address presented at the symposium "Understanding the Hull-House Legacy: Biography and Autobiography," Rockford College, Rockford, Illinois, October 20–22, 1989).

14. Vida Scudder, *On Journey* (New York: E. P. Dutton, 1938), pp. 139–40. See also Jackson Lears, *No Place of Grace: Antimodernism and the Transformation of American Culture, 1880–1920* (New York: Pantheon, 1981; reprint, Chicago: University of Chicago Press, 1994), pp. 209–15.

15. Wald, *The House on Henry Street*, pp. 1–7.

16. Addams, *Twenty Years*, p. 2. Her stance of naïveté was particularly misleading since she had spent eight years in intensive studies in Europe and America and came to Halstead Street with a great deal of cultural and intellectual baggage.

17. Kathryn Kish Sklar's *Florence Kelley and the Nation's Work: The Rise of Women's Political Culture* (New Haven: Yale University Press, 1995) provides a great deal of new information and raises important new questions about Florence Kelley. See also *The Autobiography of Florence Kelley: Notes of Sixty Years*, edited and with an introduction by Kathryn Kish Sklar (Chicago: Charles H. Kerr, 1986). See also Rebecca Sherrick, "Their Fathers' Daughters: The Autobiographies of Jane Addams and Florence Kelley," *American Studies* 27 (Spring 1986): 39–53.

18. Victoria Bissell Brown, introduction to Jane Addams, "Why Women Should Vote," in Marjorie Spruill Wheeler, ed., *One Woman, One Vote: Rediscovering the Woman Suffrage Movement* (Troutville, Ore.: NewSage Press, 1995), pp. 182–95. More critical of Jane Addams is Harriet Hyman Alonso, "Nobel Peace Laureates: Jane Addams and Emily Greene Balch," *Journal of Women's History* 7 (Summer 1995): 6–26; Rivka Lissak, *Pluralism and Progressives: Hull House and the New Immigrants* (Chicago: University of Chicago Press, 1989).

19. Allen F. Davis, *American Heroine: The Life and Legend of Jane Addams* (New York: Oxford University Press, 1973); Jill Conway, "Jane Addams, An American Heroine," in Robert J. Lifton, ed., *The Woman in America* (Boston: Houghton Mifflin, 1964), pp. 247–66. James Hurt, editor of a new edition of *Twenty Years,*

comments, "There would have been no Jane Addams if she had not created Hull House in an extraordinary act of among other things self-making"; James Hurt, introduction to *Twenty Years at Hull-House* (Urbana: University of Illinois Press, 1990), p. xi.

20. Alan Mayne, *The Imagined Slum: Newspaper Representation in Three Cities, 1870–1914* (Leicester: Leicester University Press, 1993). See also William Dean Howells, *A Hazard of New Fortunes* (New York: Harper and Brothers, 1890), pp. 241–44, in which the middle-class hero views working-class urban life "from the Elevated."

Excellent recent work on this topic includes Mark Pittenger, "A World of Difference: Constructing the 'Underclass' in Progressive America," *American Quarterly* 49, no. 1 (March 1997): 26–65; Maurine W. Greenwald, "Visualizing Pittsburgh in the 1900s: Art and Photography in the Service of Social Reform," in Maurine Greenwald and Margo Anderson, eds., *Pittsburgh Surveyed: Social Science and Social Reform in the Early Twentieth Century* (Pittsburgh: University of Pittsburgh Press, 1996), pp. 124–52.

21. The "devil baby" incident is described in *Second Twenty Years*, pp. 49–79.

22. In a typical passage, Addams claims that the social worker, "living in the midst of divers groups whose history, language, and customs show the tremendous variability of human nature . . . can find clues to new life patterns" (*Second Twenty Years*, pp. 47–48).

23. "That objectifying elite gaze" (Fox-Genovese, "Between Individualism and Fragmentation," p. 24). See also Kathryn Kish Sklar, *The Social Survey in Historical Perspective, 1880–1940* (New York: Cambridge University Press, 1991). For an example of reform writing about the slums that conflates moral contagion with public-health danger, see *Twenty Years*, p. 172.

24. Taylor, *Pioneering on Social Frontiers*; Hamilton, *Exploring the Dangerous Trades*. "Missionaries in the heart of Africa" is quoted in Louise G. Wade, *Graham Taylor: Pioneer for Social Justice* (Chicago: University of Chicago Press, 1964), p. 119.

25. "The neighborhood evoked an imagined feudal past of social harmony and well-understood obligations"; Ruth Crocker, *Social Work and Social Order: The Settlement Movement in Two Industrial Cities, 1889–1930* (Urbana: University of Illinois Press, 1992), p. 17. See also Stanton A. Coit, "The Neighborhood Guild Defined," in Lorene M. Pacey, ed., *Readings in the Development of Settlement Work* (New York: Association Press, 1950), pp. 21–28; Patricia Mooney Melvin, *Urban Definition and Neighborhood Organization, 1880–1920* (Lexington: University Press of Kentucky, 1987), pp. 11–26; Jean Quandt, *From the Small Town to the Great Community: The Social Thought of Progressive Intellectuals* (New Brunswick, N.J.: Rutgers University Press, 1970); Kenneth Scherzer, *The Unbounded Community: Neighborhood Life and Social Structure in New York City, 1830–1875* (Durham: Duke University Press, 1992). Of course, "restoring order" took different forms in different political contexts. In some of the Indiana settlement narratives it involved drawing racial lines more sharply, in others it required proselytizing immigrants, in all it involved uplift and Americanization. See Crocker, *Social Work and Social Order*.

26. Wald, *The House on Henry Street*; Simkhovitch, *Neighborhood*.

27. On the fate of the women's movement after 1920, see Nancy Cott, *Grounding of Modern Feminism* (New Haven: Yale University Press, 1987).

28. For Jane Addams's self-representation, see Davis, *American Heroine*.

29. Kelley translated Friedrich Engels, *The Condition of the Working Class in England* (New York: John W. Lovell, 1887). She opposed American entry into World War I and in the 1920s continued to advocate an extension of the welfare state in conservative times. Critics alternately denounced Kelley and Addams as Bolsheviks and lampooned them as ridiculous old maids. See Clarke A. Chambers, *Seedtime of Reform: American Social Service and Social Action* (Ann Arbor: University of Michigan Press, 1967); Kathryn Kish Sklar, "Coming to Terms with Florence Kelley," in Sara Alpern et al, eds., *The Challenge of Feminist Biography: Writing the Lives of Modern American Women* (Urbana: University of Illinois Press, 1992).

30. Robert H. Bremner, *From the Depths: The Discovery of Poverty in America* (New York: New York University Press, 1956), pp. xii–xiii. Contemporary with Bremner, other significant "discoveries of poverty" were Michael Harrington, *The Other America: Poverty in the United States* (New York: Macmillan, 1962), and Harry Caudill, *Night Comes to the Cumberlands: A Biography of a Depressed Area* (Boston: Little, Brown, 1963).

31. Bremner, *From the Depths*, pp. 60–66.

32. Davis, *Spearheads for Reform*, p. xii; Allen F. Davis, "Spearheads for Reform: The Social Settlements and the Progressive Movement, 1890–1914" (Ph.D. diss., University of Wisconsin, 1959).

33. Former settlement residents who became prominent New Dealers included Frances Perkins, Harry Hopkins, Henry Morgenthau, Jr., and Gerald Swope; Davis, *Spearheads for Reform*, pp. 242–45; Chambers, *Seedtime of Reform*.

34. Richard Wade, foreword to Davis, *Spearheads for Reform*, p. ix. See also Staughton Lynd, "Jane Addams and the Radical Impulse," *Commentary* 32 (July 1961): 54–59. Another link between the Progressive Era settlements and the War on Poverty is explored in Michael J. Austin and Neil Betten, "Intellectual Origins of Community Organizing, 1920–1939," *Social Service Review* 51 (March 1977): 155–70.

35. Christopher Lasch, *The New Radicalism in America* (New York: Knopf, 1965), pp. 3–37.

36. Christopher Lasch, introduction to Christopher Lasch, ed., *The Social Thought of Jane Addams* (Indianapolis: Bobbs-Merrill, 1965), p. xxvi; Jane Addams, "The Subjective Necessity for Social Settlements," in Jane Addams et al., *Philanthropy and Social Progress* (New York: Thomas Y. Crowell, 1893), pp. 1–26.

37. These "other settlements" were analyzed in my study of settlements of Gary and Indianapolis, Indiana, *Social Work and Social Order*. See also Raymond A. Mohl and Neil Betten, "Paternalism and Pluralism: Immigrants and Social Welfare in Gary, Indiana, 1906–1940," *American Studies* 15 (Spring 1974): 5–30; Howard J. Karger, *Sentinels of Order: A Study of Social Control and the Minneapolis Settlement House Movement, 1915–1950* (Lanham, Md.: University Press of America, 1987).

38. For example, although there were by one estimate 2,500 Catholic settlements by 1915, they were not included in Davis's *Spearheads for Reform*, on the grounds that

"these were more like missions than settlement houses and contributed little to reform" (pp. 14–15). For the history of one Catholic settlement house in Gary, Indiana, that became a force in postwar antiradicalism, see Crocker, *Social Work and Social Order*, pp. 111–32.

Historian Nancy Robertson has noted the tendency to associate religious institutions with "being backward" and the secular with the "progressive." Her work on
the YWCA suggests "that those women's groups that were religiously identified were
more likely to address race issues and take on interracial concerns"; Robertson, personal communication to the author.

39. Don S. Kirschner, "The Ambiguous Legacy: Social Justice and Social Control
in the Progressive Era," *Historical Reflections* 2 (Summer 1975): 69–88; Daniel
Rodgers, "In Search of Progressivism," *Reviews in American History* 10 (1982):
113–32. Liberal-Progressive accounts in addition to Davis, *Spearheads for Reform*,
are Louise G. Wade, *Graham Taylor: Pioneer for Social Justice* (Chicago: University
of Chicago Press, 1964); Judith Ann Trolander, *Settlement Houses and the Great Depression* (Detroit: Wayne State University Press, 1975) and *Professionalism and Social
Change: From the Settlement House Movement to Neighborhood Centers, 1886 to the
Present* (New York: Columbia University Press, 1987). See also Daniel Levine, *Jane
Addams and the Liberal Tradition* (Madison: University of Wisconsin Press, 1971).

Typical of the tendency to let settlement workers "off the hook" while being
critical of other Progressives was John Higham's remark in *Strangers in the Land:
Patterns of American Nativism, 1860–1925* (New York: Atheneum, 1965) that "the
settlement workers did more to sustain the immigrant's respect for his own culture
than to urge him forward into the new one" (p. 236). See also Michael B. Katz,
Poverty and Policy in American History (New York: Academic Press, 1983), p. 201.

40. Clarke A. Chambers, more than anyone, created a scholarly history of social
work in America. His perspective is informed by a commitment to social work as
well as to historical scholarship, and his readership is in both fields. A valuable
overview is his article, "Toward a Definition of Welfare History," *Journal of American History* 73 (September 1986): 407–33. See also Walter I. Trattner, *From Poor Law
to Welfare State: A History of Social Welfare in America*, 5th ed. (New York: Free
Press, 1994), pp. 163–92; John J. Ehrenreich, *The Altruistic Imagination: A History of
Social Work and Social Policy in the United States* (Ithaca: Cornell University Press,
1985); James S. Leiby, *A History of Social Welfare and Social Work in the United States*
(New York: Columbia University Press, 1978); Leslie Leighninger, *Social Work:
Search for Identity* (Westport, Conn.: Greenwood Press, 1987); Esther Lucile Brown,
Social Work as a Profession (New York: Russell Sage Foundation, 1936); Stanley
Wenocur and Michael Reisch, *From Charity to Enterprise: The Development of Ameri-
can Social Work in a Market Economy* (Urbana: University of Illinois Press, 1989).

41. In the world of the Progressive Era settlements, social science still served reform ends, professionalization was incomplete, and sympathy for the poor and a capacity for self-sacrifice (qualities ascribed as natural to women) were still assumed
to be the major qualifications for the social worker. See Regina Kunzel, "The Professionalization of Benevolence: Evangelicals and Social Workers in the Florence
Crittenton Homes, 1915–1945," *Journal of Social History* 22, no. 1 (Fall 1988): 21–43,

and *Fallen Women, Problem Girls: Unmarried Mothers and the Professionalization of Benevolence, 1890–1945* (New Haven: Yale University Press, 1993). The story is carried forward into the 1920s in Daniel J. Walkowitz, "The Making of a Feminine Professional Identity: Social Workers in the 1920s," *American Historical Review* 95, no. 4 (October 1990): 1051–75. See also Lela Costin, *Two Sisters for Social Justice: The Biography of Grace and Edith Abbott* (Urbana: University of Illinois Press, 1983).

42. Trolander, preface to *Professionalism and Social Change*.

43. Ibid., especially pp. 93–95. My own work attempts to place the settlements within the history of race relations in the North before 1930; see *Social Work and Social Order*, chapters 3 and 7. Also important was Howard Karger, *The Sentinels of Order: A Study of Social Control and the Minneapolis Settlement House Movement, 1915–1950* (Lanham, Md.: University Press of America, 1987).

44. This is often a problem of lack of evidence rather than unwillingness to present clients as actors. While most social work historians agree that it would be desirable to document client reactions, few research designs make this possible. Notable exceptions are Linda Gordon, *Heroes of Their Own Lives: The Politics and History of Family Violence, Boston, 1880–1960* (New York: Viking Penguin, 1988); Michael B. Katz, "Families and Welfare: A Philadelphia Case," in *Poverty and Policy in American History* (New York: Academic Press, 1982), pp. 17–56; and (though the setting is England) Ellen Ross, *Love and Toil: Motherhood in Outcast London* (New York: Oxford University Press, 1993). See also Peter Mandler, "Poverty and Charity in the Nineteenth-Century Metropolis: An Introduction," in Mandler, ed., *The Uses of Charity* (Philadelphia: University of Pennsylvania Press, 1990), pp. 1–37.

45. Roy Lubove, *The Professional Altruist: The Emergence of Social Work as a Career* (Pittsburgh: University of Pittsburgh Press, 1965). Lubove identifies the Charity Organization Society (COS) movement, not the settlements, as the ancestor of modern social work. Richard Hofstadter, *The Age of Reform: From Bryan to F.D.R.* (New York: Vintage Books, 1955), was condescending toward moralizing Progressives, though since he universalized the Progressive as "he," Hofstadter was apparently unable to see how gender might have made a difference to his account (p. 211). See also Arthur S. Link and Richard L. McCormick, *Progressivism* (Arlington Heights, Ill.: Harlan Davidson, 1983). These works all elide the class and gender identities of social workers and pay little or no attention to gender as a category of analysis. See also Barbara Laslett's essay in this volume.

46. Wenocur and Reisch, *From Charity to Enterprise*, pp. ix, 12.

47. Harry Specht and Mark Courtney, *Unfaithful Angels: How Social Work Has Abandoned Its Mission* (New York: Free Press, 1994).

48. For a statement of the promise of social-scientific history at an early, optimistic phase, see Robert P. Swierenga, ed., *Quantification in American History: Theory and Research* (New York: Atheneum, 1970), especially William Aydelotte, "Quantification in History," and Lee Benson, "Quantification, Scientific History, and Scholarly Innovation." Milestones in the development of quantitative history as a subfield were the establishment of the Inter-University Consortium on Political Research (1962), the *Historical Methods Newsletter*, the Social Science History Association, and its journal, *Social Science History*.

Declining interest in empiricist history may have been the reason why the American Historical Association's 1990 survey of historical writing in the United States had no entry on social science history; the 1980 survey *The Past before Us* included J. Morgan Kousser's essay "Quantitative Social Scientific History." See Foner, *The New American History*, pp. 163–84. See also Eric Monkonnen, "Lessons of Social Science History," *Social Science History* 18, no. 2 (Summer 1994): 161–68.

49. Examples are Judith Ann Trolander, "Twenty Years at Hiram House," *Ohio History* 78 (Winter 1969): 25–37; Ruth Crocker, "Christamore: An Indiana Settlement House from Private Dream to Social Agency," *Indiana Magazine of History* 88 (June 1987): 113–40; Ronald J. Butera, "A Settlement House and the Urban Challenge: Kingsley House in Pittsburgh, Pennsylvania, 1893–1920," *Western Pennsylvania Historical Magazine* 66 (January 1983): 25–47; Jon A. Peterson, "From Social Settlement to Social Agency: Settlement Work in Columbus, Ohio, 1898–1958," *Social Service Review* 59 (1965): 191–208. For the rhetoric of generalizability, see Megill, "Recounting the Past."

50. Davis, "Spearheads for Reform." An exception is Rivka Lissak, who effectively marshals quantitative data in her study of the Hull-House neighborhood; *Lissak, Pluralism and Progressives*, pp. 79–138.

51. James Henretta, "Social History as Lived and Written," AHR Forum, *American Historical Review* 84 (December 1979): 1293–1330. For a critical view, see Elizabeth Fox-Genovese, "The Political Crisis of Social History," in Eugene Genovese and Elizabeth Fox-Genovese, *Fruits of Merchant Capital: Slavery and Bourgeois Property in the Rise and Expansion of Capitalism* (New York: Oxford University Press, 1983), pp. 179–212. More recently, Christopher Shannon, in "A World Made Safe for Differences: Ruth Benedict's *The Chrysanthemum and the Sword*," *American Quarterly* 47, no. 4 (December 1995), argues that scholarly preoccupation with "agency" impoverishes our understanding of power relationships (p. 676).

52. Stephan Thernstrom, *The Other Bostonians: Poverty and Progress in the American Metropolis, 1870–1930* (Cambridge: Harvard University Press, 1973); James Borchert, *Alley Life in Washington: Family, Community, Religion, and Folklife in the City, 1850–1970* (Urbana: University of Illinois Press, 1980).

53. Rivka Lissak, "Myth and Reality: The Pattern of Relationship between the Hull House Circle and the 'New Immigrants' on Chicago's West Side, 1890–1919," *Journal of American Ethnic History* 2 (Spring 1983): 21–50. Michael B. Katz, *Poverty and Policy in American History* (New York: Academic Press, 1983), pp. 17–54, focuses on the poor as they deal with private charities. Ross, *Love and Toil*, is sensitive to the voices of poor mothers and also to the charity providers.

In such social history, a critic recently noted, "the rich, the powerful, the learned appear only as the given world with which the modest must deal"; Arthur Quinn, "Lives of the Modest," review of *Women on the Margins*, by Natalie Davis, *New York Times Book Review*, December 10, 1995, p. 18.

54. "Among the life members of Kingsley House in Pittsburgh (those who had contributed $1,000 or more by 1911), were three Carnegies, four Fricks, and five Mellons"; John F. McClymer, *War and Welfare: Social Engineering in America, 1890–*

1920 (Westport, Conn.: Greenwood Press, 1980), p. 22. The financial dependence of the Pittsburgh settlements on the city's business leaders "guaranteed their immunity from radicalism" (p. 23). I found the same situation in Gary, Indiana; Crocker, *Social Work and Social Order*.

55. Robert A. Woods, "The University Settlement Idea," in Addams et al., *Philanthropy and Social Progress*. See also Herman F. Hegner, "The Scientific Value of the Social Settlement," *American Journal of Sociology* 3 (September 1897): 171–82. On the tie-in between social settlements and social science, see Jo Anne Deegan, *Jane Addams and the Men of the Chicago School, 1892–1918* (New Brunswick, N.J.: Transaction Books, 1988); Crocker, *Social Work and Social Order*, pp. 20–28; Davis, *Spearheads for Reform*, pp. 30, 65–68; Karger, *Sentinels of Order*; and Kirshner, "The Ambiguous Legacy."

Much more sympathetic to the purposes of social-scientific investigation is Kathryn Kish Sklar, "Hull-House Maps and Papers: Social Science as Women's Work in the 1890s," in Martin Bulmer, Kevin Bales, and Kathryn Fish Sklar, eds., *The Social Survey in Historical Perspective, 1880–1940* (New York: Cambridge University Press, 1991), pp. 111–47.

56. "First generation of social engineers"; McClymer, *War and Welfare*, p. 217. Magali Sarfatti Larson, "The Production of Expertise and the Constitution of Expert Power," in Thomas Haskell, ed., *The Authority of Experts: Studies in History and Theory* (Bloomington: Indiana University Press, 1984), pp. 28–82. Earlier critics of social welfare spoke in terms of social control. See Frances Fox Piven and Richard Cloward, *Regulating the Poor: The Functions of Public Welfare* (New York: Pantheon, 1971), a study that was very influential. For its application to social work history, see Walter Trattner, *Social Welfare or Social Control? Some Historical Reflections on Regulating the Poor* (Knoxville: University of Tennessee Press, 1983).

57. Carson, *Settlement Folk*. Biographies include Davis, *American Heroine*; Sklar, *Florence Kelley and the Nation's Work*; Doris Groschen Daniels, *Always a Sister: The Biography of Lillian Wald* (New York: Feminist Press at CUNY, 1989); Lela Costin, *Two Sisters for Social Justice: A Biography of Grace and Edith Abbott* (Urbana: University of Illinois Press, 1983); Barbara Sicherman, *Alice Hamilton: A Life in Letters* (Cambridge: Harvard University Press, 1984); Ellen Fitzpatrick, *Endless Crusade: Women Social Scientists and Progressive Reform* (New York: Oxford University Press, 1990). See also Mina Carson, "Agnes Hamilton of Fort Wayne: The Education of a Christian Settlement Worker," *Indiana Magazine of History* 80 (March 1984): 1–34; Barbara Sicherman, "Working It Out: Gender, Profession, and Reform in the Career of Alice Hamilton," in Noralee Frankel and Nancy S. Dye, eds., *Gender, Class, Race, and Reform in the Progressive Era* (Lexington: University Press of Kentucky, 1991): 127–47.

58. Addams, "Subjective Necessity," pp. 1–26. This famous piece was originally a speech given to the Ethical Culture Society, Plymouth, Massachusetts, in 1892. It was subsequently published in *Philanthropy and Social Progress* (New York: Crowell, 1893) and later included as a chapter in *Twenty Years at Hull-House* (New York: Macmillan, 1910). See also Jane Addams, "The College Woman and the Family

Claim," *Commons* 3 (September 5, 1898), pp. 3–5; Joyce Antler, "'After College, What?': New Graduates and the Family Claim," *American Quarterly* 32 (Fall 1980): 409–34. In a companion essay, "The Objective Necessity for Social Settlements," Addams enumerated the social and industrial problems that the settlements attempted to solve.

59. There is a large literature on Progressive Era women's activism. Female reformers made the most gains in areas such as legislative protection of women, workers, and infant and child health, though this was partly as a result of an abdication of interest in these areas by male reformers. See Robyn Muncy, *Creating a Female Dominion in American Reform, 1890–1935* (New York: Oxford University Press, 1991); Nancy Cott, *The Grounding of Modern Feminism* (New Haven: Yale University Press, 1987), and her "What's in a Name? The Limits of Social Feminism, or, Expanding the Vocabulary of Women's History," *Journal of American History* 76 (December 1989): 809–29.

60. Estelle Freedman, "Separatism as Strategy: Female Institution Building and American Feminism, 1870–1930," *Feminist Studies* 5, no. 3 (Fall 1979): 512–29. John P. Rousmaniere anticipated this line of interpretation with his early essay "Cultural Hybrid in the Slums: The College Woman and the Settlement House, 1889–1894," *American Quarterly* 22 (Spring 1970): 45–66. See also Jill Kerr Conway, "Women Reformers and American Culture, 1870–1930," *Journal of Social History* 5 (Winter 1971–1972): 164–77; Antler, "After College, What?" pp. 409–32.

For "narratives of emergence," see Linda Kerber, "Separate Spheres, Female Worlds, Woman's Place: The Rhetoric of Women's History," *Journal of American History* 75, no. 1 (June 1988); Mary P. Ryan, *Women in Public: From Banners to Ballots* (Baltimore: Johns Hopkins University Press, 1981); Ruth Bordin, *Women and Temperance: The Quest for Power and Liberty* (Philadelphia: Temple University Press, 1981).

61. Martha Vicinus, *Independent Women: Work and Community for Single Women, 1850–1920* (London: Virago Press, 1985), p. 1. Her work, though focused on England, was influential in helping scholars reconceptualize the American scene. For example, Kathryn Kish Sklar titles her chapter on Hull-House "A Colony of Efficient and Intelligent Women" (*Florence Kelley and the Nation's Work*, p. 171). The classic statement that paid work outside the home would liberate (middle-class, white) women was of course from Betty Friedan, *The Feminine Mystique* (New York: Norton, 1963).

62. Carroll Smith-Rosenberg, "The Female World of Love and Ritual: Relations between Women in Nineteenth-Century America," *Signs* 1 (Autumn 1975): 1–30; Blanche Wiesen Cook, "Female Support Networks and Political Activism: Lillian Wald, Crystal Eastman, Emma Goldman," *Chrysalis* 3 (1977): 43–62; and "Women Alone Stir My Imagination: Lesbianism and the Cultural Tradition," *Signs* 4 (Summer 1979): 718–39.

63. Davis, *American Heroine*, pp. 12–13, 29–30, and passim. Mary Rozet Smith also provided substantial funding for the settlement between 1893 and 1934, including more than $116,000 between 1906 and 1934 alone. The financial basis of this relationship is better documented than its emotional side. See Kathryn Kish Sklar,

"Who Funded Hull House?" in Kathleen McCarthy, ed., *Lady Bountiful Revisited: Women, Philanthropy, and Power* (New Brunswick, N.J.: Rutgers University Press, 1990), pp. 94–115.

64. Lillian Faderman, *Odd Girls and Twilight Lovers: A History of Lesbian Life in Twentieth-Century America* (New York: Columbia University Press, 1991), p. 13. On companionate marriage, see Elaine Tyler May, *Great Expectations: Marriage and Divorce in Post-Victorian America* (Chicago: University of Chicago Press, 1980). For single women at the turn of the century, see Joanne Meyerowitz, *Women Adrift: Independent Wage Earners in Chicago, 1880–1930* (Chicago: University of Chicago Press, 1988).

For a searching and critical analysis of the contradictory uses by women (and women's history) of the concept of women's culture, see Elizabeth Fox-Genovese, *Feminism without Illusions: A Critique of Individualism* (Chapel Hill: University of North Carolina Press, 1991), and, from a different perspective, Lise Vogel, "Telling Tales: Historians of Our Own Lives," *Journal of Women's History* 2, no. 3 (Winter 1991): 88–101.

65. John D'Emilio and Estelle Freedman, *Intimate Matters: A History of Sexuality in America* (New York: Harper and Row, 1988), pp. 190–91; Faderman, *Odd Girls and Twilight Lovers*, pp. 24–26; Laura Engelstein, "What's in a Name?" review of *Odd Girls and Twilight Lovers*, by Lillian Faderman, *Radical History Review* 54 (1992): 153–57.

66. For "politics before the vote," see Paula Baker, "The Domestication of Politics: Women and American Political Society, 1780–1920," *American Historical Review* 89 (June 1984): 620–47. Maureen A. Flanagan, "Gender and Urban Political Reform: The City Club and the Woman's City Club of Chicago in the Progressive Era," *American Historical Review* 95, no. 4 (October 1990), shows how ambitious was the claim of Progressive Era women to be "municipal housekeepers." These white middle-class clubwomen "were asserting their right to involve themselves in every decision made by the Chicago city government, even to restructure that government" (p. 1050). See also Kathryn Kish Sklar, "The Historical Foundations of Women's Power in the Creation of the American Welfare State, 1830–1930," in Seth Koven and Sonya Michel, eds., *Mothers of a New World: Maternalist Politics and the Origins of Welfare States* (New York: Routledge, 1993); Sara Monoson, "The Lady and the Tiger: Women's Electoral Activism in New York City before the Suffrage," *Journal of Women's History* 2, no. 2 (Fall 1990): 100–135.

67. Essays by Carroll Smith-Rosenberg and Ellen Carol Du Bois in "Politics and Culture in Women's History: A Symposium," *Feminist Studies* 6, no. 1 (Spring 1980): 26–57. Helen Horowitz added a material culture emphasis to the analysis of space with her "Hull House as Women's Space," *Chicago History* 12 (Winter 1983–1984): 39–53. See also Dolores Hayden, *The Grand Domestic Revolution: A History of Feminist Designs for American Homes, Neighborhoods, and Cities* (Cambridge: MIT Press, 1981).

By the 1980s, scholars were rejecting the earlier "public/private" schema as an ideological construction that tended only to reify the separatism that it described. Linda Kerber and others urged a move away from metaphors of space to other descriptors of difference; Kerber, "Separate Spheres, Female Worlds, Woman's Place"; Gisela Bock, "Challenging Dichotomies: Perspectives on Women's History," in Karen Offen, Ruth Pierson, and Jane Rendall, eds., *Writing Women's History: International Perspectives* (Bloomington: Indiana University Press, 1991), pp. 4–5; Joan Scott, "Deconstructing Equality-Versus-Difference: Or, the Uses of Poststructuralist Theory for Feminism," *Feminist Studies* 14, no. 1 (Spring 1988): 33–50.

68. Foundational studies are Theda Skocpol, *Protecting Soldiers and Mothers: The Political Origins of Social Policy in the United States* (Cambridge: Harvard University Press, 1992); Michel and Koven, *Mothers of a New World*; Sklar, *Florence Kelley and the Nation's Work*; Linda Gordon, *Pitied But Not Entitled: Single Mothers and the History of Welfare, 1890–1935* (New York: Free Press, 1994); Eileen Boris, *Home to Work: The History of Industrial Homework in the United States* (Urbana: University of Illinois Press, 1994); Ann Shola Orloff, *The Politics of Pensions: A Comparative Analysis of Britain, Canada, and the United States, 1880–1940* (Madison: University of Wisconsin Press, 1993). The subfield even had its own new journal, *Social Politics*.

69. See, for example, Suzanne Lebsock, "Women and American Politics, 1880–1920," in Louise A. Tilly and Patricia Guerin, eds., *Women, Politics, and Change* (New York: Russell Sage Foundation, 1990), pp. 45–49.

In my own study of seven Midwestern settlements, only one (Christamore settlement in Indianapolis) resembled Hull-House in being a community of women reformers, though women social workers, charity workers, missionaries, and teachers were employed, along with men, in all the others, under male direction; Crocker, *Social Work and Social Order*, pp. 19–40. See also Louise W. Knight, "Jane Addams and the Settlement House Movement," in *American Reform and Reformers* (forthcoming).

70. Robyn Muncy, *Creating a Female Dominion in Progressive Reform, 1890–1940* (New York: Oxford University Press, 1991). Molly Ladd-Taylor, *Mother-Work: Women, Child Welfare, and the State, 1890–1930* (Urbana: University of Illinois Press, 1994). For a less sanguine view of the power of organized womanhood, see Kriste Lindenmeyer, *"A Right to Childhood": The U.S. Children's Bureau and Child Welfare, 1912–1946* (Urbana: University of Illinois Press, 1997).

71. Ralph E. Luker, *The Social Gospel in Black and White: American Racial Reform, 1885–1914* (Chapel Hill: University of North Carolina Press, 1991). The quotation is from Jacquelyn Dowd Hall, introduction to *Jessie Daniel Ames and the Women's Campaign against Lynching* (New York: Columbia University Press, 1993), p. xxxii. John Patrick McDowell discusses Southern Methodist settlements in his *Social Gospel in the South: The Woman's Home Mission Movement in the Methodist Episcopal Church, South, 1886–1939* (Baton Rouge: Louisiana State University Press, 1982).

72. But two recent special issues of the *Journal of Urban History* on the topic "The New African-American Urban History," edited by Kenneth W. Goings and Raymond A. Mohl (*Journal of Urban History* 21, no. 3 [March 1995] and no. 4 [May 1995]), illustrate a multivocal social history rendered more complicated by attention to gender and class as well as race and cross-fertilized with anthropology. Here, specialization had enriched, not impoverished, social history.

73. Clarke A. Chambers, "Toward a Redefinition of Welfare History," *Journal of American History* 73 (September 1986): 407–33. For the development of this sub-field, see Elliott Rudwick, "Black Urban History: In the Doldrums," *Journal of Urban History* 9 (February 1983): 251–60; Kenneth L. Kusmer, "The Black Urban Experience in American History," in Hine, *The State of Afro-American History*, pp. 91–121, and "Black History at the Crossroads," *Journal of Urban History* 13 (August 1987): 460–70; see also Walker, *Deromanticizing Black History*.

74. Even though Addams and Wald were among the founders of the NAACP by the standards of their day they were racial liberals. Influential also was a Foucauldian framework in which institutions, even (and perhaps especially) "helping institutions," become the means of sustaining the power of the state through the creation of discourses of difference.

75. Trolander, *Professionalism and Social Change*. Bremner made almost no mention of blacks in *From the Depths*. Allen Davis, in his introduction to the 1984 edition of *Spearheads for Reform* (New Brunswick, N.J.: Rutgers University Press, 1984), notes the virtual omission of blacks from the earlier edition. Carson calls the race issue one of the settlement movement's "blind spots." She writes: "In its first forty years, the settlement movement did not ameliorate, or even directly address, white society's systematic discrimination against black Americans. Though several of the white founders of the NAACP had settlement connections, institutionally the settlements failed to make any significant contribution to white Americans' consciousness of racism or to furthering black people's rights and opportunities" (*Settlement Folk*, p. 195).

76. Rayford Logan, *The Negro in American Life and Thought: The Nadir, 1877–1901* (New York: Dial Press, 1954), later revised as *The Betrayal of the Negro: From Rutherford B. Hayes to Woodrow Wilson* (London: Collier Books, 1965).

77. Crocker, *Social Work and Social Order*, pp. 68–93.

78. Darlene Clark Hine, "We Specialize in the Wholly Impossible: The Philanthropic Work of Black Women," in McCarthy, *Lady Bountiful Revisited*, pp. 70–93; Dorothy Salem, *To Better Our World: Black Women in Organized Reform* (Brooklyn: Carlson Publishing Company, 1990); Adrienne Lash Jones, *Jane Edna Hunter: Case Study in Black Leadership, 1910–1950* (Brooklyn: Carlson Publishing Company, 1990); Anne Meis Knupfer, "'Toward a Tenderer Humanity and a Nobler Womanhood': African-American Women's Clubs in Chicago, 1890–1920," *Journal of Women's History* (Fall 1995): 758–76; Evelyn Brooks Higginbotham, *Righteous Discontent: Black Women in the Baptist Church, 1880–1930* (Cambridge: Harvard University Press, 1993); Cynthia Neverdon-Morton, *Afro-American Women of the South and the Advancement of the Race* (Knoxville: University of Tennessee Press, 1989); Jacqueline Rouse, *Lugenia Burns Hope: Black Southern Reformer* (Athens: University of Georgia Press, 1988); Gerda Lerner, "Early Community Work of Black Club Women," *Journal of Negro History* 59 (April 1974): 158–67.

A brilliant essay that shows the transformative effects of new scholarship on gender, race, and region is Mary Frederickson, "'Each One Is Dependent upon the Other': Southern Churchwomen, Racial Reform, and the Process of Transformation, 1880–1940," in Nancy Hewitt and Suzanne Lebsock, eds., *Visible Women: New Essays on American Activism* (Urbana: University of Illinois Press, 1993), pp. 296–324.

79. Lasch-Quinn surveyed a number of black settlements, community centers, schools, and similar agencies, both North and South; see *Black Neighbors: Race and the Limits of Reform in the American Settlement House Movement, 1890–1940* (Chapel Hill: University of North Carolina Press, 1993).

80. Gordon, *Pitied But Not Entitled*, p. 290. Gordon showed how the power of educated, professional women in the Children's Bureau and the social work and settlement networks in the 1910s and 1920s produced some policies that were disadvantageous to poor women. See also Eileen Boris, "The Power of Motherhood: Black and White Activist Women Redefine the 'Political,'" in Koven and Michel, *Mothers of a New World*, pp. 213–45; Lori Ginzberg, *Women and the Work of Benevolence: Morality, Politics, and Class in the Nineteenth-Century United States* (New Haven: Yale University Press, 1990); Nancy A. Hewitt, "Beyond the Search for Sisterhood: Women's History in the 1980s," *Social History* 10, no. 3 (October 1985): 299–321; Christine Stansell, *City of Women: Sex and Class in New York, 1789–1860* (New York: Knopf, 1986).

81. For settlement domestic work agencies, see Crocker, *Social Work and Social Order*, pp. 86–93, 131, 149, 160. See also Elizabeth Clark-Lewis, *Living In, Living Out: African American Domestics in Washington, D.C., 1910–1940* (Washington, D.C.: Smithsonian Institution Press, 1994); Evelyn Brooks Barnett, "Nannie Burroughs and the Education of Black Women," in Sharon Harley and Rosalyn Terborg-Penn, eds., *The Afro-American Woman: Struggles and Images* (Port Washington, N.Y.: Kennikat Press, 1978), pp. 99–105; Phyllis Palmer, "Housework and Domestic Labor: Racial and Technological Change," in Karen Brodkin Sacks and Dorothy Remy, eds., *My Troubles Are Going to Have Trouble with Me: Everyday Trials and Triumphs of Women Workers* (New Brunswick, N.J.: Rutgers University Press, 1984).

82. Personal communication from Rivka Lissak to the author, October 1989. Ruth Crocker, "The Settlements: Culture and Ideology in the Progressive Era," *History of Education Quarterly* 31, no. 2 (Summer 1991): 253–60.

83. Kathryn Kish Sklar, "Hull House in the 1890s: A Community of Women Reformers," *Signs: Journal of Women in Culture and Society* 10, no. 4 (1985): 658–77.

84. Virginia Yans McLaughlin, *Family and Community: Italian Immigrants in Buffalo, 1880–1930* (Ithaca: Cornell University Press, 1977); Roy Rosenzweig, *Eight Hours for What We Will: Workers and Leisure in an Industrial City, 1870–1920* (New York: Cambridge University Press, 1983); Lissak, *Pluralism and Progressives*.

85. Although one of the very few narratives about Hull-House by a client (a Jewish immigrant from Poland), Hilda Satt Polacheck's *I Came a Stranger: The Story of a Hull-House Girl* (Urbana: University of Illinois Press, 1989) is an uncritical account of the beginnings of Hull-House that reveres Jane Addams.

86. She writes: "I shall consider here the realities behind the myth created around [Jane Addams]"; *Pluralism and Progressives*, p. 9.

87. Lissak defined a settlement as a service agency that was a member agency of

the National Federation of Settlements and that conformed to what she called "the settlement idea."

88. Mary Lynn McCree Bryan and Allen F. Davis, eds., *One Hundred Years at Hull-House* (Bloomington: Indiana University Press, 1990). This was in a series of volumes in the tradition of Jane Addams's *Twenty Years* (1912) and *Second Twenty Years* (1929), and culminating in *The Second Twenty Years at Hull-House: September 1909 to September 1929* (New York: Macmillan, 1930); Allen F. Davis, *Eighty Years at Hull House* (Chicago: Quadrangle Books, 1969). Macmillan also published Jane Addams, *Forty Years at Hull House, Being Twenty Years at Hull House and the Second Twenty Years at Hull House* (New York: Macmillan, 1935).

89. *Second Twenty Years*, p. ix. *Twenty Years* was not a firm, unchanging account, Jane Addams insisted, but an impression, limited by "the essential provisionality of everything" (p. 116). At the same time, Bryant and Davis somewhat undermine their demonstration of the open-endedness of their inquiry by rhetorically situating Hull House in America's urban-policy debate of the 1980s.

90. Zunz, introduction to *Reliving the Past*, pp. 5–6, 8.

91. "America without a metanarrative, an America of endless multiplicity" is the goal of a multicultural society; Gerald Early, "American Education and the Postmodernist Impulse," *American Quarterly* 45 (June 1995): 221. See also Nell Irvin Painter, "Bias and Synthesis in History," *Journal of American History* 74 (June 1987): 109–12.

92. Nancy Fraser and Linda J. Nicholson, "Social Criticism without Philosophy: An Encounter between Feminism and Postmodernism," in *Feminism/Postmodernism*, ed. Linda J. Nicholson (New York: Routledge, 1990), p. 23.

93. Lisa Emmerich, "Right in the Midst of My Own People: Native American Women and the Field Program," *American Indian Quarterly* 15 (Spring 1991): 201–12.

94. The famous quip ends: "offering cocoa and sponge cake as a sort of dessert to the industrial system"; *New Republic* 5 (January 8, 1916), quoted in Davis, *Spearheads for Reform*, pp. 17, 32.

95. "Creative solution" is Davis's term; see *Spearheads for Reform*.

96. James Livingston, *Pragmatism and the Political Economy of Cultural Revolution, 1850–1940* (Chapel Hill: University of North Carolina Press, 1994), p. 76.

97. Bender, "Wholes and Parts," p. 129.

RANDOLPH ROTH

IS THERE A DEMOCRATIC ALTERNATIVE
TO REPUBLICANISM? THE RHETORIC AND
POLITICS OF RECENT PLEAS FOR SYNTHESIS

A number of historians have called for syntheses of American history that would draw the findings of social and cultural historians over the past twenty-five years into a coherent whole and reverse "the declining significance of history in the general intellectual culture of our time." Advocates of synthesis blame that decline on the fragmented nature of professional scholarship and on the unwillingness of social and cultural historians to move beyond the histories of less powerful peoples (women, blacks, workers) and engage the history of the entire society.[1] There is, however, a more important plea implicit in many calls for synthesis: a plea for a democratic reinterpretation of American history that can help historians of the left understand and transform the United States in the 1990s and beyond.[2] These calls also contain an appeal for a neo-Progressive theodicy and a vision of community that can inspire faith in Americans' possibilities (if not their most recent achievements) as a people — that can recapture the tragic sense and profound hope of Walt Whitman's *Democratic Vistas* (1871) and Charles and Mary Beard's *Rise of American Civilization* (1927).[3]

These masterpieces resonate with historians of the left for many reasons. They were written, like the syntheses proposed by Herbert Gutman, Eric Foner, and others, to sustain faith in the democratic struggle during the periods of reaction that followed periods of popular upheaval and egalitarian protest. Like Whitman, an uncompromising Radical Republican in an era of Redemption, and like the Beards, unreconstructed Progressives in an era of corporatism, left proponents of synthesis hope to build upon the achievements of democratic movements in which they have participated and to learn from their failures. It is no coincidence that many of the synthetic monographs they admire study the legacy of either the Revolution or Emancipation. They ponder allegorically the legacy of the movements of the 1960s.[4]

Democratic Vistas and *The Rise of American Civilization* also resonate with proponents of democratic syntheses because their authors recognized the "ambiguities of historical outcomes"— the counter-Progressive truths that irony, tragedy, and pathos are enduring elements of history and that popular triumphs have not always diminished evil.[5] These truths have often troubled fervent democrats as they confronted the failings of the popular movements in which they had placed their hopes. Although the advocates of democratic syntheses recognize these truths, they are convinced, as were Whitman and the Beards, that the struggle for democracy has made the world a better place, that common people can profoundly affect the course of history, and that humanity's search for purpose and happiness finds its best inspiration in democratic visions of community.

The first pleas for synthesis by historians of the left appeared late in 1981, as President Reagan's eloquent reinterpretations of American history persuaded more and more voters to reject liberalism and as the impact of the Reagan revolution on the civil rights and antiwar movements became apparent. In "The Missing Synthesis," which appeared in the *Nation*, Herbert Gutman acknowledged that social historians had done excellent work on "segments" of society and "on the diverse and competing traditions that shaped the country's history." Social history had helped revitalize the traditions of oppressed peoples and had provided alternative visions of the future. But because social history often ignored "pattern and context," it left its readers — especially blacks, workers, and women — ill-equipped to address the changing economic, social, and political structures of the post–World War II era. "We need to go beyond the heap of broken historical images to live more decently and humanely in the late twentieth century."[6]

Eric Foner touched upon the same themes in "History in Crisis," which appeared in *Commonweal*. Echoing a complaint made by Elizabeth Fox-Genovese and Eugene Genovese five years before, Foner attributed the failure of social and cultural historians to achieve a "new synthesis" largely to their neglect of politics. Their failure to consider "the ways in which power in civil society is ordered and exercised . . . left social history bereft of the larger context which alone could have imparted broader meaning to its findings." He feared that the depoliticization of social history in the 1970s and early 1980s represented "a retreat from the political impulse which . . . spawned labor, women's, and black history in the first place." He also worried openly that radical historians had succumbed to the blandishments of the "me decade" and the demoralizing effects of the New Right's ascendancy. The political climate of the 1980s raised anew "the question of the role of the radical academic," he wrote, "especially at a time with little prospect for far-reaching social change. If the divorce of academic history from the general reading public has been disastrous, the separation of radical historians from any larger social movement has been equally debilitating." Radical historians needed a politicized synthesis that would "make history once again a way of illuminating the present" and serve as "a mode of collective self-education" and "a vehicle for social change."[7]

Michael Zuckerman was even more bold. In "Myth and Method," which appeared in *The History Teacher* in 1984, Zuckerman asked that social and cultural historians do nothing less than "re-mythify and re-mystify" American history. "We must create America once more, this time in images of inclusiveness and complexity." He had no nostalgia for consensus history. He recognized the importance of studies of particular communities and social groups, which revealed "an intricate array of desires" and experiences among the American people. But he asked, "How do we speak seriously of the general after years of indulgence in the delights of the particular?" Upset by the left's weak response to Reaganism, he observed:

> If we abandon all ambition of a wider public discourse, we leave all power to the special interests which are so certain to prevail in a "politics of pluralism" in which "warring groups, emptied of any vision of the social whole and guided only by the residuum of their private concerns, quarrel over the spoils." . . . It is a veritable concession of dominion to the great corporations, which are free to disconnectedly dictate policy, each in its own realm, as long as lawmakers feel no public pressure to the contrary. A historiography of anarchic parochialism facilitates private piracy and plunder, precisely by perpetuating a fragmented society incapable of mounting any countervailing moral initiative. . . . It has conceded to the celebrants of the military, financial, energy, and espionage bureaucracies the appropri-

ateness and, indeed, inevitability of their assumptions of scale, specialization, and centralization.

Zuckerman urged historians to "forge the regulative fictions we need for the purposes of our time"— to construct master narratives that could reconstruct American culture and society. He acknowledged "the unsavory uses to which the old myths and mystifications were put," and he acknowledged that those myths were fashioned "out of fables as much as from facts . . . out of imagination as much as by scrupulous empirical investigation." But he recognized too the achievements of the myth-making historians of previous generations. "They shaped vast visions and fashioned faiths for a people. . . . They instructed a democracy." Zuckerman asked that contemporary historians, with greater regard for evidence and common people, do likewise.[8]

Thomas Bender professionalized the plea for democratic synthesis in "Wholes and Parts: The Need for Synthesis in American History," which appeared in the *Journal of American History* in 1986. That essay won a wide audience among academic historians because it embraced the rhetoric of disinterested criticism and eschewed contemporary politics. But it drew its strength from Bender's commitment to democracy. In political commentaries in *Democracy* and *Dissent* and in *New York Intellect* (1987), Bender describes democracy as "capacious . . . with different emphases . . . for different people at different historical moments." "Sometimes," he writes, "it is social equality that is most salient, or political access, or engagement with the diversity and changes of [modern] life, or an assault on established institutions and restrictive policies, or a broad commitment to justice — and more." But democracy is above all an "ongoing" struggle to create a genuinely pluralistic community committed to the ideals of diversity and inclusion. Those ideals require that groups suffering oppression and discrimination gain not only wealth and civil rights but an effective voice in shaping the community's economy, polity, and culture. Bender believes, however, that the democratic struggle is at present stymied by "the absence of an adequate social or intellectual basis for contact and conflict" among society's parts. "The problem of our culture today is not a lack of consensus, a lack of unity," as conservatives would have it, but the inability of subordinated peoples to work together to contest the power of dominant groups.[9]

Bender's professional complaint in "Wholes and Parts" that the new social history has failed to achieve an "architectonic vision" of American history can thus be read allegorically as an indictment of the failure of the left to achieve a compelling vision of the struggle for democratic community. When Bender, for example, laments "the proliferation of intensely parochial, nearly hermetic [scholarly] discourses around a series of social units far smaller than either societies or nations" and warns that monographs on women, blacks, and workers "will not fall" by themselves "into an interpretive synthesis, any more than bricks will fall into a facade," his criticism can be read allegorically as an indictment of the failure of the remnants of the left to move beyond what he perceives as a parochial interest group politics that lacks a vision of community as a whole and offers no real challenge to power relationships that continue to make life difficult for oppressed peoples. He refuses to center his synthesis on the working class or the black nation or the female sphere, because he doubts that a democratic community will emerge simply from the struggles of oppressed classes, races, and genders. Bender's focus on "the making of public culture" thus represents a desire for a politics capable of realizing a genuine pluralism among and within the communities that make up America.[10]

Bender's plea for synthesis is thus part of a broad effort by left historians to sustain democratic protest in a conservative era by fashioning new master narratives of American history. The proponents of democratic syntheses do not wish to establish a single, orthodox interpretation of American history. Indeed, they themselves are politically diverse. For instance, the authors of the synthetic monographs that Bender praises — Jean Baker, Iver Bernstein, Eric Foner, Mary Ryan, and Sean Wilentz — and the historians who responded directly to Bender's plea — Richard Fox, Alice Kessler-Harris, Nell Painter, and Roy Rosenzweig — are not politically homogeneous. Ryan, who has written for *Democracy*, embraces a political economy rooted in social democracy and cooperation, whereas Wilentz, who has written for *Radical History* and *History Workshop*, acknowledges the influence of socialist and Marxist principles on his thought. Some, like Kessler-Harris and Painter, have been greatly influenced by the feminist and Black Power movements, others less so. And as we might expect, Baker and Fox, whose work reveals a deep-seated ambivalence toward ideology and its impact on American politics, do not identify with the left politically, although they are sympathetic to its aims. These historians share, however, a commitment to a genuine democratic pluralism, a discontent with gender, class, and race relationships in contemporary America, and a desire to democratize those relationships and redistribute power.[11]

Of course, not every plea for synthesis has come from the left. Liberals, like Bernard Bailyn and Arthur Schlesinger, Jr., moderates, like Gordon Wood, and conservatives, like Oscar and Lilian Handlin, have written synthetic histories and essays in recent years that oppose those produced by left historians.[12] These pioneers of social and cultural history have integrated the findings of social and cultural historians into syntheses that focus on the unique contributions of the American experiment to human progress, contributions they believe are sometimes neglected or endangered by the left: for the Handlins, the gift of liberty, threatened by license, intolerance, and complacency; for Wood, the gift of equality of condition, threatened by a failure to appreciate its radicalism and by an obsession with equality of result; and for Bailyn and Schlesinger, the gifts of an encompassing national identity, threatened by separatism, and of opportunity, threatened by a failure to appreciate how widely merit has been rewarded in American history.

These historians have won a wide audience outside academia by revitalizing interpretations from the 1950s and early 1960s that celebrate the difference of the United States from Europe and that appreciate what for these historians is the central problem of republican life: finding "the means of ordered liberty in a world condemned to everlasting change."[13] They insist that every democratic impulse must be balanced by a countervailing impulse if it is to lead to genuine progress: that diversity cannot thrive unless Americans surrender to some extent their particular identities for a common identity; that equality cannot advance unless Americans accept inequalities that arise from differences in merit; that oppression cannot diminish unless liberty is in some way constrained. They offer a republican alternative to democracy that defends the proposition that some people are more deserving of honor and power — the means of effective citizenship — than others and that insists that the balance of democratic and antidemocratic forces can be maintained only by ensuring that people get the recognition and authority they deserve. They also believe that religion and ethnic identity should remain private matters and should not intrude into the public arena, except as a demand for freedom and equal rights for people of all faiths, races, and nationalities, lest the republic be dominated by contentious factions.

In their effort to defend what they find valuable in America, republican historians run the risk of turning against democracy. The terms upon which republics distribute honor and power, and differentiate private and public matters, can be arbitrary and antidemocratic. Honor can serve the powerful by defending the conduct of elites, however brutal or imperious it might be, and by questioning the capacity of the oppressed to act honorably. Privacy can serve the privileged by denying oppressed minorities the right to fight for their values and beliefs in the public arena.

Democratic historians have used these insights to criticize republican historians and to accuse them of serving entrenched interests. The problem is that democratic historians have questioned the republicans' use of words like "honor" and "dishonor," "public" and "private," only to resurrect them on terms favorable to themselves. Most democratic historians underestimate the challenge that republican rhetoric and political theory pose for democratic history. They are more easily criticized than escaped.[14]

Democratic historians have not won or monopolized the debate over synthesis. The republicans inaugurated the debate in the early 1970s (when the left appeared ascendant) and have made important contributions. But the fact that pleas for democratic synthesis are political should not discredit them. Political activity, compelling prose, and careful scholarship need not be incompatible, and the authors of these pleas pursue the struggle for democracy and synthesis in a self-critical way. Democratic historians should, however, ask further questions about their politics — about their reasons for seeking synthesis, about the character of their faith in people and progress, and about the nature of the democracy they envision — before they can assess their readiness to write syntheses that offer an alternative to republican interpretations of American history. And they must be aware of the rhetorical problem inherent in synthesis: that any effort to create a master narrative of America's social and cultural history will make it hard for competing narratives — and for the peoples they represent in the past and present — to win a fair hearing.

The fears that Nell Painter expressed in her response to Bender's plea may be justified — that blacks, women, and workers will be given short shrift in future syntheses. Painter predicts that most syntheses will unwittingly ignore or degrade subordinated peoples or will deny the communitarian visions of the dispossessed.[15] Bender rightly criticizes Painter for accusing him falsely of resurrecting the consensus history of Louis Hartz.[16] But Painter also worries that Bender's rhetoric contains a subliminal indictment of Black Power, unionism, and feminism, and of the alternative narrative traditions they represent — an indictment that Zuckerman hands down openly in his attack on the "historiography of anarchic parochialism." Painter worries that Bender's narrative and political effort to bind genders, races, and classes into families, communities, and a nation will be no less exclusive or oppressive than those that preceded it. He appeals to aesthetics, to the superiority of wholes to parts, of synthesis to fragmentation. He also appeals to the perception, widely held among academic historians, that the peoples studied by social and cultural historians are at present too disparate, parochial, and unaware of the complexities of modern life to launch an effective democratic movement. The historian must provide guidance and a forum for public debate that these groups cannot themselves provide. Painter rightly fears the will-to-power and the drive for ideological clarity that lie embedded in appeals for democratic synthesis. Unexamined, they can subvert the democratic vision that she and the advocates of synthesis hope to realize.

The synthetic narratives that Bender admires in his essays on synthesis — Jean Baker's *Affairs of Party*, Iver Bernstein's *New York City Draft Riots*, Eric Foner's *Nothing But Freedom*, Mary Ryan's *Cradle of the Middle Class*, and Sean Wilentz's *Chants Democratic* — and Bender's own synthetic narrative, *New York Intellect* — evince the justice of Painter's concerns. Despite their great achievements, these histories fail to give competing narratives, and the peoples whose histories such narratives represent, free play within their master narratives. These works pursue one of two basic strategies: either they exclude subordinated peoples and their stories or they divert attention from cultural differences between subordinated and dominant peoples that could lead to political antagonism and narrative complication. In short, they purchase narrative and political unity at a price that subordinated peoples might not want to pay. Bender makes no claim, of course, that these works are representative. But the influential works that Bender cites illustrate the problems that democratic syntheses can encounter.[17]

The shortcomings of these outstanding histories do not stem from a failure of democratic commitment, nor are they inevitable. Indeed, other works by two of the authors Bender discusses — Foner and Ryan — avoid them.[18] However, democratic historians, most of whom belong to the historical profession and to the upper-middle reaches of the middle class, can find themselves enveloped in class-bound rhetorical strategies and authorial identities that draw them away from their democratic and scholarly purpose. The authors of these syntheses portray themselves in their narratives either as skilled cosmopolitans or as mediators among contending groups — identities that professionals have often assumed since their appearance as a "new class" in the late nineteenth century. There is much to commend in these identities. But democratic historians should not forget the lesson of many studies of professionalism: professionals embraced these identities in part to gain power over people they deemed unskilled, parochial, or incapable of resolving differences.[19]

Two widely admired synthetic narratives that adopt a democratic rhetoric of inclusion and uplift, yet largely exclude African Americans, are Sean Wilentz's *Chants Democratic* and Thomas Bender's *New York Intellect*. That exclusion stems from the focus of their respective narratives on "the working class" and "intellectuals," terms that despite their inclusive intent function as metaphors that identify the historical actors in these studies with contemporary professionals and that exclude workers and intellectuals from the past who cannot be identified with today's professionals.

From 1790 to 1820, blacks made up nearly 10 percent of New York City's population and a larger portion of its wage earners. But in *Chants Democratic*, blacks receive notice only twice. They are mentioned in a footnote, and they are shown being victimized on two pages where racial violence is described.[20]

As David Roediger observes, African Americans do not appear in most studies of the American working class, particularly those that center on the politics and social condition of male artisans.[21] It is surprising, however, given Wilentz's historiographical purpose, that he did not consider the role of African Americans or race consciousness in forging the distinctive class consciousness of New York's male workers. Wilentz argues strenuously "against exceptionalism." He rejects the idea that racism and the peculiarities of American politics and class formation precluded the rise of a European-style class consciousness among American workers.[22] But he does not explore the impact of race or the black community on political institutions, class formation, or the consciousness of the city's white artisans, and thus he falls short of offering an alternative to exceptionalism.

Wilentz discusses only in passing the abolition of slavery in New York (1799–1827) and the concomitant rise of negrophobia in the Jeffersonian party, even though the appearance of 2,500 former slaves on the free labor market and the drift toward racism of the party that most white artisans supported were pivotal events in the history of class formation and politics in the early Republic.[23] He does not compare class relationships in New York City with those in Philadelphia, where blacks were not excluded from carting or forced gradually out of seafaring, or with those in cities of the Upper and Lower South, where skilled trades were more open to free black artisans and apprentices.[24] Nor does he examine the impact on class politics of New York's election law of 1821, which by 1825 had disfranchised all but sixteen African Americans in Manhattan and had forced black seamen, the most radical and assertive black workers, to struggle outside the political process against discrimination and exploitation.[25]

Because Wilentz does not encompass these stories in his narrative, he cannot answer two crucial questions: whether black workers shared the class consciousness of white artisans and whether the association of blacks with manual labor and vice versa, coupled with the denial of black voting rights and the relegation of the majority of blacks to basement apartments, intensified the class consciousness and solidarity of white artisans and made them more jealous of the privileges and standing they enjoyed as workers who engaged in skilled labor.[26] Thus *Chants Democratic*, despite its magnificent achievements, falls short of its historiographical and democratic purpose.

Thomas Bender's *New York Intellect*, a study of intellectual life in New York City, is another outstanding synthetic narrative that largely excludes African Americans. New York City was the birthplace of the first black newspaper in the United States (1827) and of the first black literary society (1833). It was home to (or a way station for) generations of black artists and social critics. By 1850, its private and public schools enrolled three-fifths of all school-age black children — one of the highest rates in urban America. Yet Bender mentions New York's African American journalists, intellectuals, and readers only once, in a two-page discussion of the Harlem Renaissance.[27]

In that passage, Bender introduces the intellectuals who promoted the Harlem Renaissance in its early years, known as the Six — Alain Locke, Charles S. Johnson, James Weldon Johnson, Jessie Fauset, Walter White, and Casper Holstein — as "a small group of educated blacks." That phrase segregates African American intellectuals from their white counterparts (whose education is taken for granted), suggests that New York's blacks were largely uneducated, and implies that substantial formal education rather than white skin was the fundamental prerequisite for acceptance in New York's intellectual circles.[28] And whereas Bender painstakingly locates the roots of the American Renaissance in the political journalism of radical Democratic Party nationalists in the late 1830s, he ignores the political journalism of radical African American nationalists and internationalists in the 1920s, which inspired many Harlem artists.[29]

Bender proclaims the American Renaissance, which started in the late 1830s, a success because it inspired Walt Whitman and Herman Melville in the 1850s. But he proclaims the Harlem Renaissance, which began in the 1920s, a failure because it produced few enduring literary works in the 1920s[30] — an interpretation that ignores the continuity of the Renaissance from the 1920s into the early 1950s and neglects the masterpieces of Zora Neale Hurston, Richard Wright, and Ralph Ellison, all of whom spent formative years in New York.[31]

Bender's neglect of African Americans, like Wilentz's, is surprising, given his broader purpose. Bender argues that New York City offers America's best hope for creating the "trans-national" American culture that Randolph Bourne called for in the *Atlantic* in 1916 — a democratic, cosmopolitan culture that combines "an acceptance of persistent particularism with a sense of common and public discourse." The failure of African Americans to find a place in New York's "federation of cultures" represents perhaps the greatest failure of that ideal.[32] But Bender, rather than exploring the sources of that failure or the peculiar dilemmas that African American intellectuals faced, examines the Harlem Renaissance as part of a broad movement toward international modernism in the 1920s, which in his opinion abandoned "the rich interweaving of politics and culture" of the prewar years and led to "a striking shrinkage of the literary imagination and a diffusion of literary life into particular locales and coteries." He writes that "in an exploitative, even colonial, situation that should have suggested the impossibility of separating art, politics, and economics, the Harlem Renaissance was relentlessly and single-mindedly artistic. It represented an attempt to invert the order of economics and art, and to substitute art for politics."

Harlem intellectuals, like their white counterparts, allowed literature's "public dimension" to contract. They identified art with "the artist's expression of his or her private self" and fell prey to "that characteristic tendency of New York coteries to translate their own parochialism into a putative universalism." Bender alleges that black intellectuals made the same mistakes that white intellectuals made. He acknowledges that Langston Hughes was an exception, but only an exception.[33]

The early Harlem Renaissance had its limits. But Bender neglects substantial evidence that black intellectuals faced challenges and made choices that were distinctive — evidence suggesting that Bender must look further for an explanation of why a "trans-national" American culture did not develop in New York City after World War I. For example, "the rich interweaving of culture and politics" represented by Bourne may not have survived the war among white intellectuals. But the war and the race riots and the peace treaty that followed politicized black intellectuals. Garveyism, socialism, and Pan-Africanism won tremendous support until 1924–25, and many artists, editors, and critics, including Walter White, Charles S. Johnson, W. E. B. Du Bois, Paul Robeson, and A. Philip Randolph, considered culture and politics inseparable.[34]

White artists may have lost touch with working people in New York. But Bender can argue that "the literature of the Renaissance had no organic relation to everyday life in Harlem" only by neglecting Rudolph Fisher's humorous depiction of the denizens of Patmore's Pool Parlor and the employees of Isaacs Transportation Company in *The Walls of Jericho*, Claude McKay's portraits of dock and railroad workers in *Home to Harlem*, and Nella Larsen's moving account of storefront religion and spiritual awakening in *Quicksand*.[35] To argue that the Renaissance refused "to associate itself with the black masses," Bender must dismiss Hubert Harrison as an intellectual and forget the hope with which Ernestine Rose launched her reading circle at the 135th Street Library.[36] The evidence suggests that black intellectuals may have been, by choice and by racial predicament, peculiarly aware of the importance of power and politics in cultural life and unusually close to people from other walks of life. That is, they may have come closer to fulfilling the ideals of Randolph Bourne than their white counterparts did.

Bender also misses evidence from the black experience that can illuminate the experience of intellectuals from other impoverished, migrant peoples. For example, Bender is right from a certain perspective to criticize Renaissance artists for dwelling too much in the 1920s on "romantic images of rural black life" and too little on the pressing problems of urban black life. But we should not ignore the profound need of African American intellectuals to come to terms with the past, or as Nathan Huggins put it, to "find one's roots in the homeland, the South, and to claim it as one's own . . . to look into the fullness of the past without shame or fear. To be, and to relive the slave and the peasant and never be separated from that reality." [37]

It is hard to claim that Renaissance intellectuals shrank into their own narrow circle, given the efforts of Paul Robeson to unite the nations of the world through folk music, or Claude McKay's attempt to awaken racial pride in Africa and the West Indies, or Rudolph Fisher's effort to reach (and confound) white readers with his glossary of the language of Harlem (e.g., "fay. ofay. A person who, so far as is known, is white").[38] The leaders of the Renaissance did take "a chance, thinking they could exploit . . . white patrons for their own purposes." It was, as Bender says, "a dangerous game." But it is hard to say that "they lost," given that Langston Hughes, Zora Neale Hurston, Ralph Ellison, and Richard Wright not only survived pressure from philanthropists and publishers "to conform to white notions of black authenticity" but produced several of America's most profound meditations on identity and the performance of social roles.[39]

The Harlem experience could have awakened Bender to the difficulties of surviving an urban present and building a cosmopolitan future while preserving the blessings and overcoming the burdens of an oppressive rural past. It could have led him to a thorough investigation of the kinds of financial patronage that might foster a transnational culture, including a discussion of the liabilities for white intellectuals of peer review, lavish institutional support, and affluent readers. Bender, to the detriment of his argument, does not pursue these questions.

It is ironic that Bender criticizes the terms on which "black art was incorporated into the city's intellectual life" in the 1920s, for he himself forcibly incorporates black intellectuals into that life. That incorporation does reveal "a pattern of domination and subordination" by implicating black intellectuals in the failures of their white counterparts and neglecting the wider ramifications of their experience.[40] Rather than place the Renaissance in context, Bender pares off stories that do not mesh with his indictment of the intellectual "shrinkage and fragmentation" of the 1920s.

None of these criticisms diminish the achievements of Wilentz or Bender, and they are not alone in their omissions. Of the dozens of reviews of Chants Democratic and New York Intellect that have appeared, only two comment on the exclusion of blacks.[41] None were written by African Americans, and none appeared in leading African American or

African Americanist journals.[42] Whatever the cause, the silence of white reviewers and the absence of black reviewers will make it hard for democratic syntheses to flourish.[43]

There is yet another reason, however, why Wilentz's and Bender's syntheses fall short. In both cases, African Americans are disproportionately members of other social groups that suffer exclusion. *Chants Democratic* spends little time on unskilled manual laborers. *New York Intellect* only glances at intellectuals who serve ethnic or spiritual communities. These patterns of exclusion indicate that Wilentz and Bender focus rhetorically on skilled workers and cosmopolitan intellectuals, who think and behave in ways common to members of the new middle class.

That identification lies at the heart of the strengths and weaknesses of these syntheses. It helps Wilentz and Bender understand workers and intellectuals who are in fact skilled or cosmopolitan, and it makes their work accessible to its largely professional and undergraduate audience. But that identification suffuses their narratives with an ethos that distributes honor and citizenship on terms favorable to politically engaged scholars. The privileging of certain workers and intellectuals makes their narratives more republican than democratic — more intent on legitimating today's hierarchies than on challenging them.

For Wilentz, the heroes of the early Republic were skilled artisans — independent, creative, productive individuals. They were committed not merely to the accumulation of wealth but to their fellow artisans, their craft, the public good, and even their masters, as long as their masters did not exploit them. These "citizen craftsmen," intent on "imposing their own rational design on nature's fruits" and "united by a fierce pride in their skills and products,"[44] are figures through whom Wilentz speaks metaphorically about the history and destiny of middle-class professionals in America, particularly academics and college students, the implied readers of his narrative. The latter bear the responsibility for resurrecting and reinvigorating the tradition of artisan republicanism.

Wilentz is aware of similarities between artisans and professionals. Like E. P. Thompson, who refers to history as his "trade," and Karl Marx, who likened professors to master craftsmen and students to apprentices in *Das Kapital*, Wilentz considers history his "craft."[45] And like them, he draws inspiration and literary power from the metaphor, as when he criticizes "the less attractive features of eighteenth-century artisan production" — "the web of deference and clientage that governed the workshop as well as the craft economy, the marginal prospects of

the mass of independent producers," and the substitution of highly ex-
ploitable laborers, such as indentured servants, for independent journeymen. He seems to view the artisan world of the early Republic through
the eyes of a graduate student, stopping now and then to jab at the pretensions of the majordomos who at least "in principle . . . stood at the
head of their trades, as men whose skills and attention to business had
won . . . a mastery of their respective crafts," and who often "evaded or
ignored" their responsibility to train their apprentices and secure their
journeymen a just wage. Wilentz pleads, both in the old-middle-class
past and the new-middle-class present, for a transcendence of "money
grubbing" and of the urge to dominate others, for an "ideal of mutual-
ity and class pride."[46]

Wilentz does not, as some critics argue, romanticize the inner workings of the artisan world. He is aware of the artisans' shortcomings and
tergiversations. Therein lies the greatness of Chants Democratic. But
Wilentz has little time or empathy for workers who do not fit his metaphorical picture, whose labor is not elevated by the possession of socially
recognized expertise. He notes in passing, for example, the opposition
of New York artisans in 1803 to the "workshop" proposal of Mayor
Edward Livingston, who wanted new immigrants, paupers, orphans,
and ex-convicts to learn trades in municipal workshops. Livingston un-
deniably tried to help the poor at the artisans' expense. He did not offer
the unskilled a chance to compete against the city's lawyers or merchants.
But Wilentz ignores the plight of the people whom Livingston sought to
help. He neglects the discrimination that kept them out of trades, and he
never considers the fact that, according to historian Howard Rock,
many artisans viewed the workshops as "a threat to their social status
because it would identify artisans with the rabble of the city."[47] The
same is true of Wilentz's treatment of the trial in 1809 of the journeymen cordwainers who struck against a master who hired an apprentice
contrary to the regulations of the Journeymen's Cordwainers' Society. It
is natural to sympathize with the journeymen's defense of the closed
shop. But Wilentz does not consider the circumstances of the would-be
apprentice and his parents, or analyze the criteria by which the society
determined which boys merited apprenticeship and which did not.
Those criteria are important, given that many artisans, according to
Rock, felt "contempt for the moral habits and culture of those of inferior social standing."[48]

For the most part, Chants Democratic mentions unskilled workers or apprentices only when they join artisan pageants or political initiatives. It notes briefly "the social and ideological barriers that had long separated the skilled from the unskilled" when those barriers deliquesced in the mid-1830s. But it never looks at the early Republic through the eyes of the unskilled. Whenever the narrative threatens to reveal that the artisans' "benevolent hierarchy of skill" subordinated and devalued manual laborers — whenever it might expose the antidemocratic implications of professional pride and solidarity — it breaks off.[49]

Bender claims a special place in his narrative for cosmopolitan intellectuals like Randolph Bourne. He echoes Whitman's plea for a class of "native authors . . . sacerdotal, modern . . . permeating the whole mass of American mentality, taste, belief, breathing into it a new breath of life, giving it decision . . . radiating, begetting appropriate teachers, schools, manners, and, as its greatest result, accomplishing . . . a religious and moral character beneath the political and productive and intellectual bases of the States."[50] As the Beards put it, the public-spirited intellectual — apotheosized for them in the democratic historian — is "an instrument of civilization," bound to oppose all that is "materialistic, primitive, and indifferent to culture," destined to "give new direction to self-criticism and creative energy, aid in generating a richer 'intellectual climate,' and help in establishing the sovereignty of high plan, design, or ideal."[51] These intellectuals are the saving remnant who will keep democracy alive in eras of reaction and guide it in eras of upheaval.

Bender's indictment of the privatism and sycophancy of many modern, cosmopolitan intellectuals is persuasive, as is his heroic account of the democratic writers of the American Renaissance. His identification with these intellectuals makes him sensitive to the problems of New York's most powerful intellectual communities. He makes an implicit assumption, however, that nonintellectuals think less well than intellectuals about public matters, and equally troubling, he largely ignores ethnic and religious intellectuals who could be branded traditional or "parochial," and with them their contributions to a "transnational" culture. He uses a wide range of terms to cast insufficiently perspicacious and creative souls into the hellfire of intellectual provincialism: "appallingly vacuous," "third-rate," "undiscriminating, fact-laden, intellectually vacant," "by no means" great.[52] African Americans are not the only people who do not measure up in these invidious, unspecified, canonical terms: Margaret Fuller does, but a writer like Sara Parton, who produced her most famous works as a sentimental Christian does not; Lionel Trilling and Alfred Kazin do, but a believing Jew like Rabbi Stephen Wise does not.[53]

Thus, even though *Chants Democratic* and *New York Intellect* adopt a rhetoric of inclusion, they exclude or devalue African Americans, unskilled workers, and ethnic and religious intellectuals. The traditions of artisan republicanism and cosmopolitan intellect that they celebrate are unfortunately no more respectful now than they were then of people who find themselves for whatever reason without socially prized or recognized skills or with inferior skills. They deny such people honor and citizenship. When these traditions are invoked to debunk the claim of capitalists and of co-opted professionals to a disproportionate share of wealth, power, and honor in society, they are democratic. But when they sit in judgment of blacks, manual laborers, and intellectuals rooted in less powerful communities — when they do not acknowledge the existence or achievements of such people — they risk becoming antidemocratic.

There is much to admire in the traditions of artisan republicanism and cosmopolitan intellect, which have helped professional historians fashion their own identity. But there is an antidemocratic side to these traditions, just as there is to the traditions of professional history. Most academic historians have heard colleagues make derogatory remarks about students, the public, and historians that they do not respect (a skill that all too many students acquire in their first year of graduate school), to indicate that in their view, people without certain skills, without certain kinds of insight or creativity or flexibility, are people without honor, noncitizens of a sort, incapable of participation in the polity. Most professional historians who teach consider themselves successful insofar as their students avoid lives of manual labor and emancipate themselves from traditional communities.

Perhaps that is why so few complain when democratic historians unintentionally exclude the unskilled and the provincial from their narratives. After all, these narratives embrace a definition of citizenship and a code of honor that serves and flatters professionals, both literally and allegorically. Professionals make up the social sphere — admired, skilled, secular, urbane — into which people will be uplifted. As Whitman observed in *Democratic Vistas*, "ungracious as it may sound, and a paradox after what we have been saying, democracy looks with suspicious, ill-satisfied eye upon the very poor, the ignorant, and those out of business. She asks for men and women with occupations, well-off, owners of houses and acres, and with cash in the bank — and with some cravings for literature, too; and must have them, and hastens to make them." Whitman was speaking of the democracy of the old middle class. Will the democracy of professionals prove more gracious, less presumptuous and paradoxical? [54]

Wilentz and Bender are at their best when they are true to their democratic selves, when they assail the theory and practice of republicans who invoke the fictive dichotomies of honor/dishonor and citizen/noncitizen to confer privilege upon themselves and oppress others. Unfortunately, it remains relatively easy in the historical profession to ignore the criticisms of people who are not professionals or who follow different traditions and to neglect their stories.

Not all democratic syntheses that Bender praises exclude subordinated peoples. For example, Eric Foner's *Nothing but Freedom*, Mary Ryan's *Cradle of the Middle Class*, and Jean Baker's *Affairs of Party* are inclusive. [55] That quality does not, however, prevent these works from subtly circumscribing the autonomy and vision of subordinated peoples. Each draws diverse individuals into social solidarities (families, communities, parties) and the public arena at a cost that must be acknowledged. They place struggles between dominant and subordinated peoples over wealth, status, and power at the center of their narratives by asking each group to surrender part of its claim to that center. That means that subordinated peoples enter the narrative arena in these synthetic works with fewer internal divisions, less-distinctive values and aspirations, and more-moderated behavior than they have when they enter the narrative arenas of studies devoted to their own people.

In the synthetic works cited above, the authors are not purveyors of a restrictive conception of honor and citizenship. They present themselves instead as mediators who legitimate in civic terms the demands of excluded and oppressed peoples for equal shares of the stuff of human happiness — wealth, status, power (and affection) — and who delegitimate the claim of the privileged to have provided for the happiness of the subordinated. That stance has long been congenial, as Robert Wiebe argues in *Search for Order*, to middle-class professionals. Many perceive themselves as negotiators, as civic-minded citizens who help resolve conflicts among contending social groups peacefully, so that public and private interests can be better served. [56] The difficulty is that the criteria by which these authors differentiate what is public from what is private, what is good from what is self-interested, remain largely unarticulated, even though the criteria determine the extent to which a subordinated people's values, aspirations, behaviors, and disagreements can enter the public arena and be recognized, affirmed, or contested.

Eric Foner, for example, centers *Nothing but Freedom*, a comparative study of emancipation, on the struggle of freed peoples for parity in matters public, "for equality in social relations, access to the resources of the earth, and the fruits of one's labor."[57] That focus gives his narrative clarity and purpose. It allies him with the struggle of subordinated peoples for wealth, status, and power. But Foner achieves clarity by sidestepping the work of Barbara Fields, Herbert Gutman, and Nell Painter, which reveals that the distinctive customs, values, and aspirations of freed people challenged not only the privileges of the master class and the master race but at times the norms that the majority of European Americans believed should govern families, businesses, and political associations.

Nothing but Freedom does not confront the political questions raised by narratives that emphasize the distinctiveness of African Americans. What if freed men and women perceived themselves, as Barbara Fields argues, not as aspiring middle-class Americans eager for economic and community development in the South but as "a subsistence-oriented peasantry" with severe reservations about the capitalist system and worldly ambition? What if, as Herbert Gutman believed, African Americans formerly held as slaves wanted not only to protect members of their nuclear families from the abuse of gang labor and apprenticeship but to defend a diverse array of family and kinship structures, some of which many European Americans found objectionable? What if freed people, as Nell Painter asserts, believed in a consensual political system that empowered blacks in part by limiting the political independence of African American dissenters and assimilationists?[58] If freed people were indeed distinctive in these ways, they threatened prevailing middle-class European American understandings of how families, economies, and political parties should be organized.

These findings present Foner with a problem. How can he incorporate a diverse yet distinctive people into his narrative and integrate them politically into American society? He could do so by discussing the historic roots of African American distinctiveness, by refuting racists who devalue those distinctive qualities and who deny the diversity of African Americans, and by reminding European American readers that they are not as capitalistic, traditional, homogeneous, or appreciative of dissenters and culturally marginal people as they might suppose. That strategy, however, is politically and rhetorically difficult.

In *Nothing but Freedom*, Foner avoids discussion of African American distinctiveness. He champions the right of the oppressed to self-determination in family and community life.[59] But he relegates those lives to the private sphere and suggests that they pose no threat to common understandings of the public good, because freed peoples shared the nation's public understanding of how communities and families should be organized. "Small farms, thrifty villages, free schools," traditional families — freed peoples in the postbellum South wanted the same way of life that other small-town and rural Americans wanted. He notes that freed people in the South Carolina and Georgia low country retained their "cultural autonomy," but he confines that autonomy to the preservation of distinctive dialects and religious practices — an autonomy that most European Americans accept. He describes in detail the hostility of black workers who struck against rice plantations along the Combahee and Ashepoo Rivers in South Carolina in 1876 toward blacks who refused to strike, but he only hints that the coercion and violence that broke out among black workers was rooted not only in labor militance but in the emergence of an African American political culture that sometimes circumscribed dissent.[60] Foner thus incorporates freed people into his narrative by repressing or privatizing what was distinctive about them, a strategy that not only restricts their autonomy and denies the singularity of their visions of community but fails to recognize the political and cultural conflicts that precluded the creation of genuinely plural democratic communities in postbellum America.

Nell Painter's synthetic history of the Gilded Age and the Progressive Era, *Standing at Armageddon*, ironically embraces the same privatizing narrative and political strategy. So does Iver Bernstein's *New York City Draft Riots*, another excellent synthesis.[61] Jean Baker and Mary Ryan pursue a different course. They examine private as well as public life. They show how private purposes manifested themselves in public causes and how public decisions sharpened or engendered private discontents. Baker and Ryan remain wary, however, of allowing the subjects of their narratives to claim anything other than an equal share of wealth, status, and power in the public arena.

Jean Baker's *Affairs of Party* is a remarkable study of the political culture of the Democratic Party in mid-nineteenth-century America. Its engaging case studies of partisan commitment demonstrate that personal and family concerns — a rebellion against an oppressive or negligent father, an attachment to a strong family — often outweigh public concerns in determining party loyalties. Baker, however, often overlooks the subcommunities (regional, ethnic, class, and so on) that stood between private citizens and the Democratic Party. Her narrative absorbs individuals and families into a coherent party culture by lessening conflict within the party over whose way of life the party would defend.

For example, Baker notes that Hunterdon, New Jersey, a heavily Democratic agricultural community, did not fit "the model developed for midwestern counties that voted Democratic because their farms were marginal, their soil infertile, and their origins southern."[62] Her words satirize the efforts of some political historians to reduce the determinants of party loyalty to ethnocultural and economic factors in regression equations. But Baker does not capitalize on her point. She fails to humanize and give a prominent place to the voices of hard-pressed Midwestern farmers of Southern heritage. She thereby relegates the distinctive values, aspirations, and customs of these farmers to the private realm, where they have no power to threaten the unity of the Democratic Party or authoritative interpretations of its mission.[63]

The same could be said of Baker's portrait of the Dutch inhabitants of Pella, Iowa. For the most part she reduces the community's aspirations to inclusion in public life and autonomy in private life, reflected in Pella's opposition to nativism and Prohibition. The reduction deprives readers of an understanding of Dutch culture and of the difficulties that Pellans encountered as they tried to realize their aspirations in an alien political culture. Baker notes, for example, that Henry Scholte, who led Pellans out of the Democratic Party and into the Republican Party in the 1850s, made his decision "on the high ideological ground of choosing freedom over slavery and did not mention any mundane concerns — an ethnic grudge, local grievance, or private advantage — that might have influenced him."[64] But why must Scholte's concerns have been abstract or mundane, public or private? Could they not have emerged from his participation in a Dutch culture? Could historic commitments to religious toleration and Calvinist communitarianism, to empire and antislavery principles, have left many Dutch immigrants peculiarly dissatisfied with both parties? Perhaps their distinctiveness left them outsiders in both parties; perhaps they might have become power brokers (and hence major architects of party culture) in closely contested states.[65]

Baker comes closest to recognizing the distinctiveness and diversity of subcommunities and their challenges to party culture in her discussion of the labor movement through the experience of William Sylvis, an

ironworker and union activist from Pennsylvania. She does not, however, confront the full implications of Sylvis's class-conscious challenge
to the capitalist political economy. "In moving from a traditional party
commitment to interest-group politics and finally to a labor party,"
she writes, Sylvis had "adopted a nonpartisan, interest-group approach
to public life."[66] Baker does not depict Sylvis as an increasingly class-
conscious, militant, and disruptive Democrat with distinctive values
and aspirations. She depicts him as an increasingly privatistic special-
interest advocate who abandoned the party when it declined to champion his economic cause. Class conflict (and the cultural conflict it represents) thus never enters the Democratic Party or its culture. The
concerns of class-conscious workers within the party remain by definition private or shaped by self-interest. Class-conscious workers thereby
lose their power to destabilize the Democratic Party or shape its culture.[67]

In short, "the primary focus" of Baker's study "is attachment to
party — not class, occupation, residency, or religious denomination."[68]
Therein lies the problem with her narrative. Where attachments to
less-inclusive communities are given lower priority and relegated to the
private sphere insofar as they cannot be represented publicly through
interest-group politics, the narrative and the politics embedded in it become less democratic.

Mary Ryan, in her study of the making of middle-class society in
Oneida County, New York, offers the most powerful treatment of both
public and private life. Like Eric Foner, she writes with clarity and conviction about the public struggle of oppressed people for wealth, status,
and power, and about the deleterious effects of society's decision to rele-
gate women to a separate and unequal sphere centered on the family.
Ryan laments that middle-class women "remained shackled by the limitations and contradictions of the doctrine of spheres" and that "the
myriad ways in which women contributed to the maintenance of society" went "usually without just reward, public authority, or a sense of individual achievement."[69] She details the sufferings caused by the exclusion of women from full participation in public life — low wages, poverty,
dependence on male authority, inferior status. But unlike Foner, Ryan
also explores the private consequences of the separate-and-unequal doctrine, particularly the emotional distance that it placed between men
and women, which disrupted marriages and strengthened bonds among
women, especially between mothers and daughters.

Ryan concludes that "sex segregation cut an especially deep rift through American life in the nineteenth century, dividing culture, society, and even human emotions into male and female domains."[70] But *Cradle of the Middle Class* shies away from a direct discussion of the challenge that female values, aspirations, and customs posed to a male-dominated public culture. Ryan does address the issue in "Beyond the Family Crisis," a political essay that appeared in *Democracy* in 1982. She asserts that "the principle success of the domestic ideology was to produce a return of the long-repressed politics of social-political life, a politics that renounced the family as a haven and sought to change the world." She calls for a politics, grounded in "the family's cherished values of love, sharing, and caring," that would "take as its aim the humanizing of the extrafamilial worlds of government, work, education, and social life."[71] But *Cradle of the Middle Class*, despite the fact that it provides the evidence upon which "Beyond the Family Crisis" rests, concludes with a plea for gender-neutral domestic arrangements and ideologies that would facilitate the integration of women into the public sphere and men into the private sphere, rather than with a demand for the transformation of public culture and the recognition of women as a distinctive people with distinctive visions.

Ryan might agree with Carroll Smith-Rosenberg, Suzanne Lebsock, Alice Kessler-Harris, or other historians of women's culture. She may concur with Smith-Rosenberg's assertion that in women's culture prostitution and the sweatshops of the clothing trades functioned as metaphors through which women attacked the corruption and exploitation of a male-dominated urban, capitalist society. Ryan may support Lebsock's contention that women embraced a distinctive ethic of "personalism" that placed less importance on material possessions and greater importance on personal relationships and obligations than did the ethic of male society. She may also agree with Kessler-Harris that women's distinctiveness presented the labor movement with particular opportunities and challenges.[72] But unlike Smith-Rosenberg, Lebsock, and Kessler-Harris, who center their narratives on women, Ryan does not gather the elements of female distinctiveness that she discovers in Oneida County into a women's culture that challenged male culture and presumption.

Ryan does not do so in part because of her ambivalence toward participation in male and female cultures and her fear of fostering debilitating stereotypes of women. She admires Nancy Chodorow's psychological study of the reproduction of mothering and gender, and in *Cradle of the Middle Class* she shows how deeply gender divisions differentiated the temperaments of women and men.[73] Yet in one summation she notes only that "gender lines cut deep into the temperaments ascribed to male and female and into the process of socialization as well" — not necessarily into character — and she emphasizes that many women heroically and painfully "skirted the borders of their assigned sphere" and resisted social pressures toward feminization. She mocks the male delusion of self-creation and self-mastery and speaks ironically of women's roles as "nurturers of male careers, the selfless supporters of self-made men," yet she establishes "strength and self-sufficiency" as women's ideal. She observes time and again that women probed with greater depth and clarity the moral failings of their society, yet she repudiates "the nineteenth-century doctrine of the moral superiority of women" — a doctrine that included many of the same claims when it was articulated by women. Ryan rightly fears the Cult of True Womanhood, which portrayed women as emotional, pure, maternal, and unsuited to public life.[74] But she clearly admires the passion, the moral vision, the capacity for nurture, and the receptivity to nurture of many nineteenth-century women, even though she does not ask or expect women to champion distinctive values in public life. Indeed, she suggests that middle-class women in Oneida County shared male understandings of capitalism, nativism, materialism, benevolence, and evangelism with few reservations and little modification.

Ryan's synthesis echoes W. E. B. Du Bois's account of the predicament of African Americans in a separate-and-unequal society. She has a special feeling for the middle-class women of Oneida County, for their distinctive achievements, strengths, failings, and sufferings behind the veil of discrimination. But in the public arena she places her hopes on integration and the struggle of a vanguard of exceptional women — who in Oneida County included authors Mary Clemner Ames and Emily Chubbuck, physician Caroline Brown, educator Urania Sheldon, and feminist and reformer Paulina Kellogg — for a rightful share of wealth, status, power, and affection. Certainly, a humane nationalism (acknowledging diversity among women and sympathetic to other oppressed nationalities) and an antiimperial internationalism (recognizing that all human beings are kindred) are embedded in her account, as they were in DuBois's. But the narrative success and political appeal of her synthesis rests on her willingness to subordinate those impulses in the here-and-now to her integrationist purpose and to legitimate women's struggle as a quest for inclusion and autonomy on terms that the dominant culture can accept, rather than as a quest for social transformation and female self-determination that the society as presently constituted is bound to reject (even if the readers of *Democracy* are not).

Democratic historians must certainly remain conscious of the impact of dominant groups and cultural imperatives on subordinated, enclaved peoples. Identity and difference are determined not only by heritage, culture, compromise, and choice but also by power. Ryan and Baker are right to remind us of the commonalities between subordinated peoples and the powerful communities with which they must contend or make their peace.[75] Democratic historians must also remain wary of gathering subordinated peoples into wholes that are more coherent and distinctive than evidence justifies. Feminist critics such as Elizabeth Spellman, Eleanor Maccoby, Carol Jacklin, Linda Kerber, and Barbara Johnson warn eloquently of the dangers of subsuming diverse people under such rubrics as "women," of reducing differences to binary oppositions, and of ignoring the fact that "questions of difference and identity are always a function of a specific interlocutionary situation" and that the answers to those questions depend as much on authorial strategy and intent as they do on evidence.[76] But these dangers cannot free historians from the responsibility to discuss differences that are narratively or politically disruptive.

The syntheses of Foner, Baker, and Ryan promote a powerful vision of democracy. Their emphasis on public culture and on struggles for wealth, status, and power gives voice to the basic needs of subordinated peoples, if not always to their particular aspirations. These works widen readers' sympathies and heighten their sense of identity with excluded or devalued peoples, even if they do not test the limits of readers' sympathies or heighten their sense of difference.[77] These authors launch powerful critiques of the republican propensity to draw a rigid and impermeable divide between public and private life. That divide often excludes and oppresses less-powerful peoples and diminishes the quality of private life by segregating it from public life instead of offering it public recognition and protection. These authors also reveal the antidemocratic implications of the republican opposition between public goods and private interests. They unmask the subjective and self-interested character of definitions of the public good offered by dominant groups and demonstrate that the public good can also be embedded in the seemingly self-interested quest of subordinated groups for wealth, status, and power.

Synthesizing authors risk implicating themselves in republicanism's program, however, whenever they embrace the rhetoric of mediation — whenever they curb freedom and difference in the name of a higher liberty or unity. *Nothing but Freedom, Affairs of Party*, and *Cradle of the Middle Class* open the public arena to claims by subordinated groups for wealth, status, and power, but subsume other claims under a claim for autonomy in private life. They embrace a politics of civility that civilizes the discontents of subordinated peoples. The politics of civility allows citizens to struggle in the public arena for equal rights and just rewards. But it demands that citizens not struggle for public acceptance of values, aspirations, or customs that might be deemed parochial, self-interested, offensive, divisive, or imperial by other groups.

The politics of civility, like John Cuddihy's religion of civility, can be invasive, transformative, and oppressive.[78] It is rooted historically in a fear that people will not tolerate dramatic differences between themselves and their neighbors, that they will become violent as arguments over values, aspirations, and the public good intensify. It reflects a belief that people are not capable of civilized behavior, and therefore asks only that people be civil. It asks subordinated peoples to embrace an etiquette of political combat that requires they give no offense to dominant peoples — that they be less zealous, demanding, and distinctive — less "African," "rural," "Dutch," "working-class," or "female" than they might be. Such is the price of orderly admission to the public arena in these narratives, which mediate conflict by melding people together, downplaying differences, and avoiding confrontation. By failing, in the words of political theorist J. Peter Euben, to recognize fully voices that are "otherwise marginalized, silenced, or denied," they fall short of showing readers "what it means to choose and think about choice" when choices are painful.[79]

At its best, as in these narratives, mediation serves justice, diminishes prejudice, and lessens violence. The rhetoric of mediation helps Foner, Baker, and Ryan reach their largely middle-class audience, which, whatever its feelings about democracy, is deeply committed to negotiation and the nonviolent resolution of domestic conflict. Most professionals, including academic historians, share the civic values of Foner, Baker, and Ryan, as long as those values do not portend a radical transformation of society; they appreciate diversity, as long as it does not threaten other values or interests; and they too believe themselves well situated, as occupants of the upper-middle reaches of the social order, to understand and judge all sides in social conflicts. However, the price of mediation is sometimes silence about what matters most.

In sum, the pleas of left historians for democratic syntheses are timely. With a few notable exceptions, social and cultural histories have yet to help readers understand how they might integrate society's parts into narrative or political wholes. Their recommendations on theory and technique can improve social history, as can an appreciation of the great democratic historians, for whom political engagement and a tragic sensibility were the touchstones of narrative achievement.[80] But social and cultural historians must also consider the implications of pleas for synthesis. As professional historians, they have an obligation to write coherent narratives of American history that can help people understand the nation's problems along with its potential. But as social and cultural historians, they have an additional obligation: to understand pleas for synthesis as bids on behalf of the members of a particular social group for the power to transform the nation's culture and society. As the great tragedians of ancient Athens attest, the drive for clarity that makes knowledge possible contains the seeds of tyranny and anarchy. It can lead to visions of the future that privilege and silence. It can also dissolve the ties to place, community, and tradition from which democracy draws its strength.[81]

Is democratic synthesis then impossible? Consider the example of three democratic syntheses, one recent and two not: Eric Foner's *Reconstruction* (1988), W. E. B. Du Bois's *Black Reconstruction in America* (1935), and C. Vann Woodward's *Origins of the New South* (1951).[82] These are not dispassionate histories; they are works of multiple identification and advocacy. They give voice to blacks and to poor and middling whites in the postbellum South, and let them struggle among themselves and against each other. They give the distinctive stories of these peoples fair hearing and allow them to compete with each other to determine the shape and meaning of the encompassing narrative. Their histories explore the commonalities and universalities of black and white experiences and reveal the blindnesses and failings of both communities. They summon up the passions that threaten to destroy the South (and the nation) as a moral and political community and yet remain the source of its energy, patriotism, and dignity. These tragic histories thus reclaim the South's legacy, "however cursed it may be," by finding, in J. Peter Euben's words on Greek tragedy, a "place and hearing for different voices within the whole" and by establishing an ideal of reciprocity and reconciliation.[83]

What makes these democratic syntheses great is that they are true tragedies.[84] They confront evil, suffering, and defeat to the point of despair, yet they affirm the struggle for democracy. Like the tragedians of ancient Athens, as described by Euben, they place a nation's "dearly bought cultural accommodations on trial." At the same time, they help citizens understand democracy and gain the wisdom they will need to achieve it. By exposing the moral failures and blindnesses of postbellum Americans, these histories demonstrate that beliefs and institutions considered "normal and natural" more often than not violated the ideals Americans shared. But by juxtaposing the ideal and the real, as *Origins* does in its stark depictions of Southern Redeemers, Progressives, and Democrats, or as *Black Reconstruction* does in its empathetic portrait of President Andrew Johnson, they point the way toward redemption, progress, and democracy.[85]

Foner's, Du Bois's, and Woodward's multivocal, multistoried narratives force readers to acknowledge that they are bound "by and to" their history. History is the source of the energy, passion, and loyalty that draw the members of a human community together as peoples, despite their divisions, and make them thirst for greatness. Yet history makes it nearly impossible for humans to live together and to realize democratic ideals. History furthers, yet limits, self-understanding and understanding of others. It empowers humans, yet traps them in webs partly of their own "inadvertent devising" and commits them to solutions that deepen their problems. Foner's, Du Bois's, and Woodward's histories confront human limitation, but in so doing yield insights that are prerequisites for creating a genuine democratic community.

Origins, Black Reconstruction, and *Reconstruction* cannot inspire democratic faith where there is none. That the Populist struggle ended in disfranchisement and mutual recrimination and that the Radical Republican struggle ended in debt peonage and the destruction of Reconstruction governments only gives doubters further reason to doubt. But for the faithful — and Foner, Du Bois, and Woodward, as a socialist, a Marxist, and a populist devoted to the struggle for racial equality, are to be counted among that group — these reversals did not mark the final triumph of evil, nor did they render futile the democratic struggles that preceded them. Foner quotes the Reverend Peter Randolph, a former slave, who said, "The river has its bend, and the longest road must ter-

minate." The defeat of Reconstruction did not diminish the determina-
tion of many of Reconstruction's architects to carry on. Nor could it
undo the "framework of legal rights" that Reconstruction had "enshrined
in the Constitution" or crush "the institutions created or consolidated
after the Civil War"— the black family, school, and church — that "provided the base from which the modern civil rights revolution sprang."
Because they recall the struggles of democrats in the past, tragic narratives like *Reconstruction*, *Black Reconstruction*, and *Origins of the New
South* are powerful theodicies that give solace in reactionary times. They
help contemporary democrats identify with their predecessors, no less
frail and no more influential than themselves, who made the world a
better place and left a legacy on which future democrats could build.
They encourage contemporary democrats to write the next chapter of
democracy's ascent.[86]

Woodward's portraits of poor and middling Southern whites are admittedly more fully realized than his portraits of Southern blacks; the
opposite is the case for Foner. Du Bois's portraits of freed people and
poor whites are psychologically acute, yet abstract and impersonal. Their
works doubtless reflect both the relative strengths of the historical literatures at the times they wrote and complicated patterns of personal identification.[87] Each history falls short, perhaps inevitably, of the "poly-
vocal" or "open" ideal articulated by Elsa Barkley Brown and Edward
Ayers.[88] But none of these historians privileges a particular group's understandings of honor and citizenship. Their narratives criticize the inner and outer workings of all human communities, including that of the
nation at large. And they offer multivalent theodicies of the democratic
struggle, because they examine the sufferings of several peoples and find
evil in much more than the failure of a particular social group to uphold
what is best in its traditions. They thus can reach broad audiences.[89]

The strength of these narratives is also attributable in part to their
length. It takes many thoughtful words to realize a democratic vision of
history. Unlike the tragic plays of ancient Greece, democratic syntheses
must see the world through the eyes of legions of characters, not a handful, and must bring them onto the historical stage in full voice.

The narratives are strong also because they rest on clear yet subtle
theories of how power is distributed and of how politics, economics,
and culture interact. *Origins* and *Reconstruction* revolve around social
theories familiar to contemporary readers. Woodward does not embrace the Beards' economic determinism; Foner does not impose Marx's

dialectical schemes on the past. The reputations of these historians rest in part on the care with which they rework these theories, altering them so that they address questions of race and culture. Yet the Beards and Marx remain embedded in their narratives. Their theories help readers, particularly those on the left, feel at home amid a mass of information and interpretation and help them follow the twists and turns of Foner's and Woodward's plots, which are driven by conflict between popular forces and ruling elites.

The need for theoretical clarity poses problems, however, for historians — especially feminist scholars — who wish to rest democratic syntheses on social theories that are not widely accepted or understood. As Mary Ryan proves in her recent theoretical essays, which extend and clarify the arguments of *Cradle of the Middle Class* on the relationship between public and private, attention to theory can help democratic historians transcend the limits of time-honored rhetorical strategies (like mediation) and confront the troubling implications of their findings.[90] But theory, when novel and explicit, leads away from narrative and costs readers. One reviewer complained, "If this . . . represents the new Mary Ryan, I would prefer the old Mary Ryan of *Cradle of the Middle Class*."[91] The synthetic enterprise will need both Ryans if it is to improve upon the syntheses of Foner and Woodward, which neglect the fundamental role that gender relations played in shaping postbellum Southern politics — a role that Ryan has made clear in an elegant analysis of the resistance of Confederate women in New Orleans to the Union soldiers who occupied the city in 1862.[92] Theoretical essays can clarify the thought of synthetic authors and remind them of power relationships (such as those among whites and blacks in New York City) that are crucial to relationships they want to discuss.

Finally, democratic syntheses can profit from a clearer understanding of republicanism and its relationship to democracy, both ancient and modern. Democracy first arose as a critique of the theories and practices of the republicans of ancient Greece, who were perhaps the first members of a settled agricultural society to seek alternatives to government by nobles or monarchs. The social crises that besieged the city-states of the Greek world from the ninth through the fifth centuries revealed the inadequacy of those forms of government, as well as the undesirability of the alternatives. No one wanted factional strife or tyranny. But it proved difficult to create new governments that could avert anarchy, class conflict, and rebellion. On an abstract level, by the sixth and fifth centuries many Greeks believed that the general welfare and social harmony could be advanced in a just community (*eunomia*) dedicated to common moral principles and ruled by its citizens, who would hold equal shares in its government (*isonomia*). In practice, however, such polities were difficult to create. Who deserved citizenship? What issues were too divisive for citizens to decide? Would citizens care more about the community than about themselves?[93]

Ancient republicans had to answer these questions if they were to resolve the social crisis of the Greek world. They first defined citizenship. They divided people into natives and foreigners, the civilized and the barbarian, the honored and the dishonored, males and females, the free and the slave; they divided the material world into persons and property, humanity and nature; and in each case, they gave the former preeminence over the latter. The resulting hierarchies together defined the citizen: human, person, free, male, honored, civilized, native.

Next, ancient republicans put certain issues beyond the reach of citizens. They divided society into public and private spheres and restricted the citizens' right to interfere in such divisive "private" matters as the economy and household government. Finally, they tried to limit the power of selfish factions. They divided values and aspirations into goods and interests and deemed only the former to be worthy of entering politics. Ancient republicans thus understood their world through fictive (yet meaningful) dualisms, which they then transformed into hierarchies. They sustained those hierarchies through a rhetoric of disinterest and sacrifice, which promised that the common good would be served if each person and thing took its proper place and complemented its counterpart.[94]

Modern republican historians like Bailyn, Schlesinger, Wood, and the Handlins of course reject many of the beliefs and practices that ancient republicans embraced. They would never restrict political participation to a minority of all adults. They fear the intrusion of religious and ethnic antagonisms into public life far more than they fear the intrusion of government into business and family life. And they believe that economic and intellectual ambition can serve the public interest. Yet modern republican historians embrace the central assumptions of ancient republicans: that effective citizenship best belongs in the hands of the honorable, that private and public matters should remain separate for the sake of social peace, and that selfish interests should not be allowed to subvert the public good.

Democracy, as understood by ancient democrats and modern democratic historians, challenges the dualisms and hierarchies that ancient republicans and modern republican historians have created and raises questions about whether those dualisms and hierarchies serve the common good. Sometimes democratic historians ask that people transcend dualisms — such as those that differentiate the honored and the dishonored, or men and women — and acknowledge the dignity and solidarity of humanity. Sometimes democratic historians invert hierarchies, by championing the cause of noncitizens or by reminding readers that masters can be slaves or the honored dishonorable. Sometimes democratic historians subsume one dualistic term in another, as when they claim that property is not a thing but a fiction through which persons claim the partial or exclusive right to control portions of the human and nonhuman world, or when they assert that privacy is a fiction through which privileged peoples preserve their privileges and oppressed peoples protect their autonomy and community. Sometimes democratic historians suggest that terms penetrate each other, that gender can be ambiguous, for instance, or that interests are often valued because they represent goods and that goods are often valued because they represent interests. Democratic social and cultural history, at its best, participates in democracy's ongoing critique of the dualisms and hierarchies of republicanism.[95]

It is important to remember, however, that this critique depends upon republicanism. It does not abolish fictive dualisms or hierarchies. It recasts dualisms and rejects the invidious, debilitating hierarchies that past republics have created.[96] But it leads to the creation of new republics, with their own divisions, repressions, and silences. Democratic epiphanies like *Origins of the New South*, *Black Reconstruction in America*, and *Reconstruction*, which reveal postbellum America's "dearly bought" accommodations, can help readers progress toward democratic ideals. But these epiphanies break off at a critical moment, historically and politically. They end before a more democratic republic can take shape — before that republic's own accommodations become clear. Republican historians like Bailyn, Schlesinger, Wood, and the Handlins may be wrong to suggest that citizens should in some instances embrace these accommodations willingly, but they are right to insist that citizens embrace them knowingly. Democratic historians must be wary of using the rhetoric of disinterest and sacrifice, lest they become enmeshed in the latest antidemocratic programs of republicanism.

Greater self-awareness can be a political good. It can help citizens appreciate the limitations of their political beliefs and the political implications of their rhetoric. But greater self-awareness can be a scholarly good as well. It can help historians understand the ways in which the struggle between democracy and republicanism has shaped America's social and cultural history, and it can help them find better words to tell that story.

NOTES

1. Thomas A. Bender, "Wholes and Parts: The Need for Synthesis in American History," *Journal of American History* 73 (1986): 120–21. See also Thomas Bender, "Images of the Past," *Partisan Review* 3 (1983): 459–63; Thomas Bender, "The New History — Then and Now," *Reviews in American History* 12 (1984): 612–22; and Thomas Bender, "Making History Whole Again," *New York Times Book Review*, October 6, 1985, p. 1. Bender's essays participate in the contemporary debate in Great Britain and the United States over the decline of narrative and the need for synthesis in historical literature. See Richard T. Vann, "The Rhetoric of Social History," *Journal of Social History* 10 (1976): 221–36; Lawrence Stone, "The Revival of Narrative: Reflections on a New Old History," *Past and Present* 85 (1979): 3–24; Jack Hexter, "The Rhetoric of History" and "Garrett Mattingly, Historian," in *Doing History* (Bloomington: Indiana University Press, 1971), pp. 15–76, 157–72; C. Vann Woodward, "A Short History of American History," *New York Times Book Review*, August 8, 1982, p. 3; J. Morgan Kousser, "The Revival of Narrative: A Response to Recent Criticisms of Quantitative History," *Social Science History* 8 (1984): 133–49; Olivier Zunz, "The Synthesis of Social Change: Reflections on American Social History," in Olivier Zunz, ed., *Reliving the Past: The Worlds of Social History* (Chapel Hill: University of North Carolina Press, 1985), pp. 53–114; William H. McNeill, "Mythistory, or Truth, Myth, History, and Historians," *American Historical Review* 91 (1986): 1–10; Eric H. Monkkonen, "The Dangers of Synthesis," *American Historical Review* 91 (1986): 1146–57; Peter Novick, *That Noble Dream: The "Objectivity Question" and the American Historical Profession* (New York: Cambridge University Press, 1988), pp. 622–25; and George M. Frederickson, "Commentary on Thomas Bender's Call for Synthesis in American History," in Günther Lenz, Harmut Keil, and Sabine Bröck-Sallah, eds., *Reconstructing American Literary and Historical Studies* (New York: St. Martin's, 1990), pp. 74–81.

On the professionalization of history and the diminished role of history in public discourse, see Casey Blake, "Where Are the Young Left Historians?" *Radical History Review* 28–30 (1984): 114–23; Thomas Bender, "Erosion of Public Culture: Cities, Discourses, and Professional Disciplines," in Thomas L. Haskell, ed., *The Authority of Experts* (Bloomington: Indiana University Press, 1984), pp. 84–106; Susan Porter Benson, Stephen Brier, and Roy Rosenzweig, eds., *Presenting the Past: Essays on History and the Public* (Philadelphia: Temple University Press, 1986); Russell Jacoby, *The Last Intellectuals: American Culture in the Age of Academe* (New York:

Basic Books, 1987); Theodore S. Hamerow, *Reflections on History and Historians* (Madison: University of Wisconsin Press, 1987); and Novick, *That Noble Dream*, pp. 573–92.

2. Important references include Herbert G. Gutman, "The Missing Synthesis: Whatever Happened to History?" *Nation*, November 11, 1981, pp. 521, 553–54; Eric Foner, "History in Crisis," *Commonweal*, December 18, 1981, pp. 723–26; and Michael Zuckerman, "Myth and Method: The Current Crises in American Historical Writing," *The History Teacher* 17 (1984): 219–45. Allan Megill observes in "Fragmentation and the Future of Historiography," *American Historical Review* 96 (1991): 693–94, that "all calls for synthesis are attempts to impose an interpretation." On the political implications of calls for synthesis in the United States and Great Britain, see Harvey J. Kaye, *The Powers of the Past: Reflections on the Crisis and Promise of History* (New York: Harvester/Wheatsheaf, 1991).

3. Whitman, *Democratic Vistas*, pp. 301–59; and Charles A. Beard and Mary R. Beard, *The Rise of American Civilization*, rev. ed. (New York: Macmillan, 1933). Thomas Bender discusses his political vision in *New York Intellect: A History of Intellectual Life in New York City* (New York: Knopf, 1987), pp. xiii–xix.

4. See especially Bender, "Wholes and Parts: The Need for Synthesis," 132–35; and the unpublished version of that paper presented at the Ninety-ninth Annual Meeting of the American Historical Association, Chicago, 1984. For a list of the studies that Bender admires, see n. 11.

5. Eric Foner, *Nothing but Freedom: Emancipation and Its Legacy* (Baton Rouge: Louisiana State University Press, 1983), p. 110; and Gene Wise, *American Historical Explanations*, 2d ed. (Minneapolis: University of Minnesota Press, 1980), pp. 223–95.

6. Gutman, "Missing Synthesis." Gutman delivered his remarks at a meeting of the American Writers Congress in October 1981. He participated in a panel on the question "Have writers disregarded history?"

7. Foner, "History in Crisis." On the place of politics in social history, see Elizabeth Fox-Genovese and Eugene Genovese, "The Political Crisis of Social History: A Marxian Perspective," *Journal of Social History* 10 (1976): 205–20; Geoff Ely and Keith Nield, "Why Does Social History Ignore Politics?" *Social History* 5 (1980): 249–71; Gertrude Himmelfarb, "History with the Politics Left Out," in *The New History and the Old* (Cambridge: Belknap Press, 1987), pp. 13–32; and Novick, *That Noble Dream*, pp. 438–45.

8. Zuckerman, "Myth and Method," pp. 236, 225, 235–36, 239, 219. See also Michael Zuckerman, "Puritans, Cavaliers, and the Motley Middle," in Michael Zuckerman, ed., *Friends and Neighbors: Group Life in America's First Plural Society* (Philadelphia: Temple University Press, 1982), pp. 3–25; and McNeill, "Mythistory."

9. Bender, *New York Intellect*, pp. xvii, 5; Thomas Bender, "The End of the City?" *Democracy* 3 (1983): 8–20; and Thomas Bender, "New York as a Center of 'Difference': How America's Metropolis Counters America's Myth," *Dissent* 34 (1987): 429–35. For complementary visions of democracy, see Beard and Beard, *Rise of American Civilization*, p. 725; Whitman, *Democratic Vistas*, pp. 317–19; and Nell Irvin Painter, *Standing at Armageddon: The United States, 1877–1919* (New York: Norton, 1987), pp. xiii, xlii–xliv.

10. I recognize the need for caution when putting forward allegorical interpretations of documents that are otherwise clear and salient. My case is circumstantial, based on the rhetoric of Bender's plea, the political opinions he expresses in other writings, and the politics of Herbert Gutman's and Eric Foner's pleas for synthesis, whose influence Bender acknowledges.

11. Bender praised the following synthetic monographs in "Wholes and Parts" (pp. 132–35), and in the unpublished paper on which it was based: Jean H. Baker, *Affairs of Party: The Political Culture of Northern Democrats in the Mid-Nineteenth Century* (Ithaca: Cornell University Press, 1983); Iver Charles Bernstein, "The New York City Draft Riots of 1863 and Class Relations on the Eve of Industrial Capitalism" (Ph.D. diss., Yale University, 1985), which has since appeared as *The New York City Draft Riots: Their Significance for American Society and Politics in the Age of the Civil War* (New York: Oxford University Press, 1990); Foner, *Nothing but Freedom*; Mary P. Ryan, *Cradle of the Middle Class: The Family in Oneida County, New York, 1790–1865* (New York: Cambridge University Press, 1981); and Sean Wilentz, *Chants Democratic: New York City and the Rise of the American Working Class, 1788–1850* (New York: Oxford University Press, 1984). The following scholars have responded directly to Bender's plea for synthesis: Richard Wightman Fox, "Public Culture and the Problem of Synthesis," *Journal of American History* 74 (1987): 113–16; Alice Kessler-Harris, "Social History," in Eric Foner, ed., *The New American History* (Philadelphia: Temple University Press), 177–80; Nell Irvin Painter, "Bias and Synthesis in History," *Journal of American History* 74 (1987): 109–12; and Roy Rosenzweig, "What Is the Matter with History?" *Journal of American History* 74 (1987): 117–22.

12. Bernard Bailyn, "The Challenge of Modern Historiography," *American Historical Review* 87 (1982): 1–24; Bailyn, *The Peopling of British North America: An Introduction* (New York: Knopf, 1986); Bailyn, *Voyagers to the West: A Passage in the Peopling of America on the Eve of the Revolution* (New York: Knopf, 1986); Arthur M. Schlesinger, Jr., *The Cycles of American History* (New York: Houghton Mifflin, 1986); Schlesinger, *The Disuniting of America: Reflections on a Multicultural Society* (New York: Norton, 1992); Gordon Wood, "Star-Spangled History," *New York Review of Books*, August 12, 1982, pp. 4–9; Wood, *The Radicalism of the American Revolution* (New York: Knopf, 1992); Fredric Smoler, "The Radical Revolution: An Interview with Gordon Wood," *American Heritage* (1992), pp. 51–58; and Oscar Handlin and Lilian Handlin, *Liberty in America*, 4 vols. (New York: Harper and Row, 1986–).

13. Schlesinger, *Cycles of American History*, p. 422.

14. I hope to discuss republican syntheses of American history more fully in a future essay. I have developed the opposition between democracy and republicanism at greater length in *The Democratic Dilemma: Religion, Reform, and the Social Order in the Connecticut River Valley of Vermont, 1791–1850* (New York: Cambridge University Press, 1987). My work has been influenced by Michael Kammen, *People of Paradox: An Inquiry Concerning the Origins of American Civilization* (New York: Knopf, 1972). Kammen emphasizes the importance of "biformities," or paired oppositions, in shaping American culture and politics. Most American historians, how-

ever, have been more deeply influenced in recent years by the so-called republican interpretation of American history, which defines republicanism differently than I do in this essay. That interpretation emphasizes the role in American history of ideas drawn from dissenters in eighteenth-century England who embraced the "commonwealth" tradition and its antecedents. On that interpretation, see Daniel Rodgers, "Republicanism: The Career of a Concept," *Journal of American History* 79 (1992): 11–38; Robert E. Shalhope, "Toward a Republican Synthesis: The Emergence of an Understanding of Republicanism in American Historiography," *William and Mary Quarterly* 29 (1972): 49–80; and Shalhope, "Republicanism and Early American Historiography," *William and Mary Quarterly* 39 (1982): 334–56.

15. Painter, "Bias and Synthesis in History," 109–12.

16. Thomas Bender, "Wholes and Parts: Continuing the Conversation," *Journal of American History* 74 (1987): 124–25.

17. Harold Mah, "Suppressing the Text: The Metaphysics of Ethnographic History in Darnton's Great Cat Massacre," *History Workshop Journal* 31 (1991): 1–20; and William Cronon, "A Place for Stories: Nature, History, and Narrative," *Journal of American History* 78 (1992): 1347–76, use a similar analytic strategy. Like Mah and Cronon, I focus on influential works by prominent scholars, nearly all of whom have won major prizes in American history and have served on the editorial boards of major journals.

18. I am referring to Eric Foner, *Reconstruction: America's Unfinished Revolution, 1863–1877* (New York: Harper and Row, 1988); and Mary P. Ryan, *Women in Public: Between Banners and Ballots, 1825–1880* (Baltimore: Johns Hopkins University Press, 1990). I will discuss them below.

19. The literature on professionalism and the new class is voluminous. My understanding has been shaped by C. Wright Mills, *White Collar: The American Middle Class* (New York: Oxford University Press, 1951); Samuel P. Hays, "The Politics of Reform in Municipal Government in the Progressive Era," *Pacific Northwest Quarterly* 55 (1964): 157–69; Lawrence R. Veysey, *The Emergence of the American University* (Chicago: University of Chicago Press, 1965); Robert H. Wiebe, *The Search for Order, 1877–1920* (New York: Hill and Wang, 1967), pp. 111 ff.; David T. Bazelon, *Power in America: The Politics of the New Class* (New York: New American Library, 1967); Anthony Giddens, *The Class Structure of Advanced Societies* (New York: Harper and Row, 1975), pp. 167–97; Burton J. Bledstein, *The Culture of Professionalism* (New York: Norton, 1976); Thomas L. Haskell, *The Emergence of Professional Social Science: The American Social Science Association and the Nineteenth-Century Crisis of Authority* (Urbana: University of Illinois Press, 1977); Barbara Ehrenreich and John Ehrenreich, "The Professional-Managerial Class," in Pat Walker, ed., *Between Labor and Capital* (Boston: South End Press, 1979); Alvin Ward Gouldner, *The Future of Intellectuals and the Rise of a New Class* (New York: Seabury Press, 1979); Paul Fussell, *Class: A Guide through the American Status System* (New York: Summit Books, 1983); Thomas L. Haskell, ed., *The Authority of Experts* (Bloomington: Indiana University Press, 1984); Andrew D. Abbott, *The System of Professions: An Essay on the Division of Expert Labor* (Chicago: University of Chicago

Press, 1988); Novick, *That Noble Dream*; Barbara Ehrenreich, *Fear of Falling: The Inner Life of the Middle Class* (New York: Pantheon, 1989); and Dorothy Ross, *The Origins of American Social Science* (New York: Cambridge University Press, 1991).

20. Wilentz, *Chants Democratic*, pp. 48 n, 264–65.

21. David Roediger, "'Labor in White Skin': Race and Working-Class History," in Mike Davis and Michael Sprinker, eds., *Reshaping the U.S. Left: Popular Struggles in the 1980s* (London: Verso, 1988), pp. 287–308. Exceptions include Alexander Saxton, "Blackface Minstrelsy and Jacksonian Ideology," *American Quarterly* 36 (1984): 211–35; William J. Rorabaugh, *The Craft Apprentice: From Franklin to the Machine Age in America* (New York: Oxford University Press, 1986); and the works cited in Roediger, "'Labor in White Skin,'" p. 288 n. 6. See Clarence E. Walker, *Deromanticizing Black History: Critical Essays and Appraisals* (Knoxville: University of Tennessee Press, 1991), pp. xi–33, for a critical view of Marxist approaches to the problem of race in American history.

22. Sean Wilentz, "Against Exceptionalism: Class Consciousness and the American Labor Movement," *International Labor and Working Class History* 26 (1984): 1–24; and *Chants Democratic*, pp. 9–19, 101–3.

23. Wilentz, *Chants Democratic*, pp. 30, 30 n, 34, 36, 74; Shane White, "'We Dwell in Safety and Pursue Our Honest Callings': Free Blacks in New York City, 1783–1810," *Journal of American History* 75 (1988): 445–70; Shane White, *Somewhat More Independent: The End of Slavery in New York City, 1770–1810* (Athens: University of Georgia Press, 1991); Gary B. Nash, "Forging Freedom: The Emancipation Experience in the Northern Seaport Cities, 1775–1820," in Ira Berlin and Ronald Hoffman, eds., *Slavery and Freedom in the Age of Revolution* (Charlottesville: University Press of Virginia, 1983), pp. 3–48; Howard B. Rock, *Artisans of the New Republic: The Tradesmen of New York City in the Age of Jefferson* (New York: New York University Press, 1979), p. 38; and Graham Russell Hodges, *New York City Cartmen, 1667–1850* (New York: New York University Press, 1986), pp. 102–5.

24. Rock, *Artisans of the New Republic*, p. 224; Gary B. Nash, *Forging Freedom: The Formation of Philadelphia's Black Community, 1720–1840* (Cambridge: Harvard University Press, 1988), pp. 149–50; Hodges, *New York City Cartmen*, pp. 25, 35, 109, 152, 158–59; W. Jeffrey Bolster, "'To Feel Like a Man': Black Seamen in the Northern States, 1800–1860," *Journal of American History* 76 (1990): 1178; Leonard P. Curry, *The Free Black in Urban America, 1800–1850* (Chicago: University of Chicago Press, 1981), pp. 15–36; and Ira Berlin, *Slaves without Masters: The Free Negro in the Antebellum South* (New York: Pantheon, 1974), pp. 217–49.

25. Phyllis F. Field, *The Politics of Race in New York: The Struggle for Black Suffrage in the Civil War Era* (Ithaca: Cornell University Press, 1982), pp. 19–42; Curry, *The Free Black in Urban America*, pp. 217–18; and Bolster, "Black Seamen in the Northern States," p. 1192.

26. Rock, *Artisans of the New Republic*, pp. 3, 279, 311. Jonathan Glickstein, *Concepts of Free Labor in Antebellum America* (New Haven: Yale University Press, 1991), contains a brilliant discussion of the prejudices against manual labor in a putatively free labor society. David Roediger, in *The Wages of Whiteness: Race and the Making*

of the American Working Class (New York: Verso, 1991), argues that race was central in forging the consciousness of American male workers in the nineteenth century.

27. James Weldon Johnson, *Black Manhattan* (New York: Knopf, 1930), pp. 29–30, 20–26; Curry, *The Free Black in Urban America*, pp. 205, 168–69; and Bender, *New York Intellect*, 253–55.

28. Bender, *New York Intellect*, p. 253; and David Levering Lewis, *When Harlem Was in Vogue* (New York: Knopf, 1981), pp. 119–55.

29. Bender, *New York Intellect*, pp. 140–56; and Theodore G. Vincent, ed., *Voices of a Black Nation: Political Journalism in the Harlem Renaissance* (San Francisco: Ramparts Press, 1973).

30. Bender, *New York Intellect*, pp. 253–55. Bender bases his interpretation on Johnson, *Black Manhattan*; Harold Cruse, *Crisis of the Negro Intellectual* (New York: Morrow, 1967); Nathan Irvin Huggins, *Harlem Renaissance* (New York: Oxford University Press, 1971); and David Levering Lewis, *When Harlem Was in Vogue* (New York: Knopf, 1981). The evidence and arguments in Cruse's, Huggins's, and Lewis's books, however, do not support Bender's characterization of the Harlem Renaissance. As the notes below reveal, I draw on that evidence and those arguments in shaping my alternative interpretation of the Renaissance.

31. Bender, *New York Intellect*, pp. 253–55. Zora Neale Hurston attended Barnard College from 1925 to 1927. She wrote in New York City from 1930 to 1932 under the patronage of Charlotte Mason and returned in 1935–36 as a drama coach for the Works Progress Administration. She resigned to accept a Guggenheim Fellowship. Ralph Ellison moved to New York City in 1936 to study sculpture. He worked for the Federal Writers Project from 1938 to 1942 and edited the short-lived *Negro Quarterly* in 1942–43, before joining the merchant marine. He received a Rosenwald Fellowship upon his return from the war, with which he started *Invisible Man*. Richard Wright moved to New York City in 1937 to become the Harlem editor of the *Daily Worker*. He published *Uncle Tom's Children*, *Native Son*, and *Black Boy*, and received a Guggenheim Fellowship, before moving to Paris in 1947. See Robert E. Hemenway, *Zora Neale Hurston: A Literary Biography* (Urbana: University of Illinois Press, 1977); Harold Bloom, ed., *Ralph Ellison* (New York: Chelsea House Publishers, 1986), pp. 173–74; Robert Felgar, *Richard Wright* (Boston: Twayne, 1980), pp. 14–15.

For interpretations of the Renaissance that extend it temporally beyond the 1920s, see Houston A. Baker, Jr., *Modernism and the Harlem Renaissance* (Chicago: University of Chicago Press, 1987); and Michael Awkward, *Inspiriting Influences: Tradition, Revision, and Afro-American Women's Novels* (New York: Columbia University Press, 1989). Huggins anticipated these interpretations (*Harlem Renaissance*, pp. 190, 303). In his opinion, the opening of the 1930s marked the end only of "that promoted culture called the 'Harlem Renaissance'" and of "the innocent Harlem Renaissance."

32. Bender, *New York Intellect*, pp. 246–49; and Randolph S. Bourne, "Trans-National America," *Atlantic* 118 (1916): 86–97. According to Bender, Bourne "celebrated diversity and difference." His ideal "implied a proliferation of vital subcultures — ethnic, but also aesthetic, geographical, and political." Bourne hoped that

"the geographical contiguousness of the metropolis would deny each group the privilege of provinciality" and breed tolerance and conversation.

33. Bender, *New York Intellect*, pp. 253–55.

34. On art and politics in Harlem, see Lewis, *When Harlem Was in Vogue*, pp. 115–18; Huggins, *Harlem Renaissance*, pp. 7, 26–56; Vincent, *Voices of a Black Nation*; Edward E. Waldron, *Walter White and the Harlem Renaissance* (Port Washington: Kennikat Press, 1976); Robert Earl Williams, "Three Pioneers of Black Sociology" (Ph.D. diss., Washington State University, 1976); Arnold Rampersad, *The Art and Imagination of W. E. B. DuBois* (Cambridge: Harvard University Press, 1976); Rampersad, *The Life of Langston Hughes*, vol. 1 (New York: Oxford University Press, 1986); and Jervis Anderson, *A. Philip Randolph: A Biographical Portrait* (New York: Harcourt Brace Jovanovich, 1973). Lewis and Huggins criticize Harlem Renaissance art for being at times politically heavy-handed, and they sometimes question the efficacy of the political programs of Renaissance leaders. Their findings, however, suggest that Bender's portrait of the relationship between art and politics in Harlem is inadequate. Walter White, an officer in the NAACP and an active Republican, wrote *The Fire in the Flint* (New York: Knopf, 1924), a novel on the plight of contemporary blacks in a small town in southwestern Georgia, and *Rope and Faggot* (New York: Knopf, 1928), a history of lynching based on research he had conducted for the NAACP. Both works emphasized the need for political action in the campaign for civil rights. Charles S. Johnson, a sociologist and editor of the Urban League's periodical, *Opportunity*, published the work of Harlem artists and social scientists, including E. Franklin Frazier and Ralph Bunche. W. E. B. Du Bois, a tireless political activist, produced a flagrantly political novel, *Dark Princess* (New York: Harcourt, Brace, and Company, 1928), and edited *Crisis*, which published Langston Hughes's "The Negro Speaks of Rivers." A. Philip Randolph edited a socialist and antiwar newspaper, the *Messenger*, published Claude McKay's "If We Must Die," organized a tenants' union, and founded the Brotherhood of Sleeping Car Porters.

35. See Lewis, *When Harlem Was in Vogue*, pp. 226–33, 274–77; Huggins, *Harlem Renaissance*, pp. 77–79; Rudolph Fisher, *The Walls of Jericho* (New York: Knopf, 1928), pp. 3–34, 45–55; Claude McKay, *Home to Harlem* (New York: Harper and Brothers, 1928), pp. 41–54, 123–203; and Nella Larsen, *Quicksand and Passing* (1928 and 1929; reprint, New Brunswick, N.J.: Rutgers University Press, 1986), pp. 109–14, 115–35. See also Countee Cullen, *One Way to Heaven* (New York: Harper and Brothers, 1932), pp. 1–89, 252–80. These novels are admittedly picaresque. They do not focus exclusively on the experience of the urban working class, and Nella Larsen's *Quicksand*, which explores the spiritual and cultural predicament of its mulatto heroine, Helga Crane, purposely views white and black life with detachment. But the protagonists in these novels enter a variety of social worlds, including high society and working-class society, so that readers can experience Harlem and the wider black world in its entirety.

36. Huggins, *Harlem Renaissance*, pp. 41–47; and Lewis, *When Harlem Was in Vogue*, pp. 104–5, 122.

37. Bender, *New York Intellect*, p. 254; and Huggins, *Harlem Renaissance*, p. 186.

Among the works that confront the legacy of the rural South, see White, *Fire in the Flint*; Larsen, *Quicksand*; and Jean Toomer, *Cane* (New York: Boni-Liveright, 1923).

38. Martin Duberman, *Paul Robeson* (New York: Knopf, 1988), pp. 87–214; Huggins, *Harlem Renaissance*, pp. 172–79; and Fisher, *Walls of Jericho*, p. 299.

39. Bender, *New York Intellect*, p. 254. See note 31, on the jobs, fellowships, and philanthropic support that Hurston, Ellison, and Wright received in New York City. Hughes received support from Charlotte Osgood Mason, a white patron, until 1930, and won a Guggenheim Fellowship in 1935. Lewis, *When Harlem Was in Vogue*, pp. 151–55, 175–78, 256–59; and James A. Emanuel, *Langston Hughes* (Boston: Twayne, 1967), pp. 11–12. It is also clear that not all relationships with white patrons and critics were equally patronizing. See Lewis, *When Harlem Was in Vogue*, pp. 140–41, 226–28, on Claude McKay's relationships with Louise Bryant and Sinclair Lewis.

On identity and performance in Afro-American literature, useful references include Barbara Johnson, "Thresholds of Difference: Structures of Address in Zora Neale Hurston," *Critical Inquiry* 12 (1985): 278–89; Henry Louis Gates, Jr., *The Signifying Monkey: A Theory of Afro-American Literary Criticism* (New York: Oxford University Press, 1988); and Houston A. Baker, Jr., and Patricia Redmond, eds., *Afro-American Literary Study in the 1990s* (New York: University Press Books at the New School, 1989).

40. Bender, *New York Intellect*, p. 253.

41. In the *American Historical Review* 93 (1988): 1392–93, Hamilton Cravens asks why Bender spends more time on the *Partisan Review* than on the Harlem Renaissance. Cravens is the only reviewer to question whether *New York Intellect* realizes its democratic ideals. In the *Journal of Interdisciplinary History* 15 (1985): 352–54, Gary B. Nash criticizes Wilentz's neglect of black workers. Nash had just published *Forging Freedom: The Formation of Philadelphia's Black Community, 1720–1840* (Cambridge: Harvard University Press, 1988), a study of urban blacks in postrevolutionary America. Michael Kazin, in *Nation* 239 (1984): 181–82, doesn't comment on the exclusion of blacks in *Chants Democratic* but calls for further discussion of racism in the 1850s.

For other reviews of *Chants Democratic*, see Sandra L. Albrecht, *Contemporary Sociology* 14 (1985): 228–29; Glenn C. Altschuler, *Labor History* 29 (1988): 91–92; Amy Bridges, *Political Science Quarterly* 101 (1986): 161–62; Richard W. Brown, Jr., *Historian* 48 (1986): 611–12; Mary Jo Buhle, *Times Literary Supplement*, February 1, 1985, p. 124; Patricia Cooper, *Journal of Social History* 20 (1986): 190–91; Thomas Dublin, *Reviews in American History* 13 (1985): 43–47; Melvyn Dubofsky, *Science and Society* 51 (1987): 223–26; Phyllis F. Field, *History* 13 (1984): 27–28; D. R. Jamieson, *Choice* 22 (1984): 337; Robert L. Filippelli, *Library Journal*, March 15, 1984, p. 582; Bruce Laurie, *Journal of Economic History* 45 (1985): 1009–10; Howard B. Rock, *Journal of Urban History* 12 (1985): 89–97; Daniel J. Walkowitz, *Journal of American History* 71 (1985): 862–63; David Ward, *Journal of Historical Geography* 11 (1985): 442–43; Robert Wiebe, *American Historical Review* 90 (1985): 1265–66; and Sharon Zukin, *American Journal of Sociology* 91 (1986): 1490–92.

For reviews of *New York Intellect*, see Robert Boyers, *New York Times Book Review*, July 26, 1987, p. 18; David Brooks, *National Review*, July 17, 1987, pp. 47–48; Paul A. Carter, *Historian* 51 (1988): 142–43; Robert L. Fishman, *Journal of Urban History* 16 (1989): 78–90; Richard Wightman Fox, *Commonweal* 114 (1987): 712; Herbert G. Gutman, *New Republic*, July 9, 1984, pp. 33–36; Thomas L. Haskell, *Journal of American History* 75 (1988): 586–87; D. R. Jamieson, *Choice* 25 (1987): 528; Richard La Brecque, *Educational Studies* 20 (1989): 197–204; Michael J. Lacey, *Washington Post*, August 2, 1987, p. 11; David Lehman, *Tikkun* 2, no. 4 (1987): 79–80; Ross Miller, *Los Angeles Times Book Review*, August 16, 1987, p. 8; Richard Pells, *Wall Street Journal*, July 15, 1987, p. 26; Eric J. Sandeen, *American Quarterly* 40 (1988): 259–65; Michael M. Sokal, *Isis* 81 (March 1990): 85; and Mark R. Yerburgh, *Library Journal*, May 15, 1987, p. 82.

42. Black journals and black studies journals that did not review *Chants Democratic* or *New York Intellect* include *Black Scholar, Journal of Black Studies, Journal of Negro History, Phylon, Review of Black Political Economy*, and *Urban League Review*. The *Index to Black Periodicals* (Boston: G. K. Hall and Co.) and the *Black Newspapers Index* list no review of either book.

43. Three reviewers of *Chants Democratic* who failed to discuss its exclusion of blacks had already published insightful work on race relations in New York at the time they wrote their reviews, and another had published a major study of the black family. They were doubtless constrained by length and a desire to give readers a full and fair summary of Wilentz's argument on white artisans. See note 41 for the reviews by Phyllis F. Field, Howard B. Rock, and Herbert G. Gutman. See also Field, *Politics of Race in New York*, which was published in 1982; Rock, *Artisans of the New Republic*, which appeared in 1979; and Gutman, *The Black Family in Slavery and Freedom, 1790–1925* (New York: Pantheon, 1976).

As Peter Novick demonstrates in his account of divisions between black and white historians and of the declining interest of white liberals in African American history, our profession does not always offer effective criticism on matters of race; Novick, *That Noble Dream*, pp. 472–91.

44. Wilentz, *Chants Democratic*, pp. 4, 23, 42.

45. E. P. Thompson, "Agendas for Radical History," *Radical History* 36 (1986): 37; and Karl Marx, *Capital*, quoted in Wilentz, *Chants Democratic*, pp. 4–5.

46. Wilentz, *Chants Democratic*, pp. 33–35, 37–38, 63, 94–95, 102–3.

47. Ibid., pp. 71, 73; and Rock, *Artisans of the New Republic*, pp. 3, 65–66, 197–99, 279, 311. On unskilled and semiskilled workers in the 1850s and 1860s, see Richard B. Stott, *Workers in the Metropolis: Class, Ethnicity, and Youth in Antebellum New York City* (Ithaca: Cornell University Press, 1990).

48. Wilentz, *Chants Democratic*, pp. 97–101, 57–58; and Rock, *Artisans of the New Republic*, pp. 69, 272–83, 311. On apprentices, see Rorabaugh, *The Craft Apprentice*.

49. Wilentz, *Chants Democratic*, pp. 87, 90, 289, 250–51, 102.

50. Whitman, *Democratic Vistas*, p. 304.

51. Beard and Beard, *Rise of American Civilization*, pp. vii, xii.

52. Bender, *New York Intellect*, pp. 169, 182, 334, xiv, 239, 193.

53. See Huggins, *Harlem Renaissance*, pp. 195, 200–201; Ann Douglas, *The Fem-*

inization of American Culture (New York: Knopf, 1977), pp. 90–114; Mary Kelley, *Private Woman, Public Stage: Literary Domesticity in Nineteenth-Century America* (New York: Oxford University Press, 1984); and Moses Rischin, *The Promised City: New York's Jews, 1870–1914* (Cambridge: Harvard University Press, 1962). Although Sara Parton wrote predominantly in a sentimental idiom, she could also be a satirical, feminist writer. See Fanny Fern, *Ruth Hall and Other Writings*, ed. Joyce W. Warren (New Brunswick, N.J.: Rutgers University Press, 1986), ix–xxxix; and David S. Reynolds, *Beneath the American Renaissance: The Subversive Imagination in the Age of Emerson and Melville* (Cambridge: Harvard University Press, 1989), pp. 402–7. See Thomas Bender, "Metropolitan Life and the Making of Public Culture," in John H. Mollenkopf, ed., *Power, Culture, and Place: Essays on New York City* (New York: Russell Sage Foundation, 1988), pp. 261–71; and "Lionel Trilling and American Culture," *Intellect and Public Life: Essays on the Social History of Academic Intellectuals in the United States* (Baltimore: Johns Hopkins University Press, 1993), for further evidence of Bender's interest in cosmopolitan intellectuals.

54. Whitman, *Democratic Vistas*, p. 320.

55. See note 11.

56. Wiebe, *The Search for Order*, pp. 111–63.

57. Foner, *Nothing but Freedom*, p. 110.

58. Barbara Jeanne Fields, *Slavery and Freedom on the Middle Ground: Maryland during the Nineteenth Century* (New Haven: Yale University Press, 1985), pp. 154–65, 190–91; Herbert G. Gutman, "The Black Family in Slavery and Freedom: A Revised Perspective," in Gutman, *Power and Culture: Essays on the American Working Class*, ed. Ira Berlin (New York: Pantheon, 1987), 357–79; Gutman, *Black Family in Slavery and Freedom*; and Nell Irvin Painter, *Exodusters: Black Migration to Kansas after Reconstruction* (New York: Norton, 1976), pp. 22–34.

59. Foner, *Nothing but Freedom*, pp. 19, 24, 44, 78–79.

60. Ibid., pp. 40, 78, 93–94, 102.

61. Painter, *Standing at Armageddon*; Bernstein, *New York City Draft Riots*.

62. Baker, *Affairs of Party*, pp. 45–52.

63. For a portrait of that distinctiveness, see John Mack Farragher, *Sugarcreek* (New Haven: Yale University Press, 1987).

64. Baker, *Affairs of Party*, pp. 59–63.

65. For studies that appreciate the diversity and distinctiveness of ethnic communities, see Jon Gjerde, *From Peasants to Farmers: The Migration from Balestrand, Norway, to the Upper Middle West* (New York: Cambridge University Press, 1985); Walter Kamphoefner, *The Westfalians: From Germany to Missouri* (Princeton: Princeton University Press, 1987); and Ned C. Landsman, *Scotland and Its First American Colony, 1683–1765* (Princeton: Princeton University Press, 1985).

66. Baker, *Affairs of Party*, pp. 66–70.

67. On the distinctiveness of class culture and politics, see Wilentz, *Chants Democratic*; and Jacquelyn Dowd Hall et al., *Like a Family: The Making of a Southern Cotton Mill World* (Chapel Hill: University of North Carolina Press, 1987).

68. Baker, *Affairs of Party*, p. 11.

69. Ryan, *Cradle of the Middle Class*, pp. 191, 229.

70. Ibid., p. 191.

71. Richard Busacca and Mary P. Ryan, "Beyond the Family Crisis," *Democracy* 2 (Fall 1982): 90–91.

72. Carroll Smith-Rosenberg, "Beauty, the Beast, and the Militant Woman: A Case Study in Sex Roles and Social Stress in Jacksonian America," in *Disorderly Conduct: Visions of Gender in Victorian America* (New York: Knopf, 1985), pp. 109–28; Suzanne Lebsock, *The Free Women of Petersburg: Status and Culture in a Southern Town, 1784–1860* (New York: Norton, 1984), p. xix; and Alice Kessler-Harris, "Problems of Coalition-building: Women and Trade Unions in the 1920's," in Ruth Milkman, ed., *Women, Work, and Protest: A Century of U.S. Women's Labor History* (London: Routledge and Kegan Paul, 1985), pp. 110–38.

73. Nancy Chodorow, *The Reproduction of Mothering: Psychoanalysis and the Sociology of Gender* (Berkeley: University of California Press, 1978); and Ryan, *Cradle of the Middle Class*, p. 194.

74. Ryan, *Cradle of the Middle Class*, pp. 222–23, 185, 228.

75. Fox, "Public Culture and the Problem of Synthesis," makes the same point.

76. Elizabeth Spellman, *Inessential Women* (Boston: Beacon, 1988); Eleanor Emmons Maccoby and Carol Nagy Jacklin, *The Psychology of Sex Differences* (Stanford: Stanford University Press, 1974), pp. 1–8; Linda K. Kerber, Catherine G. Greeno and Eleanor E. Maccoby, Zella Luria, Carol B. Stack, and Carol Gilligan, "On *In a Different Voice*: An Interdisciplinary Forum," *Signs* 11 (1986): 304–33; and Johnson, "Thresholds of Difference," p. 285.

77. An interesting question emerged from the discussion of an earlier draft of this essay at the Workshop on the Rhetoric of Social History at the University of Iowa. Is it a coincidence that women and minority scholars in the late 1970s and early 1980s preferred the rhetoric of mediation to the rhetoric of skilled cosmopolitanism? Participants in the workshop suggested that the rhetoric of mediation served the initial struggle for affirmative action in the academy, which sought to foster diversity without disrupting the academic community. It favored the creation of autonomous departments and disciplines for the study of women and minorities (where women and minority scholars could express themselves safely) and the promotion of women and minority scholars in mainstream departments on the basis of traditional criteria—a program that the syntheses of Baker, Ryan, and Painter support allegorically. The question merits study.

Another interesting question came forward. Is it a coincidence that white males in their thirties and early forties embraced the rhetoric of skilled cosmopolitanism in the 1980s? That rhetoric might have served young white males who were trying to make their way in a declining profession, because it saw political and professional solidarity (not affirmative action) as the ultimate means to power in the academy and the nation at large. Democratic historians who assumed the mantle of skilled cosmopolitans did not oppose affirmative action. But their ideal of solidarity, drawn as it was from the traditions of artisan republicanism and cosmopolitan intellect, was suffused with white, male preoccupations. This question also merits further study.

78. John Murray Cuddihy, *No Offense: Civil Religion and Protestant Taste* (New

York: Seabury, 1978), pp. 1–23; and John Murray Cuddihy, *The Ordeal of Civility: Freud, Marx, Lévi-Strauss, and the Jewish Struggle with Modernity* (New York: Basic Books, 1974).

79. J. Peter Euben, *The Tragedy of Political Theory* (Princeton: Princeton University Press, 1990), p. 72.

80. On the connection between political engagement, tragic sensibility, and democratic history, see the biographical information in W. Robert Connor, *Thucydides* (Princeton: Princeton University Press, 1984); C. Vann Woodward, *Thinking Back: The Perils of Writing History* (Baton Rouge: Louisiana State University Press, 1986); James Green, "Past and Present in Southern History: An Interview with C. Vann Woodward," *Radical History Review* 36 (1986): 80–100; and Gutman, *Power and Culture*, pp. 3–16, 329–31. For an eloquent statement of the heroic possibilities of social history, see the obituary of Herbert Gutman by Sean Wilentz in the *History Workshop Journal* 22 (1986): 222–25.

81. Euben, *Tragedy of Political Theory*, pp. 36, 127, 225.

82. Foner, *Reconstruction*; W. E. Burghardt Du Bois, *Black Reconstruction in America* (New York: Russell and Russell, 1956); and C. Vann Woodward, *Origins of the New South, 1877–1913* (Baton Rouge: Louisiana State University Press, 1951).

83. The quotes and several phrasings are drawn from Euben, *Tragedy of Political Theory*, pp. 88, 62, 162.

84. Laurence Shore, "The Poverty of Tragedy in Historical Writing on Southern History," *South Atlantic Quarterly* 85 (1986): 147–64; and Sheldon Hackney, "*Origins of the New South* in Retrospect," *Journal of Southern History* 38 (1972): 215; also note the tragic character of Du Bois's and Woodward's histories.

85. The literature on tragedy is voluminous. The citations in this and the following paragraph and the understanding of tragedy that they reflect are drawn from Euben, *Tragedy of Political Theory*, especially pp. 18, 29–31. Euben argues, as have a number of classicists in recent years, that tragedy helped the inhabitants of ancient Athens understand the problems of democratic life. References include John J. Winkler and Froma I. Zeitlin, eds., *Nothing to Do with Dionysos? The Social Meanings of Athenian Tragedy* (Princeton: Princeton University Press, 1990); Christian Meier, *The Greek Discovery of Politics* (Cambridge: Harvard University Press, 1990), pp. 24, 82–139; J. Peter Euben, ed., *Greek Tragedy and Political Theory* (Berkeley: University of California Press, 1986); Helene Foley, *Ritual Irony: Poetry and Sacrifice in Euripides* (Ithaca: Cornell University Press, 1986); Charles Segal, *Dionysian Poetics and Euripides' Bacchae* (Princeton: Princeton University Press, 1982); Jean-Pierre Vernant and Pierre Vidal-Naquet, *Tragedy and Myth in Ancient Greece* (Brighton: Harvester Books, 1981); James Boyd White, *When Words Lose Their Meaning* (Chicago: University of Chicago Press, 1984), pp. 59–113. These works build upon Bernard M. W. Knox, *Oedipus at Thebes: Sophocles' Tragic Hero and His Time* (New Haven: Yale University Press, 1957); and Bernard M. W. Knox, *The Heroic Temper: Studies in Sophoclean Tragedy* (Berkeley: University of California Press, 1964).

Although Euben believes the insights and narrative structure of Thucydides' great *History* were rooted in tragedy, he does not conflate theater and history. History, for example, never rivaled the theater as a vehicle for popular political education in ancient Athens. The plays of the Greek tragedians were performed in the theater of Dionysus before a wide audience (including some women, slaves, and metics) at the annual festival of Dionysus, the god "who confounded the divisions and inequalities deemed central to public life." See *Tragedy of Political Theory*, p. 29; and A. Pickard-Cambridge, *The Dramatic Festivals of Athens*, 2d ed. (Oxford: Clarendon Press, 1968). Thucydides could not count on an inclusive, devout audience in ancient Athens, whose population was largely illiterate. He could hope, however, that his *History* would in time reach future generations of readers attuned to tragedy and its oblique way of serving democracy. *Tragedy of Political Theory*, pp. 167–201.

86. Foner, *Reconstruction*, pp. 602–12. My thoughts on theodicy have been shaped largely by M. H. Abrams, *Natural Supernaturalism: Tradition and Revolution in Romantic Literature* (New York: Norton, 1971). As Hayden White observes in *Metahistory: The Historical Imagination in Nineteenth-Century Europe* (Baltimore: Johns Hopkins University Press, 1973), pp. 9, 433–34, tragedy results in "a gain in consciousness by the spectators" and an "epiphany of the law governing human existence." It is thus conducive to hope and political action, no matter how terrible the fate of the tragic hero.

87. For example, Novick, *That Noble Dream*, pp. 479, 479 n, observes that many gifted gentile historians of the 1960s and 1970s studied "white attitudes and behavior toward blacks," whereas many talented Jewish historians "wrote of blacks as subjects." Novick suggests "a partial explanation for the difference: Jews were considerably more likely to have a background in left politics — to be presocialized into identification with the oppressed."

88. Elsa Barkley Brown, "African-American Women's Quilting: A Framework for Conceptualizing and Teaching African American Women's History," *Signs* 14 (1989): 921–29; Brown, "Polyrhythms and Improvisation: Lessons for Women's History," *History Workshop Journal* 31 (1991): 85–90; and Edward L. Ayers, "Narrating the New South," *Journal of Southern History* 61 (1995): 555–66. Brown and Ayers make a powerful case for improvisational narratives that embrace a multiplicity of voices, stories, and themes and that resist closure. Robert F. Berkhofer, Jr., cautions, however, that contextualization may be inevitable in historical narratives — that a historian may have no choice but to embed multiple voices in "an appropriate Great Story," in which "the politics of historical viewpoint determines the politics of multivocality and multiple viewpoints." See Berkhofer, *Beyond the Great Story: History as Text and Discourse* (Cambridge: Harvard University Press, Belknap Press, 1995), pp. 201, 281–83.

89. Euben, *Tragedy of Political Theory*, pp. 45, 197–201, 276, cautions, however, that the tragedian's voice is omnipresent, even when many characters and peoples are given voice. He argues further, in his comparison of Thucydides' *History* with Euripides' *The Bacchae*, that the tragedian's voice is more dominant in history than in theater, where the playwright has less control (and perhaps seeks less control) over interpretation of narrative. Thucydides' *History* was a tragic response to the

corruption and dismemberment of the Athenian polity during the Peloponnesian War. As an exile despondent over the state of Athenian politics, he had no choice but to turn away from his immediate audience and hope that future readers would save democracy. As Euben puts it, the *History* offers readers "an imaginary experience of cultural reconstitution which might, under certain circumstances, contribute to political reconstitution — which is another way of saying that the community formed between writer and reader retains many of the political attributes no longer possible in times of corruption and civil war" (197–98). That relationship requires, however, that Thucydides use "his reason to show us why the reasoning of others failed" (199). His speech thus "contains the speeches of others, thereby creating a whole in which each becomes part of a dialogue and debate with all the others. Thus the work is a unity that sustains the plurality that *stasis* destroys. . . . Within its confines, leaders, cities, motives, impulses, and points of view speak to each other in ways that clarify the nature of action and thought. While it is a unity that excludes many and much (as a comparison with tragedy indicates), it is neither authoritarian nor tyrannical" (200–201). In the same way, Woodward's and Foner's voices dominate *Origins* and *Reconstruction*, but they are not dominating, as I fear Wilentz's and Bender's are at times. To the extent that Wilentz and Bender privilege a particular voice (and themselves through it), they impede their efforts as historians "to make sense of political, moral, and linguistic corruption" (201).

90. Mary P. Ryan, "The American Parade: Representations of the Nineteenth-Century Social Order," in Lynn Hunt, ed., *The New Cultural History* (Berkeley: University of California Press, 1989), pp. 131–53; and Ryan, *Women in Public*.

91. Walter Licht, "Cultural History/Social History: A Review Essay," *Historical Methods* 25 (1992): 38.

92. Ryan, *Women in Public*, pp. 3–4, 143–47.

93. Meier, *Greek Discovery of Politics*, pp. 1–9, 20–52, 157–85; Martin Ostwald, *From Popular Sovereignty to the Sovereignty of the Law: Law, Society, and Politics in Fifth-Century Athens* (Berkeley: University of California Press, 1986); and Philip Brook Manville, *The Origins of Citizenship in Ancient Athens* (Princeton: Princeton University Press, 1990). Isonomy seldom diminished the political power of noble families, nor did it enfranchise poor citizens anywhere in the Greek world before the fifth century. But it pointed the way toward popular sovereignty and the rule of law. Together with eunomy, it established what we know today (via the Roman Republic) as the republican tradition.

Today most American historians draw their understandings of republicanism from Renaissance humanists, who themselves drew upon the classical republicanism of Aristotle. See J. G. A. Pocock, *The Machiavellian Moment: Florentine Political Thought and the Atlantic Republican Tradition* (Princeton: Princeton University Press, 1975).

94. Euben, *Tragedy of Political Theory*, pp. 29, 35–36, 154–56. These dualisms and hierarchies are most clearly defined in Aristotle, *The Politics*, trans. T. A. Sinclair, rev. ed. (New York: Penguin Books, 1981). The republican tradition was well established in Greece by the late fourth century, when Aristotle composed *The Politics*.

95. See Segal, *Dionysian Poetics and Euripide's Bacchae*; Froma Zeitlin, "Playing the Other: Theatre, Theatricality, and the Feminine in Greek Drama," *Representations* 11 (1985): 63–94; and Euben, *Tragedy of Political Theory*, pp. 27–29, 35–36, 137–39, 154–56, 298, on the dissolution and refiguring of dualisms and hierarchies in Greek theater, history, and political theory. Gender, ethnicity, and class were not issues for democratic thinkers in ancient Athens in the ways they are for modern democratic social historians. But those thinkers did probe the boundaries, as is evident in Euripides' *Bacchae*, Aristophanes' *Ecclesiazusae* and *The Wasps*, and Ephialtes' reform campaign in 462/461 B.C. to give genuine power to the Athenian thetes, the poorest class of Athenian citizens, who supplied the manpower for the Athenian navy.

96. Euben, *Tragedy of Political Theory*, pp. 35–36, 154–56, 306–8.

Daud Ali lectures in early Indian history at the School of Oriental and African Studies in London. His recent work is on courtly and monastic practices in early India.

Florence S. Boos, professor of English at the University of Iowa, has published two critical studies: *The Poetry of Dante G. Rosetti* and *The Design of William Morris's "The Earthly Paradise."* She has edited several collections of texts, including a *Victorian Poetry* centenary issue on William Morris and a forthcoming scholarly edition of *The Earthly Paradise*, and is now preparing a manuscript on Victorian women working-class poets.

Jeffrey Cox is professor of history at the University of Iowa and author of *The English Churches in a Secular Society: Lambeth, 1870–1930*. He has published several articles on British and American missionary work in India and is completing a book titled *Imperial Fault Lines: Christianity and Colonial Power in Punjab, 1830–1940*.

Ruth Crocker, associate professor of history at Auburn University, received her training in British history at Oxford University and in American history and American studies at Purdue. She is the author of *Social Work and Social Order: The Settlement Movement in Two Industrial Cities* and a forthcoming study of Victorian women and money, *Splendid Donation: A Life of Margaret Olivia Sage*.

Charles W. Hayford is an independent scholar and associate of the Department of History, Northwestern University. In recent years he has taught at Northwestern, the University of Illinois at Chicago, Stanford University, the University of Illinois at Urbana-Champaign, and the University of Iowa. He has published *To the People: James Yen and Village China* and *China*, a comprehensive, annotated bibliography, as well as a number of articles on Sino-American relations. He is now working on *America's China*, a study of how Americans construed China from the 1840s to Tienanmen.

Barbara Laslett is professor of sociology at the University of Minnesota. She has written extensively on the historical sociology of gender, social reproduction, and the family and on the history of American sociology and feminist scholarship. She is currently working on a collaborative study (with M. J. Maynes and Jennifer Pierce) investigating the uses of personal narratives in the social sciences.

Adriana Méndez Rodenas, an associate professor in Spanish and comparative literature at the University of Iowa, specializes in nineteenth- and twentieth-century Latin American literature. Her book *Gender and Nationalism in Colonial Cuba: The Travels of Santa Cruz y Montalvo, Condes de Merlin* is forthcoming from Vanderbilt University Press. She is currently working on a book on the travels of European women to Spanish America during the crucial period of national formation at mid-nineteenth century.

Randolph Roth is associate professor of history at Ohio State University. The author of *The Democratic Dilemma: Religion, Reform, and the Social Order in the Connecticut River Valley of Vermont, 1791–1850*, he is currently completing a study of violent crime and violent death in New Hampshire, Vermont, and Maine, titled *Death Is God's Work: A History of Why Northern New Englanders Seldom Commit Murder*.

Shelton Stromquist is professor of history at the University of Iowa. His publications include *A Generation of Boomers: The Pattern of Railroad Labor Conflict in Nineteenth-Century America*; *Solidarity and Survival: An Oral History of Iowa Labor in the Twentieth Century*; and (edited with Marvin Bergman) *Unionizing the Jungles: Labor and Community in the Twentieth-Century Meatpacking Industry*.

Stephen Vlastos is professor of history at the University of Iowa. He is the author of *Peasant Protests and Uprisings in Tokugawa, Japan* and "Opposition Movement in Early Meiji" in *The Cambridge History of Japan*. He is also the editor of and a contributor to *Mirror of Modernity: Invented Traditions of Modern Japan*. He is currently writing a book on radical agrarian movements in prewar Japan.

INDEX